De Witt Colony of Texas

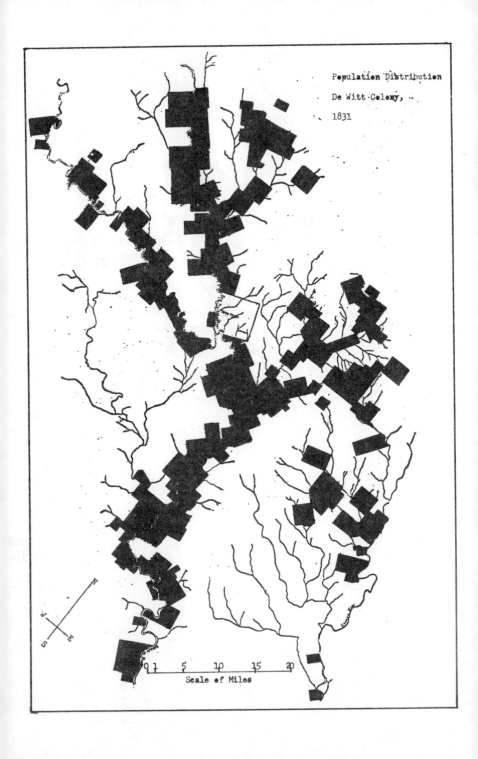

Population Distribution
De Witt Colony,
1831

Scale of Miles

De Witt Colony of Texas

Edward A. Lukes

Jenkins Publishing Company
The Pemberton Press
Austin, Texas / 1976

De Witt Colony of Texas

The beginnings of the counties of:

Caldwell

De Witt

Fayette

Gonzales

Guadalupe

Jackson

Lavaca

Victoria

Contents

Maps and Illustrations

Preface

The colonization of Texas was similar in many respects to other areas of the advancing frontier of the 1820's and 1830's. In relating the history of the De Witt Colony, this study hopes to represent, in microcosmic form, those similarities which made the Texas frontier an extension of the entire Anglo-American line of settlement.

What has made the history of Texas during that period so dynamic and colorful has been the distinctive rather than the similar features of that frontier, however. The obvious distinctions, even to the most casual observer, are, of course, the Texas Revolution and Independence. Another distinction was the manner in which colonization was encouraged. The first phase of Anglo-American colonization of Texas was occasioned by events and decisions occurring outside the traditional pattern of frontier expansion. Until that time all significant migrations occurred within the national boundaries of the United States. With Anglo-American migration to Texas the first, large scale movement onto foreign soil occurred. The policy which fostered this migration originated during the Spanish period and was carried out by Mexico a short while later. The policy sought to protect the northeastern frontier of New Spain, or Mexico, by gaining a respectable population for Texas. Slight Mexican modification of the policy resulted in the creation of a number of "empresario" colonies so as to speed the process. The De Witt Colony, like most other Anglo-American settlements in Texas, was one of these colonies.

Once colonization began, as in the case of the De Witt Colony, the distinctive features of the Texas frontier end and similarities to other areas of the Anglo-American frontier developed. When these colonists entered Texas they brought with them the traits shared, in one degree or another, by all Anglo-Americans. A major trait was the quest for land. Land that would be utilized either for agricultural production or for speculative purposes, or for both. As the history of the United States public lands attest, this was a dominant feature of the Anglo-American frontier. The same was true for Texas. As the Anglo-American frontier had its large, as well as small scale, land promotions, so to in Texas with the leading promoters, or empresarios, and descending to the lowliest settler.

As the Anglo-American frontier expanded, the inevitable clash with the native Americans occurred time and again. It was no different on the Texas frontier. The colonists, as shown with the history of the De Witt Colony, continually experienced Indian

12

raids, sometimes imagined, but at other times quite
real. The docile, coastal tribes of Texas, more an-
noying than threathening, were eventually subdued.
The relations with these Indians offer a contrast to
those relations that developed when the colonists encountered the more formidable Plains Indians. Interestingly, the Texas colonists encountered the Plains
Indians some two to three decades before other
Anglo-Americans did. This was especially true of the
De Witt colonists. That colony sustained more raids
than any other Anglo-American settlement in Texas,
at that time, because of its exposed location. The colony was in the path of the southward advance of the
Comanche and Wichita Indian frontier.

Similarities to the Anglo-American frontier
continue when patterns of population distribution are
considered. As the population of the De Witt Colony
increased it distributed itself throughout the area. In
conjunction with population increases and distribu-
tions recognizable social and economic patterns
emerged. In Texas as in the United States the initial
phase of the frontier economy was subsistence. The
hope, of course, was to move from the mere subsistence level to a level of a market economy. In order to
achieve this transition the role of an urban center was
vital. The primary function of the urban center, as
applied in Texas by the Spanish-Mexican experiment,
was administrative and political. Anglo-Americans in
Texas attempted to modify the urban function so as
to coincide with their own experiences. The pattern of
similarity again comes to the forefront. As in the
United States, Texas urban development went beyond the simple administrative phase and was viewed
as a stimulator of the economy. The urban center, as
seen with the development of the only town in the De
Witt Colony, would hopefully become a thriving
commercial area.

The Anglo-Americans' regard for government provides another example of the similarities of the two frontiers. Rugged individualism went so far, but when assistance was needed the frontiersmen did not find it contradictory to call upon the government for aid. When the government, whether local, state or national, promoted banking and credit facilities, internal improvements, favorable tariff policies, or an Indian pacification program the frontiersmen cheered. So also in Texas, the Anglo-Americans, when faced with the need of greater governmental assistance, expected the same response from the Mexican government. When that government would not, or could not, provide the desired assistance, and attempts for separate statehood for Texas were frustrated, the Anglo-Americans reacted. The De Witt colonists were the first to precipitate the reaction that led to revolution and independence. The conditions, however, where already there, and these colonists merely acted as a catalyst to set the chain of events into motion.

The history of the De Witt Colony deals with one of the empresario settlements. Further studies should be done for the others. Eugene C. Barker, in his *Life of Stephen F. Austin*, has treated the Austin Colony, but by way of an excellent biography. Histories of the Austin Colony, with its various settlements, remain to be written. Through the study of other empresario colonies and settlements a greater understanding may be obtained of the Mexican empresario system; of Mexican foreign and domestic policy, particularly after 1830; and of the economic history of Texas between the years 1825 to 1836. Above all, further investigation would add to greater understanding of the similarities as well as the differences of the entire Anglo-American frontier.

Edward A. Lukes

1

Formation
of a Policy:
An Introduction

During the closing years of the seventeenth century, more than half of the eighteenth century, and some twenty years into the nineteenth century, the land nominally referred to as "Tejas" played a strategic role in the defense of the northeast frontier of the Spanish possessions of North America. Although making no serious attempts to establish permanent settlements northeast of the Rio Grande River, Spain found it necessary to do so after 1690 because of the westward encroachments of the French from Louisiana.[1] Aside from the French threat the Spaniards were forced to contend with the ever-present problem of the savage and hostile natives of central and eastern Texas.[2]

The only way to deal with the Indian problem, as well as the one posed by the French, was to increase the population. However the Spanish population was small in proportion to the area comprising the entire northern fringe of New Spain, and the economic inducements in these provinces were few.[3] Therefore, some means other than colonization had to be employed.

The method chosen to halt the French advance and to convert Texas into a fortified buffer zone was of a three-fold nature: the mission, the presidio, and the pueblo. Theoretically the mission would provide for the spiritual well being of the natives and would also serve as a method of changing them from their nomadic and warlike tendencies to a more civilized and stable way of life. Rather than roaming the vast countryside, the natives would be settled into towns or pueblos. To provide for the protection of the mission and pueblo, a presidio, or armed, garrisoned outpost was established. That the mission was the primary institution which was protected and supplemented by the presidio is evident from the fact that when a mission was moved, as in the case of Espiritu Santo and Xavier missions, the presidio was also moved. The mission with its corresponding pueblo and presidio, then, went hand in hand and served the single purpose of holding the area of Texas for Spain.[4]

This mission system proved to be a benefit, for not only was Texas relatively secured within the empire but also Spain, unwillingly, fell heir to the French province of Louisiana just prior to the end of the Seven Years' War. The end of the French threat signified the end of Texas' role as a bulwark. Texas became another interior province. This is demonstrated to some degree by the fact that no new missions were established after 1762 while many of the existing ones were being abandoned.[5]

The fortunes of war had changed the role which Texas played within the empire. The first concrete efforts to reorganize the frontier military establishments of that province occurred in 1772. Since Louisiana was no longer a French possession, but a sister province, it was suggested and eventually put into operation that all troops were either to be sent to the newest frontier, the Mississippi, or removed to San Antonio.

The reorganization which the military establishments underwent in 1772 soon befell the missions with greater ramifications. Basically the mission had no right or title to the land, either by general law or grant, but had an "easement" of the territory which it occupied.[6] It was generally held that after a ten year period, the native population would be sufficiently educated and Christianized that the mission system could give way, without much difficulty, to the pueblo system. By 1793 most of the missions were secularized, which means that the missions along with the property attached to them were transferred from the Franciscan Order to diocesan control. The land holdings were then distributed to the neophytes and the communal life gave way to individual dwellings and plots. The agricultural produce was no longer stored in a common granary.[7]

In effect, Texas became the "neglected province," for Spain's policy of protecting New Spain focused now upon the newly-acquired Louisiana. Perhaps unjustly critical, the comments of Francois Barbe-Marbois, Napoleon's Treasury minister, partially reflect Spain's role for Louisiana: ". . . Spain, by uniting Louisiana in 1763 to her vast American states, was not actuated by any intention of extending her navigation or augmenting her treasures. She still followed the ancient policy of those barbarous nations, who only think their frontiers secure when vast deserts separate them from powerful nations . . ."[8]

With the acquisition of Louisiana, Spain found herself in a new and different situation. Aside from the fact that it was her first experience in North America with a colony previously occupied by Europeans, she found it necessary to make some departures in her traditional policy. One was fostered by the nature of the Indian element encountered in the vastness of Louisiana. Since the various tribes were powerful and warlike, Spanish policy did not and probably could not employ the mission system as a method of control. Instead she relied upon the easier French method of chartering trading companies and sending fur traders among the various tribes.[9] Another departure, one that would have great and lasting consequences for Spain's offspring, Mexico, was the emphasis and reliance upon colonization.[10]

The problem of holding the northeastern frontier became acute, for, as has been mentioned previously, the Spanish population, proportionately small in comparison to the areas needed to be colonized, was now even smaller with the addition of the extensive Louisiana province. As early as 1780, Spanish apprehensions were heightened at the rapid increase of Anglo-American settlements being established opposite her.[11] She soon saw that there was this habit among western Anglo-Americans to continue to move. However, Spain looked upon them, at this time, not as a direct threat, but as a useful element, providing the existence of one important factor: that this westward movement be under Spanish control. Therefore, why not encourage immigration since it would be better to have them move as Spanish citizens than as citizens of another power, a power which might be hostile.[12] Spain viewed the westerners as a product of their environment. The westerners were unruly because of their great distance from any formal government, their dislike in general for any form of restrictive government, and their economically depraved situation, i.e. the closure of the Mississippi resulting in the lack of markets for their produce. It was felt that these problems could easily be solved and the aggressive tendencies neutralized if the westerners were under direct Spanish control.[13]

The attitude regarding the westerners was formulated, in part, by Spanish informants within the United States. It was believed that the people of the "western waters" were completely indifferent to the government of the United States since many of them were either foreigners, French, German, and Irish, or fugitives from the United States government, loyalists, debtors, and criminals. The situation which existed in the Natchez district led Count Floridablanca, Charles III's Minister of Foreign Affairs, to believe that these westerners, once under a stable government, such as that of Spain, would be docile in nature.[14]

It is of interest to note the colonial policy and immigration regulations which were developed in Louisiana by Spain bear a striking resemblance to those which were inaugurated in Texas some years later. This policy can readily be seen in the various official dispatches and reflections of the governors and intendants of the province of Louisiana.[15]

The immigration policy regarding Louisiana was formalized with the Royal Decree of December 1, 1788. It provided for the granting of land, equal commercial privileges and religious toleration, providing the oath of allegiance was taken and the immigrant became a bonafide settler. The principal objectives of this policy were to placate the volatile western element of the United States and to obtain a respectable population for the province of Louisiana. However, the spirit of the decree was revolutionary in nature, since it had liberalized Spanish immigration policies.

Formerly, only Roman Catholics were allowed to settle in the provinces.[16]

The attempt to increase the population of Louisiana and, at the same time to deplete the population east of the Mississippi was, however, an unfortunate failure for Spain. The policy failed because the religious and political advantages offered by Spain were already enjoyed by a majority of the western Anglo-Americans, with the added advantage of relative security. It was generally believed by Anglo-Americans that, at any time, Spain might revoke these privileges and compel the settlers to accept the monarchial form of government and the Roman Catholic faith, or suffer the consequences of confiscation of property and expulsion. The ever-present Indian menace was not relieved even though the settlers were under Spanish jurisdiction. It is also of interest to note that as soon as Spanish authority, in the form of garrison troops, was established in any area where the settlers had already established themselves, immigration to that sector declined.[17]

The colonization problem was soon joined by a financial one for Spain in Louisiana. The six percent export and import duties were netting less than $100,000 per year while the annual expense for Spain in maintaining the province was $537,000, coming mainly in the form of aid to the colonists. Clearly the province was becoming a financial liability and was placing a severe strain upon the treasury.[18]

Some solution had to be found and it soon came in the form of the French desire to obtain Louisiana. In May, 1798, Talleyrand sent a representative to Madrid and instructed him to caution the Spanish against making any concessions to the United States. The instructions went on to state that the only way to curb the endless ambitions of the Anglo-Americans was by "shutting them up within the limits

Nature seems to have traced for them." However Spain was in no position to undertake this task alone since the possibility of an accord between Great Britain and the United States always loomed in the background. Therefore Spain had to seek the aid of another power, in this case France, and in return cede a small portion of her vast holdings. By a cession of certain areas, the remainder of Spanish colonial possessions would be forever secure and the power of the United States would be bounded by those limits imposed upon it by the will of France and Spain. ". . . The French Republic, mistress of these two provinces,[19] will be a wall of brass forever impentrable to the combined efforts of England and America. . . ."[20] On October 1, 1800 the secret treaty of San Ildefonso was concluded and Louisiana was ceded to France. However, France did not take actual possession until a full three years later.

Napoleon's plans for Louisiana withered with General Leclercs army in Santo Domingo, and in April, 1803, he sold the province outright to the United States. The "wall of brass" lasted twenty days, for on November 30, 1803, France finally took formal possession of Louisiana only to depart when the United States assumed control on December 20, 1803. The fears which the Spanish Intendant, Martin Navarro, had voiced earlier were now a stark reality. No longer was the Mississippi a "feeble barrier," there was no barrier at all now. Spain was thrown back and forced, once more, to defend along the only natural line available — the Sabine River. The province of Texas now became again the front line of defense.

For forty years, Texas had been relegated to a position of an interior province and, correspondingly, the colonization of that area had declined. Several explanations show why the population of Texas was neglible. One of which, as has been mentioned previously, was the conspicuous absence of any economic inducements. With the exception of the San Saba mine, the area did not provide the necessary stimulus for any large scale land developmental enterprises. What limited colonization occurred seemed to have centered in the areas of San Antonio de Bexar and La Bahia (Goliad), the only footholds in southern Texas. Each was situated on the well-watered prairie and open brush country which was highly adaptable to the traditional, Spanish ranching practices. The population consisted of a few colonists from the Canary Islands and central Mexico. The area of Nacogdoches, however, was altogether different. It lay far in the timbered region of East Texas, approximately one-hundred miles from any prairie openings. Nacogdoches failed to attract the usual Spanish colonists since traditional ranching techniques were not possible. The climate and the terrain were uninviting to those accustomed to the high dry plateaus of Mexico. Nacogdoches was never colonized, it merely accumulated adventurers, refugees from homeland authority, drifters, smugglers, Indian traders, and squatters.[21]

A second explanation for the small population lies in the fact that Spain, after 1784, prohibited the entrance of any foreigner into Texas.[22] However, as was the case with many other regulations, the restriction upon illegal entrance was not rigidly enforced by provincial authorities. After the pressures from the north-east became more intense upon the Spanish frontier, compliance with the restriction was imperative. In August, 1800, Nemesio Salcedo became the Commandant-General of the Interior Provinces and was determined to carry out the restriction upon entrance.[23]

General Salcedo saw the urgent need to develop the area under his control. The task of securing such a vast area was a sizable project. Even if a sufficient number of troops were obtained, a highly unlikely prospect, there was still the question of how these garrisons could be supplied. The supply lines from Mexico would certainly be too distant and would always be at the mercy of the marauding Indians. To supply the Texas frontier from the Floridas was not practical since any supply vessels might fall prey to Lafitte's pirates at Barataria. If hostilities were to open with the United States, the line of supply could easily be severed by privateers. Without people and supplies Texas would certainly be lost. It was apparent that the only reasonable course left to the commandant-general was to encourage immigration and enlarge the population. With a sufficient population in the province, numerous settlements could be established and the lines of supply and communication need not be so lengthy. The government could rely upon an appreciable population to provide militia service, if the need arose, and to supply food for the nearby garrison.

To diverge for a moment, it is interesting to point out that the "mission system," which had been employed earlier in Texas and had worked so well, could not be employed now, simply because time was of the utmost importance.[24] It would take years to reduce the nomadic Indians once more, while the sendentary white men could more easily be obtained and dispersed throughout the vast province.

General Salcedo now faced the problem of obtaining these colonists. His solution came with the cession of Louisiana. The settlers there petitioned him for admission into Texas. They were displeased with the change of sovereignty.[25] He did not hesitate in replying, for on May 23, 1803, he issued a decree which ruled that all desiring admittance must first prove that they had been Spanish subjects in Louisiana and demonstrate evidence of good character. Those who could not furnish absolute proof were to be settled not in Texas but further into the interior, Nueva Viscaya or Coahuila.[26] The ban on entry, it should be stressed, had not been entirely abolished because only those who were previous subjects would be admitted while others would be turned away, with force if necessary.

The following month, Salcedo seemed to be justifying his ruling of May 23, for in his report he cited the deplorable state of affairs then existing in Texas. He stated there existed only three small settlements, the capital of San Antonio de Bexar, the presidio of La Bahia and the pueblo of Nacogdoches. He continued by estimating that the population of San Antonio with 2,500, La Bahia with 618, Nacogdoches with 770, and a few small and scattered settlements all totaled not more than 4,000,[27] a number quite disproportionate to the size of the province.

As his decree was not overruled by his superiors, Salcedo continued to allow admittance to the first of many immigrants who had qualified under his ruling of May 23. These immigrants were allowed to settle anywhere in Texas, Coahuila, or Nueva Viscaya, but none could settle at Nacogdoches. The great fear of close contact with objectionable sources and the probability of illicit and contraband trade were uppermost in his mind. He suggested settling the immigrants near San Antonio. In an attempt to weaken the potential threat on the east bank of the Mississippi, he suggested that any Anglo-American deserters, who were given refuge in Spanish territory, should be brought to San Antonio and given land. Any immigrants who were found to be tradesmen should be urged to settle in Coahuila, since they would be safer there than on the frontier with its hazardous conditions.[28]

A number of large scale colonization projects for Texas were planned, but failed because of a lack of organization and funds.[29] However many settlers came in smaller groups. Their number was of a appreciable proportion since their migration did not go unnoticed by the United States officials. By June, 1806, Governor Claiborne of Louisiana was informed that, in addition to those persons who had already gone over to the Spanish province, a considerable immigration was to take place from Opelousas County, Rapides, and Nachitoches to the settlements along the Trinity River in Texas.[30]

As General Salcedo began to see his plan succeeding for strengthening Texas by means of selective colonization, i.e., only Spanish subjects, he now thought it was time to bring all available troops up to the frontier.[32] By the middle of 1805, the troops of Coahuila, aided by those of Nuevo Leon and Tamaulipas, under the command of Colonel Antonio Cordero, Governor of Coahuila, took up positions on the frontier.[33] Cordero's force was the largest ever to enter Texas and once within the province he quickly garrisoned troops at La Bahia (Goliad, Texas) and Nacogdoches, reoccupied the presidio of Orcoquisac (near Anahuac, Texas), kept constant patrols along the Camino Real,[34] and fortified Los Adaes (near Robeline, Louisiana). This sudden show of force was no doubt in conjunction with the influx of colonists who needed protection, but a better explanation lies in the fact that the United States was pressing its claim for Texas. The United States government maintained that Texas was a portion of Louisiana, and Salcedo was determined to resist all incursions. By August, 1805, he further strengthened his position by issuing an edict which was to be declared in force if hostilities with the United States should break out. The edict prohibited anyone from selling munitions or horses to any inhabitant of Louisiana. It restated an earlier decree which forbade the entrance of Anglo-Americans into Texas and prescribed the death penalty for anyone who violated the edict.[35]

As relations became strained, Salcedo's primary interests centered upon maintaining the border, while colonization, still very important in his mind, assumed a secondary role. After the province of Louisiana had been ceded to the United States, two Spaniards, Casa Calvo and Ventura Morales, remained in the area to make final settlements concerning land titles. Then during the winter of 1805, Casa Calvo made a thorough exploration of that area surrounding Nachitoches and concluded that the eastern boundary of Texas should be set at the Arroyo Hondo, a rivulet east of the Sabine River.[36] Based upon Casa Calvo's conclusion, Spain maintained that the Arroyo Hondo was the true eastern boundary. The United States, on the other hand, proposed, as early as 1804, that the area between the Sabine and the Colorado Rivers should be made into a neutral territory. The suggestion was later changed to the establishment of a neutral area between the Colorado and the Rio Grande Rivers. Spanish officialdom became concerned over these statements. Consequently a sizable detachment of Cordero's force, under the command of Simon de Herrera reached the Arroyo Hondo. He was asked to withdraw, which he did, while General James Wilkinson, commander of the United States troops, followed cautiously behind. The Spanish troops withdrew only across the Sabine to await further orders. Tension mounted as the two armies stared across at each other with only the river between them.

The crisis was finally terminated when General Wilkinson decided to go to Natchez, where he was to be rewarded and honored for his action in deterring

Burr's attempted invasion of Spanish territory. However, before he departed, both of the commanders reached an understanding that the area in question be neutralized. The "neutral ground" was to be between the Sabine River and the Arroyo Hondo.[37]

The Neutral Ground was an area where neither country exercised any jurisdiction, and in time that area became a haven for every lawless and desperate character along the entire frontier. On many occasions both governments attempted to halt the lawlessness of the area, but their efforts were hopeless.[38] However, the entire affair turned out well for Spain for it gave her time to build up a population that might resist the inevitable onslaught of the Anglo-Americans.

With the crisis over, for the time being, Salcedo's thoughts focused once more upon colonization. During 1806, slight progress was made. Villa de Salcedo (near Midway, Madison County, Texas) was established by settlers from San Antonio, but colonization was beginning to decline.[39] It was becoming evident that all the Catholic, Spanish subjects of Louisiana who were ever to come had already immigrated. Therefore, a new colonization measure had to be adopted. By 1807, this new method was to bring settlers from the interior of Mexico into Texas. In December of that year, a few families from Refugio were sent to the area of the San Marcos River. Here on January 6, 1808 the settlement of San Marcos was established where the Camino Real crossed the San Marcos River. The total population consisted of eighty-one persons, mostly from Refugio and the remainder being from San Antonio and La Bahia.[40] Unfortunately, this method did not prove as successful as Salcedo hoped, for the people of the interior had no desire to immigrate to Texas, an area which afforded nothing but hardships and dangers.

Up to this time, the immigration and colonization policy that was being employed was one of selectivity. This policy, in itself, was limited and consequently limited its immediate effectiveness. Had there been ample time, it might have proved to be the answer, but the question was how much time. More settlers were needed, and needed soon. As a result Salcedo's policy began to raise doubts in the minds of some Spanish officials. Although they did not disagree with the ultimate end of his policy, they questioned the means, namely the selectivity aspect. Cordero, Herrera and Manuel de Salcedo, the governor of Texas and the son of a former Spanish governor of Louisiana, were a few who began to question General Salcedo's approach to the problem. Their doubts soon gave rise to two distinct opinions concerning colonization. These men strongly believed that the province of Texas could best be defended by adopting a liberal policy concerning the introduction of settlers rather than a restrictive and limited one.[41] General Salcedo however, steadfastly maintained that any immigration should be restricted to those persons who were undeniably faithful subjects and who had no ties, commercially, socially, or economically, with areas or nations which might prove unfriendly to Spain. Needless to say, General Salcedo was hampered in carrying out his policy from this time on. By the end of 1808, the population did not increase since the two conflicting opinions prevented a united effort.[42]

As Napoleon's troops marched across the Pyrenees and placed his brother, Joseph, upon the Spanish throne, the problem of immigration became accentuated. Fear of Napoleon's designs upon New Spain by encouraging and fermenting revolution there, possible French invasions, and Anglo-American aggressiveness all contributed, in part, to a more extreme view which General Salcedo took regarding immigration. In January, 1809, General Salcedo had decided that all foreigners should be expelled since he believed that any one of these might be an agent of Napoleon. Officially, he based his orders for expulsion upon the grounds that these persons, especially in the Sabine River area, were objectionable because of their nationality, religion, and their failure to produce full satisfactory papers of once being Spanish subjects and good Catholics in Louisiana. There was no immediate response and almost a year later, Salcedo re-issued the order. The Governor of Texas, Manuel de Salcedo, protested this measure which would seriously weaken the position of Texas.[43]

General Salcedo, sensing the growing opposition to his policy, decided to counter any scheme that Cordero, Herrera, and Manuel de Salcedo might be planning. On April 2, 1809, he issued orders that no foreigners were to be allowed entrance into Texas. This, of course, was received by Cordero, Herrera, and Manuel de Salcedo with much displeasure. The two governors and the frontier commander were now firmly convinced that Texas should be defended by the establishment of a strong military element, especially along the frontier, and an emphasis placed upon a more liberal colonization program. Immigrants should be drawn from Spanish subjects from the interior and foreigners.[44]

They reacted vigorously to one of General Salcedo's most extreme measures, which was to retreat and consolidate along the Rio Grande. He reasoned that it would be easier to defend along that portion, with its true natural barrier, than to attempt to defend a plain. Cordero, Herrera, and Manuel de Salcedo, to the contrary, felt that if Spain were to withdraw to the Rio Grande, the Anglo-Americans would merely fill the vacuum thus created. The problem would not be alleviated at all. As a matter of fact, the problem would be worse for instead of worrying about the frontier along the Sabine, they would be worrying about the frontier along the Rio Grande. They reasoned that a retreat would be senseless, better to see the problem through as far as possible from the frontiers of Mexico.[45] Although Cordero, Herrera, and Manuel de Salcedo felt that a liberal immigration policy should be introduced, they were not naive in thinking that colonization alone would be sufficient for holding Texas. A strong military force always was needed. To them the Neutral Ground Agreement of 1806 would not long contain their neighbors to the east. Even if a sufficient amount of settlers were obtained for Texas, that province would never be safe until armed garrisons could maintain a constant vigil. General Bernardo Bonavia y Zapata reflects well the distrust which most Spanish officials had of the United States.

> . . . We can never depend upon the government of the United States with their present singular constitution, and should always dread the ambitious, restless, and enterprising character of the people, and their misconceived ideas of liberty. . . . Self interest and the lure being the only object of the Anglo-American who cares not whence it comes. Hence, even in time of peace, we must be watchful and keep our arms in our hand against that people amongst whom the scum of all nations is to be found.[46]

When the cry, "Death to the Gachupines" resounded through Mexico, neither General Salcedo nor the advocates of a liberal colonization policy had time to give much thought, if any, to the defense of Texas.

In September, 1810, the parish priest of Dolores, Miguel Hidalgo y Costilla, sounded the call for the revolutionary struggle which was to last until 1821. To go into the causes and the movement of the revolution would range far from the present discussion, but it is necessary to deal with them briefly so as to obtain a broader understanding of the problems faced by the Spanish colonial officials regarding colonization. Hidalgo's revolution was gaining momentum and soon his forces were within reach of Mexico City. However, he was defeated by loyalist forces and retreated northward, toward Texas. Before he reached the Rio Grande, he was captured and executed. When word of the revolution reached Texas, Juan Las Casas took up the cause and, on January 21, 1811, from San Antonio, proclaimed the principles of Hidalgo. Here too the revolutionists met with early success and the rebel government took command of San Antonio, La Bahia, and Nacogdoches. The Spanish officials were sent to Coahuila as prisoners. However, in Texas, as in Mexico, the rebellion was soon crushed. By March, the loyalists had gained control once more.

The movement may have been crushed but it was not destroyed. A number of Hidalgo's and Las Casas' followers took refuge across the Sabine where they found a pleasant sanctuary. At any time they were ready to re-enter Texas and, with aid from the Anglo-Americans, continue the revolution. The Spanish officials now had an even greater threat across the Sabine. They felt that the government of the United States had a perfect pretense for the invasion of Texas.

> . . . it appears the Government of the United States intends, as preliminary to its conquest, to cut off the vagabonds and revolutionists, and consummate them afterwards with their arms and taking of possessions. In fact all indicates a very considerable upturning if this Province is not attended to, from which it would be difficult to dislodge the Americans if they succeed in occupying it.[47]

Despite all of General Salcedo's precautions, the various revolts had caused Texas to fall into a very precarious state. The next question was whether meager Spanish forces in Texas could resist the impending onslaught that might burst upon them. To the east of the province of Texas were the Anglo-Americans, revolutionists, and filibusters; to the north and west were the Indians, especially the hostile Comanches; and within the very province itself were the seeds of insurrection, sown by Hidalgo and Las Casas. What was definitely needed now was a greater military factor. It would take trained infantry, artillery and lightning swift cavalry to enforce any effective control upon the province. However, at this time, all available Spanish troops were being employed against Napoleon in the Iberian campaign. All possible man-power that could be gathered had already been deployed with Cordero in 1805.

In the meantime, Miguel Ramos Arizpe, the deputy representing the provinces of Coahuila, Nuevo Leon, Santander, and Texas in the Spanish Cortes, was emphatically stressing the need for colonization in Texas. He cited various advantages and the high degree of prosperity that could be attainable in Texas. He went on to castigate the government which "never has . . . put into practice effective measures for leading men there." He concluded his presentation by strongly recommending that the population of Texas should be increased since it would be "profitable to all that may undertake it" and "advantageous to the province of Texas, that so much needs the industrious workers, and necessary to the nation for the preservation of that important province."[48]

The pressure upon the military was to become more intense within the next few years, but they reacted well to every challenge hurled upon them. In August of 1812, the first challenge came in the form of a conglomerated filibustering[49] revolutionary assault. When Hidalgo had established his revolutionary government, he had sent Bernardo Gutierrez as agent to the United States to procure much needed money and supplies. That government was unable to offer direct aid, but extended encouragement and moral support.

Gutierrez, undaunted, returned to New Orleans and began, on his own, the preparation for the invasion of Texas. He was soon to find assistance from Augustus Magee, who had just resigned from the United States Army. They set about recruiting an army of approximately five hundred frontiersmen and gathered them together in the Neutral Ground. This newly formed "Republican Army of the North" was determined to liberate Texas, attack Mexico and join with the revolutionary armies, and assist them in gaining Mexican independence. The soliders would not receive any pay, but would be rewarded for their services by receiving one league of Texas land.[50]

The Gutierrez-Magee invasion quickly crushed any notable Spanish resistance; Nacogdoches was entered easily; La Bahia fell; and by the end of March, 1813 San Antonio was in the hands of the rebels. On April 1, 1813 the Green Flag Republic of Texas was established and a few days later a declaration of independence and a constitution were proclaimed. Meanwhile, across the Rio Grande, the new Commandant General of the Eastern Interior Provinces, Joaquin de Arredondo, gathered a force of two-thousand men.

Arredondo's military action was so devastating that within a few short months he practically had depopulated Texas, and had undone any positive gains made by General Salcedo in securing a sizable population. By October, 1814 Arredondo published his "Proclamation" which was intended to prevent the entrance of any strangers who desired to inspire revolution.[51] For all purposes, Texas had reverted to a wilderness state. When Arredondo departed for his headquarters in Monterrey, there were only 457 mounted troops in the entire province. Their main task was that of defense, but, being poorly equipped, they were little more than useless. The conditions were highly auspicious for the Indian tribes to resume, with greater frequency and audacity, their raids upon the remaining settlers.

Since San Antonio and La Bahia were constantly menaced by Indians, the privations of daily needs became extreme. A sack of corn sold for three dollars, coffee was two and one-half dollars per pound, sugar was a dollar and a half per pound and tobacco sold for one dollar per ounce. Conditions were so terrible that people engaged in farming were forced to travel in squads or groups of fifteen or more when going to the fields or searching for stray oxen. While they worked, it was necessary for them to keep their firearms always at their sides. ". . . It may be counted as a miracle that no more deaths occurred than there did; because the Indians would dress themselves with the clothes of their victims, and would promenade the streets at will . . ."[52]

Because of the overall weakness of the province, it became a haven for disreputable individuals. Bandits, filibusters, and pirates plagued the coastal regions of Texas while the Indians devastated the interior. This was the drastic situation in 1817 when Antonio Martinez was appointed governor of Texas. The problems which he faced were insurmountable and his correspondence with the Viceroy, Ruiz de Apodaca, bear witness to the sorry state of affairs in Texas. Martinez was faced with the problems of an inadequate military force to defend eastern Texas, incessant Indian attacks, and a drastic need to rebuild the economy. He was in especially great need of money, soldiers, gunsmiths, physicians, horses, clothing, paper, seed, arms and ammunition, medicine, iron, and steel. But above all, and more than anything else, the province was always in dire need of food.[53]

However, the situation was growing worse for more soldiers could not be had and the condition of the troops in Texas was rapidly deteriorating. The revolutions in South America were diverting any supplies which might have been destined for Texas. The unfortunate Texas garrisons were unwillfully neglected to such an extent that the basic needs were unavailable. The condition of the company at San Antonio was the most deplorable simply because they were the farthest removed from the border and were thereby unable to engage in contraband trade to obtain their necessities. That company was so impoverished and poorly equipped that they had not been provided with any clothing and were practically naked.[54] By June, 1819, Governor Martinez, possibly seeing that reinforcements might never arrive, pleaded for immigrants and pointed out his attempts to improve Texas were fruitless because of the lack of resources available to him. He lamented that there were only 2,000 settlers left in Texas and asked to be granted permission for the introduction of colonists from Saltillo and from beyond the border.[55] Although his suggestions and pleas were not discarded, they were overshadowed by the consequences of the Adams-Onis negotiations, completed in February of that year.

From 1809 to 1815, no diplomatic communication existed between Spain and the United States since the latter did not accord recognition to the provisional government of Spain. In 1810, the provisional government sent an envoy, Luis de Onis, to Washington. He was not officially received until December of 1815.[56] He was thoroughly convinced that if a satisfactory arrangement regarding boundary and border difficulties was not reached with the United States, that country would seize Florida and Texas as soon as an opportunity was available.[57]

Terms were finally reached on February 22, 1819, in which the Floridas were ceded to the United States and Spain, in effect, obtained sole possession of Texas. The western boundary was run along the Sabine River till the 32nd parallel and from there on a line due north to the Red River; the line would run along the course of that river to the 100th meridian and along that line northward to the Arkansas River; from there it would follow the south bank of that river to its source thence to the 42nd parallel; along that parallel to the Pacific Oean.[58]

Spain had secured a diplomatic victory for now the Sabine line had been elevated to a treaty basis. She now could hold the United States diplomatically accountable for restraining its own nationals and deterring them from any aggressive incursions into Texas.

In assessing the treaty Onis maintained the Floridas were of little value to Spain. It was better to cede them now and gain something in return, rather than to wait and possibly lose them without gaining anything. He went on to cite some advantages which accrued to Spain by the treaty: the formal securing of Texas, the securing of territory west and north of the Red River, and a wide region between the boundary line and New Spain.[59]

Onis was not naive in thinking a mere line drawn on a piece of paper would bind Texas securely to the Spanish empire. He realized all of his gains would be useless unless supplemented by colonists.

By the end of 1819 then, Spain's immigration and colonization policies had not obtained a sizable population for Texas. There was still a conscious restriction of certain groups, primarily Anglo-Americans. However, by 1820, a radical change in this policy was effected. In March of that year, Ferdinand VII, under the prodding of the Spanish liberal military and political elements, proclaimed the restoration of the Constitution of 1812. The following April the king issued another decree which re-established the legality of all laws, decrees, and ordinances passed by the Cortes prior to 1814.[60]

With reference to land laws, this meant that the various ayuntamientos were legally allowed to distribute land under the law of January 4, 1813. The change in policy did not end here, for on September 28, the Cortes issued a decree which, in effect, lifted the exclusion regarding the entrance of foreigners. They were now allowed asylum, providing they respected the political constitution and the laws.[61] This liberalized colonization policy, and similar subsequent measures, would provide the most auspicious conditions for the peaceful penetration of Anglo-Americans into Texas.

2

The Empresario System and De Witt's Grant

The opening of Texas to Anglo-American immigration cannot be discussed without mention of the two men most directly responsible for laying its foundation: Moses Austin and his son, Stephen.[1] The economic situation in the United States and especially along the frontier in 1818 and 1819 caused Austin and many of his contemporaries to look for new avenues to alleviate their desperate financial position.[2] This avenue, for Austin, was found in the liberalized Spanish land policy.

Moses Austin had always been an enterprising individual and, when financial reverses caused the loss of his lead mine in Wythe County, Virginia, he journeyed to Spanish Louisiana and obtained a land grant in 1797. He established himself and his family in what is today Washington County, Missouri.[3]

There he engaged in the mining of lead and became a large shareholder in the Bank of St. Louis. Once more financial misfortune befell him, for in 1818 the bank went bankrupt and he was forced to relinquish all his holdings, property included, to satisfy his creditors. His total losses amounted to approximately $30,000.[4]

To make matters more difficult, the United States Congress, in 1820, legislated a change in the land purchasing laws. By the terms of the law the minimum price per acre was reduced to $1.25, with a minimum purchase fixed at eighty acres. In order to obtain any land from the public domain, it was necessary to deposit the entire purchase price. In principle the law abolished the credit system for land purchasing. Needless to say, land sales decreased[5] for many were suffering the effects of the depression — monetary and credit stringency — and had no way of meeting the requirement.[6] However the liberalization of the Spanish land policy and her eagerness to dispose of her public domain provided a solution for the needs of the Anglo-American frontier.

Moses Austin and most of his contemporaries were probably not aware of the lifting of the ban against Anglo-American immigration but various filibustering expeditions and especially the Adams-Onis negotiations brought Texas into the focus of public attention. However it remained for Moses and Stephen Austin, and other promoters like them, to advertise Texas land. Much relatively inexpensive land, safeguarded by bona fide title, sanctioned by the Spanish government, was available.

In October, 1820 Moses Austin journeyed to San Antonio where he petitioned the Spanish government for a land grant. He also suggested the possibility of introducing other Anglo-Americans into the province. On January 17, 1821, the petition was favorably approved by the Spanish officials and Austin was allowed to introduce 300 families.[7]

The Spanish authorities in granting the Austin petition, were acting in accordance with the decree of 1820 which allowed entrance to anyone, providing the basic requirements were met. It was not until March, 1821 however that the provincial authorities fully realized the possibility of the introduction of three hundred families. Austin's letter of January 16, 1821 to Governor Martinez of Texas, stated that since a treaty of limits had been reached between Spain and the United States, and that the Sabine River would be the boundary, a great hardship would be worked on many families. Because of this boundary situation and a law passed by the United States Congress, which by treaty with the Choctaw Indians exchanged lands on the Tennessee River and the east bank of the Mississippi River for lands on the Arkansas River, many Anglo-American families in that area would be forced to abandon their homesites by the end of May, 1821. Therefore, these families would be available if they were allowed to settle in Texas.[8]

In the early part of 1821, Moses Austin returned to the United States. However the trip from Texas exhausted his health and he died in June of that year. Upon the death of the elder Austin, Stephen fell heir to what little possessions his father had, but now included with them was the grant to establish a colony in Texas.

By the middle of August of that year, Stephen Austin was in Texas. As he approached San Antonio he was met by a rider coming from that town who jubilantly reported the news of Mexican Independence. A short while later, when Austin arrived in the town, he was officially greeted by the governor. The governor suggested that Austin survey the area and select a suitable site for the establishment of the new colony.[9] The survey situated itself around the area near La Bahia and up the Colorado and Brazos

Rivers. During the latter part of August, Austin toured the countryside and arrived at La Bahia, which was in "a state of ruin" owing to the revolution and the many Indian raids. He found the inhabitants living very poorly and without any furnishings or utensils in their homes.[10] This depressing picture of the situation in Texas had been brought to Governor Martinez's attention by the ayuntamiento of Bexar and was not lost on him.[11] The governor felt, more now than ever before, that a concentrated effort to populate Texas was indispensable to the welfare of the nation. He, along with a number of other Mexican officials, felt that the easiest and least expensive way of accomplishing this was to offer sufficient encouragements so as to quickly bring foreigners into the province.[12]

The provincial authorities, on the assumption that the news of Austin's grant in the United States would cause a wave of unauthorized immigration, decided to take precautions. In order to deter any unauthorized immigration, a large force would be needed to protect, especially, the town of Nacogdoches in order ". . . to check and keep within respectful bounds the people of the United States . . . These people shall also be prevented from settling in our territory without the consent of the government, and under the express condition of being Catholic . . ."[13] For those people who were authorized, every possible encouragement was given, including free exportation and importation with the United States for a period of ten years. Also, to encourage the mechanical arts, agriculture and industry, each Interior Province would be supplied with families of farmers, mechanics, and tradesmen.[14]

The reaction to Austin's notices in the newspapers was encouraging. Soon potential settlers became quite interested in the prospects of the low priced land. It should be emphasized that Mexican land was much cheaper than land within the United States at this time. By the end of 1821, the flow of immigration had already begun in the midst of Mexican political upheavals occasioned by the recent independence movement.

The political situation in New Spain greatly changed from the time that Moses Austin first obtained his grant. By the Plan of Iguala, February 21, 1821, Colonel Augustin de Iturbide, a loyalist commander who defected to the rebels, and Vincente Guerrero, the rebel commander, joined forces and agreed that Mexico should proclaim its independence. Correspondingly, Spain repudiated the plan and, in August of that year, sent a military force, under the command of General Juan O'Donoju, to attempt to re-establish Spanish authority. The reconquest failed and O'Donoju, by the Treaty of Cordova, surrendered all troops under his command to Iturbide. Mexican independence became a reality.

The Treaty of Cordova also provided for a temporary government or junta which would function until such time that a European prince would accept the crown of Mexico. The junta, which had been nominated by Iturbide, set its task first to the creation of a regency with Iturbide at its head. It then proceeded to call a national representative Congress and passed out of existence in February, 1822. The national Congress, containing an excellent cross sample of Bourbonists, national monarchists and republicans, with the last of these beginning to dominate, immediately took under consideration the problems of foreign affairs and a general colonization law. However, its attempts to curtail the power of Iturbide as regent, brought on a crisis which was resolved by a staged public demonstration which demanded that Congress succumb and Iturbide be proclaimed emperor. The Congress yielded to the populace, which had invaded its halls, and elected Iturbide emperor under the title of Augustin I.[15]

The difficulties in Mexico were, to a degree, compounded by the presence in Mexico City of a number of foreigners seeking grants to establish colonies, especially in Texas. Given this situation the Committee on Colonization, created by the new Congress, had its suspicions aroused and acted slowly and deliberately so as to truly assess the situation in Texas. The welfare of the Mexican nation was paramount in the minds of the members:

> The situation of Texas, its fertility, and its abundant waters make it superior to any other province of the Empire. . . . These advantages and its proximity to the United States aroused some time ago the desire of the United States to possess it — a desire which they will satisfy if we do not take steps to prevent it. . . . The committee cannot conceal from the Congress that our neglect in this matter would bring upon Texas the fate of the Floridas.[16]

On January 4, 1823 a colonization law was approved and proclaimed, but was short lived.[17] Another political upheaval occurred and resulted in the abdication of Iturbide on March 19. The Mexican Congress reconvened and, as one of its first acts, abrogated all decrees proclaimed during the previous regime, including the Colonization Law of January 4, 1823.

Although Spain was never allowed to witness the realization of its policy of colonization and assimilation for Texas, that policy was continued, with slight modifications, by Mexico. There was no reason why there should have been any change, for many of the same colonial officials under the Spanish government continued to hold their positions under the newly created Mexican government. Although any attempts at colonization were temporarily suspended between January, 1823 and August, 1824, the only exception being the reconfirmation of Moses Austin's grant to Stephen Austin, this did not indicate that Mexico was abandoning the original Spanish policy. When Mexico did finally adopt and promulgate a new colonization law, it was not motivated by any equalitarian doctrine. Mexico, like Spain before her, did not trust its northern neighbor republic, who, on occasions, still believed the true boundary of the Louisiana Purchase to be the Rio Grande River.[18] The old problems which faced Spain now faced the young Mexican Republic. The monumental project of maintaining Texas and, with it, the northern boundaries of all of Mexico now became part of the Spanish legacy which Mexico inherited.

The Mexican nation was attempting to establish a government based upon a federal system. The Federalist Constitution of 1824, which was adopted, provided for a new colonization law which was enacted on August 18, 1824. The General Colonization Law provided an invitation to any foreigner desiring to settle in the republic providing they respect the laws. The law applied to lands not held by any other individual, corporation or town. Also any lands lying within twenty leagues of the boundary of any foreign nation, or ten leagues from the coast, could not be occupied by any settlers. Congress, according to the law, would not prohibit, until 1840, the admissions of any foreigners to colonize, except when circumstances obliged it to do so. The General Colonization Law *guaranteed the contracts which speculators [empresarios and contractors] might make with those families which they conveyed at their expense,* provided that the contracts were not contrary to the laws of the land. No one who obtained possession of any lands, could legally hold them if settled out of the territory of the Republic. The new colonization law provided that each of the Congresses of the States should frame laws and regulations regarding colonization and land distribution.[19]

It is of interest to note the reversed operations of the two federal republics of North America, the United States and Mexico, in their administration of the public domain. In the former, the various states claimed ownership of the lands within their respective boundaries and surrendered them to the national government. While the latter national government claimed ownership and surrendered them to the various states, for administrative purposes.

By virtue of the provision in the General Law which provided that state governments or legislators should enact colonization laws of their own, the state of Coahuila-Texas, officially joined in May, 1824, proceeded to enact laws governing foreign immigration and land distribution. It is of some interest to point out here two underlying factors of this decentralizing provision of the General Law. The first, obviously, being the very principles or philosophy of federalism and the second being a precedent created by the Spanish Cortes in a decree issued on April 15, 1820. This decree re-enacted the law of January 14, 1813 which authorized city councils and provisional assemblies to distribute public lands to any settler desirous of them in order to develop agriculture and commerce.

Enacted on March 24, 1825, the state colonization law of Coahuila-Texas was similar to the Colonization Law of January 4, 1823 in that it attempted to procure settlers for the unoccupied regions of that state by conferring large tracts of land upon individuals, who at their own expense would introduce large numbers of families into the area. This plan or system of land distribution was generally referred to as the Empresario system. The empresario was an agent who was hired by the Government to introduce a specific number of families of a certain description within a period of six years. When the empresario introduced the families, and if they were received by the Government Commissioner as being of the description required, then, and not before, was he entitled to receive his compensation. He would receive five leagues of land (22, 140 acres) for each one-hundred families introduced. However, any land that was left vacant in the colony once all the stated settlers had been placed, reverted to the government and did not become the property of the empresario. The empresario could hold a maximum of eight leagues.[20]

There were families who might immigrate without the assistance of an empresario. However this method did not result in the best way to acquire land. Families, operating independently, were required to petition the ayuntamiento. Since a great majority of these people knew little or no Spanish, an enormous problem existed. Too, the ayuntamiento lacked the procedural ability and means of conducting surveys, issuing titles and recording them properly. Also, such free land as existed was soon divided into all encompassing empresario grants. In order to settle any area permission of the given empresario was needed. Therefore it became a matter of prudence to become a member of an empresario's colony.[21]

The state colonization law reiterated, to some extent, the national law by emphasizing the prohibition of grants in those areas which were specifically set aside as federal reserves; the prohibition of settlements within twenty leagues of the Mexican-United States boundary; and within ten leagues of the Gulf of Mexico. The law also stipulated that preference in land distribution was to be given to those elements who were continually and directly connected with the military service of the colony and to all Mexicans, even if they were not connected with the military directly. Indians were allowed to trade in the settlements, and once they had achieved a certain stage in being civilized, they were to be admitted to the colony and would receive land on the same and equal terms as all other colonists; only Mexicans were allowed to hold the maximum of eleven leagues of land.

The colonization law of Coahuila-Texas also restated the right, to be exercised by the federal government, to regulate and even to exclude immigrants from any given nation. With regard to the issue of slavery, the law only stated that the new settlers were subject to the then existing laws and any future laws which might be enacted on the subject at a later date. In anticipation of any labor shortage that might occur if the introduction of slaves or slavery itself were prohibited, the government authorized the utilization of all vagrants and criminals in the area for military service, for use on public works, and to be hired out to individuals.[22]

Contained in the state colonization law was a provision which was highly indicative of an attempt to control colonization and colonists to meet a desired end. This was the requirement that all colonists should be Catholic in faith, or should soon become so after admittance. The emphasis on Catholicism soon became a dead letter in that both the empresarios and the Mexican officials tended merely to overlook the requirement most of the time. If this provision had been strictly enforced it is almost certain that any plan as that of the empresario system certainly would have been destined to failure. The Mexican officials themselves certainly sensed that the enforcement of this provision would defeat the system.[23]

However, and probably unknown to the Mexican authorities, the religious requirement had a leveling effect upon religious extremists in the United States. The extremists were, no doubt, repelled by the requirement to be, or become Catholic, and therefore did not migrate. Those who did migrate were not moved by this stipulation. Although the overt practices of any Protestant clergy were not tolerated, the Anglo-American Protestants were seldom, if ever, exposed to any evangelizing efforts on the part of the Mexican Catholic clergy. It appears that the settlers accepted the situation with little or no anxiety.[24] Perhaps the officials felt, that since the colonists were not strongly opposed to the measure, they might in time, become assimilated into the dominant culture and eventually accept the Catholic faith. The authorities indirectly tried to promote this end by granting more land to anyone who happened to marry a Mexican woman.

The Colonization Law of the State of Coahuila-Texas laid down certain requirements and stipulations which one was to follow in order to obtain an empresario contract. The wording of the law and that of the contract were identical for all with the only exception being a general description of the boundaries of each contract.[25]

Any prospective empresario was required to present a formal petition to the state assembly asking for permission to colonize certain areas, which were open to colonization and indicate the actual number of families to be introduced. All land distribution was to be under the control of a commissioner, appointed by the state, who could make no assignments without the expressed consent and approval of the empresario. All the land that was not distributed would then revert to the public domain of the state. The empresario agreed to introduce the stipulated number of families within a period of six years. If the required families were not introduced within the time alloted, the empresario's compensations were reduced proportionately. The entire contract was declared void if the empresario failed to introduce, within the time alloted, the minimum of one-hundred families. However, the empresario was granted "premium land" which consisted of five leagues, or 22,140 acres, of grazing land and five labors, or 885 acres, of tillage land for every one hundred families he introduced. The maximum of "premium land" that an empresario could personally accumulate could not exceed the premium obtainable from the introduction of eight hundred families.[26]

Although the problems encountered by any empresario were great, the premium land which he could receive would certainly be worth the effort on his part. From the figures given above, it would seem that an empresario, who did manage to introduce the maximum amount of eight hundred families, would become the possessor of an enormous holding: 177,120 acres of grazing land and 7,080 acres of tillage land. However, according to the colonization law, no empresario could hold more than eight leagues, or 35,424 acres. Therefore the empresario would have to dispose of the excess, 148,776 acres, by means of sale. If he were unable to dispose of his excess, all or that portion which remained unsold would revert to the public domain within a period of twelve years.[27]

Once the empresario had been granted a certain area to colonize, further requirements were made of him. He was bound to recognize all legal titles existing within the geographic area of his grant. He was cautioned to admit only those who were Catholic, or who soon intended to become so, and to be aware of their moral character. He was to organize and command the militia, receiving the rank of colonel. When the empresario's colony had at least one hundred families, he was to inform the government so that the latter could appoint the much needed commissioner to issue the titles and attempt to establish a town. When the town was established, a school was to be organized where the Spanish language was to be taught. Also a Catholic Church was to be built and a priest obtained within a reasonable time.[28]

The empresario system, in theory, was an excellent means of colonization in that it made the question of success or failure of the colony a question of financial success or failure for the empresario.

When the news of Moses Austin's grant circulated in the United States there were, no doubt, men there willing to risk everything, like Austin, in the hope of success. These men, encouraged by Stephen Austin's earlier success, were soon in Mexico City and each was seeking the same goal, the procurement of a land grant. One such man was Green De Witt of Missouri.[29]

The De Witt family, like so many others from western Virginia, Kentucky, and Tennessee, were part of that phenomenon of the "moving frontier." When Green De Witt's father moved into Spanish Louisiana the brunt of the Anglo-American population was not yet formidable. The agricultural frontier, with its greater population, lay far east of the Mississippi River. But in less than a generation's time, men like the De Witts, Kerrs, Austins, and Smiths were becoming a grave threat to Mexico, a greater threat than Spain ever faced. The leading edge of the Anglo-American population was poised on the fringe of Texas by the time Green De Witt was thirty-two years of age. These farmers, stock raisers, merchants, lawyers, land speculators, and promoters, and all other forms of fortune seekers were always on the lookout for an honest dollar, and, at times, even a dishonest one. Although they were always hard pressed for credit and ready money, they were rich with tradition. They were endowed with a tradition of experience, inherited from restless pioneering ancestors. Green De Witt was one such heir, a "budding entrepreneur" of the frontier.

De Witt was born in Lincoln County, Kentucky on February 12, 1787. While he was yet an infant, the De Witt family moved to Spanish-held Missouri. Nothing is known of De Witt's father's activities there.[30] It can be assumed that the family was in possession of some means since Green De Witt was given an education beyond the mere rudimentary level.[31] When he was eighteen, he returned to Kentucky to complete his education. He remained in Kentucky for two years and then returned to Missouri. Soon after his return De Witt married Sarah Seely. She was born in 1789 in northwestern Virginia. She was a woman of refinement and culture and a descendant of a family which had fought in the Revolutionary War. Her parents migrated from Brooks County, Virginia[32] and settled in Saint Louis County, Missouri.[33]

During the War of 1812, De Witt served with the Missouri state militia. He entered that service as a private and received a number of promotions. By the end of the war, he attained the rank of lieutenant. At the time of his resignation from the state militia, he held the rank of captain. In Missouri he was active in politics, and even served as the sheriff of Ralls County.[34] By 1821, the news of the Austin grant had caused a great stir in the Mississippi Valley and primarily in Missouri. No doubt the news made an impression on De Witt for in that year he left for Mexico City to procure a similar grant.

He arrived in that capital in 1822 and his presence added to the growing number of foreigners already in Mexico City. A multitude of reasons accounted for their presence there. However, a majority of them were seeking to present petitions for land grants.[35] It does not appear that De Witt was as avid in pressing his petition as were Stephen Austin, Hayden Edwards, Frost Thorn, Robert Leftwich, or James Wilkinson. After a stay of three months, De Witt returned to Missouri without ever having presented his petition for the land grant. Although his first trip to Mexico was in vain, it introduced him to the intricate workings of Mexican politics, an entirely new experience for him. No doubt he was dismayed by the unfortunate and chaotic events occurring there and came away disillusioned. During his trip to and from Mexico City, however, he became very impressed with Texas.[36]

When the news of the Federal Colonization Law of 1824 was circulated in Missouri, De Witt returned to Texas. Once more he hoped to obtain a land grant. In Texas, he visited the few Anglo-Americans in Austin's grant. There he met a number of the prominent and influential men. Among them was Stephen Austin. He had not met Austin when both of them were in Mexico City in 1822. He was introduced to Austin by virtue of a letter of recommendation written for De Witt by Judge William Trimble in June, 1824.[37]

As has already been mentioned, the General Colonization Law provided that the various states of the Mexican republic should administer the disposal of the public domain. Accordingly, De Witt had to journey to Saltillo, the state capital of Coahuila-Texas, in order to present his petition. He arrived there by December, 1824. Upon his arrival he found that the state colonization law had not as yet been passed. While awaiting the passage of the law, he spent most of his time making acquaintances and writing Austin for advice. From their very first meeting De Witt placed great trust in Austin. Throughout his entire career as an empresario, De Witt continually sought Austin's advice and assistance ". . . and anything more that you can consistently do to insure a permission of the settlement petition for which I wish to locate somwhere in this Province; your compliance will ever be remembered by your friend and Humble Servant."[38]

Austin did comply. On January 8, 1825, he wrote the Baron de Bastrop, the representative of Texas in the state congress, and a personal friend of Austin, and informed him of De Witt's plans. He recommended De Witt and asked Bastrop to aid in any possible way. He requested Bastrop to exert his influence in order that De Witt might procure the grant.[39] Austin's recommendation and Bastrop's assistance were definitely factors in De Witt's success in obtaining a grant.

De Witt officially petitioned the government on April 7, 1825.

> . . . I, Green De Witt, a citizen of the United States of North America, appear before your excellency to make known to you that I have come to this country seeking to obtain permission to colonize with four hundred industrious Catholic families those lands of the ancient province of Texas, now an integral portion of this State, which are included within the limits that I shall here designate. These immigrants shall be required to subject themselves to the religious, civil, and political laws of the country which henceforth they adopt as their own, and in establishing themselves therein, they shall respect the rights of all previous settlers, as provided by the colonization law which the honorable congress of this state has just passed. Moreover, there shall be brought into this colony only such families as are known to be respectable and industrious. I therefore beg you to grant me, your petitioner, those lands that are included within the following limits, in order that I may settle upon them the four hundred above mentioned: Beginning on the right bank of Arroyo de la Vaca at a distance of the reserved ten leagues from the coast, adjoining the colony of Stephen Austin on the east, the line shall go up the river to the Bejar-Nacogdoches road; it shall follow this road until it reaches a point two leagues to the west of Guadalupe River; thence it shall run parallel with the river down to the Paraje de las Mosquitos; and following the inner edge of the ten league coast reservation, it shall close the boundaries of the grant at the point of beginning.
>
> We are also desirous that respectable families of this country[40] shall come to settle with us, not only in order to contract enduring friendship with them, but also in order to acquire the use of the language of the nation that we now adopt as our own and the ability to give perfect instruction therein to our children. Therefore, I humbly beg you to grant my petition.[41]

De Witt's grant was approved on April 15, 1825. It was situated in the area southwest of Austin's grant. The boundaries of the De Witt grant began on the right bank of the Lavaca River at a point ten leagues, or 30 nautical miles from the Texas coastline. The line, following the course of the river, ran in a northwesternly direction till it reached the headwater of the Lavaca, a distance of 85 miles. From there, the boundary line was projected due north till it reached the Old San Antonio Road, a distance of 28 miles. The line then followed along that road for 65 miles to a point two leagues, or six nautical miles, from where the road crossed the Guadalupe River. Then the line ran in a southeasterly direction, for 110 miles, paralleling the Guadalupe, until it reached a point ten leagues or 30 nautical miles, from the coast. From here, the closing line, 25 miles in length, was run to its point of origin on the Lavaca River.[42] (See map on page 54)

De Witt was authorized to introduce four hundred families. More than 75,000 acres were set aside for him as his "premium land."[43] One fourth of this "premium land" was obtainable after the first one hundred families were introduced. The remainder was obtained on a pro-rated basis until the maximum amount of "premium land" was reached. The confirmation of the grant carried with it certain requirements for De Witt. He was to respect the ownership rights of any individuals who might already legally possess land within his grant;[44] to introduce at least one hundred families or forfeit all of the rights and privileges; to guarantee that the colonists were not "criminals, vagrants, or persons of bad morals"; to obtain from the colonists certificates which attested to their good character; to organize a militia and command it until such time that other arrangements were made; to advise the state government when the mini-

53

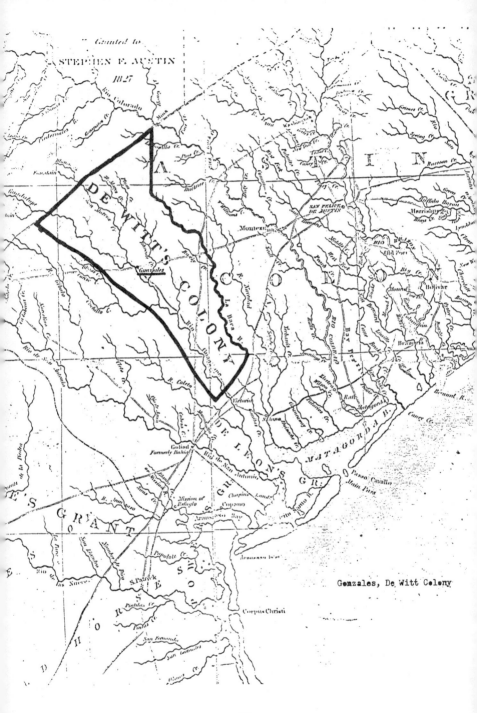

Gonzales, De Witt Colony

mum of one hundred families were introduced so that a land commissioner could be assigned to issue the titles; to establish towns; to write all official correspondence with the government and all public documents in Spanish; to establish schools where Spanish was to be taught; to erect churches in the towns; to provide the church with "ornaments, sacred vessels, and other adornments dedicated to divine worship"; to apply for the services of a priest who was to administer spiritual instructions; and to respect and be guided by the "constitution, general laws of the nation, and the specific laws of the state."[45]

It is of interest to point out that, unlike Stephen Austin, Green De Witt had not previously inspected the area of his grant. No doubt he had been encouraged by Austin to request that given area. If the De Witt colonization project were a success, it would provide, because of its geographic position, greater protection for the left flank of the Austin grant. The Mexican authorities also desired to populate that area included in the De Witt grant. General Anastacio Bustamante, commander of the Interior Provinces, recommended to Iturbide in 1822 that the Austin settlement be located in the area of the abandoned missions of San Jose and Concepcion in order to add strength to that portion of the Mexican frontier.[46] Although Austin did not locate his colony there, a sizable portion of that area was included in the De Witt grant.

With his business completed, De Witt left Saltillo by the end of April. He intended to visit and inspect the area of his grant, but was delayed. He was charged by Peter Ellis Bean[47] with having misappropriated public funds. The charges were heard by the jefe-politico at San Antonio who appointed Stephen Austin to investigate the matter. The exact nature of these "public funds" in question or what interest Bean had with them are unknown. But, in any event, De Witt was found innocent by Austin. He was exonerated from the charge on October 17, 1825.[48] Once again the influence and friendship of Austin proved beneficial to Green De Witt. With that unpleasant matter settled, De Witt proceeded with the pressing business of establishing the colony.

Green De Witt, of course, was not the only recipient of a land grant. There were twenty-eight such grants given between the years 1825 and 1832.[49] His success, and that of the other empresarios, in obtaining a grant was realized because of a given set of circumstances existing, at that time, on both the Anglo-American frontier and the Mexican frontier.

The Anglo-Americans were starving for land, cheap land, which the Mexican government had to offer in Texas. The colonists, on the other hand, had stability to offer and, it was hoped, would become the factor which was to hold the northern fringe of Mexico intact against anyone who might attempt to divest it from the Mexican nation. But was not this policy highly dangerous in itself? It seemed so to the English charge'd'affaire in Mexico, Henry G. Ward, who warned the Mexican government of the dangers inherent in allowing the immigration of Anglo-Americans into Texas. His sole aim was to arouse the Mexican government's fear and prejudices against Anglo-American immigrants and the ulterior designs of the government of the United States. He used the incident of the Floridas as an excellent example. He even had published a map of Texas, with its empresario grants, which was intended to demonstrate to the Mexican government the insatiable appetite of all Anglo-Americans for land. He predicted that the new inhabitants would, some day, attempt to place the province under the protection of the United States.[50] However, the policy which was dictated by expediency and necessity had already been decided upon.

During the Spanish period and under the Mexican empresario system, some twenty-six million acres of land in Texas were distributed. It has been estimated that 5,000 land titles were issued by Spain and Mexico. However, the records in the Texas General Land Office reveal only 4,200 titles having been issued.[51] In any event, the land grant system, primarily under Mexico, provided a substantial increase in the population of Texas. In 1821, there were only 3,334 inhabitants.[52] In just a six year period, and primarily during the years 1825 to 1827, the total population had more than tripled and amounted to approximately 12,000.[53] The population numbered well over 25,000 by 1830.[54] Although the overall number of inhabitants was increasing the Mexican population remained relatively the same as in 1821 and was definitely in the minority by 1827. The Mexican population, centered around the areas of San Antonio and La Bahia, accounted for less than one-third of the entire population. The entire eastern portion of Texas was solely inhabited by Anglo-Americans and the English language and customs were dominant.[55] Of the Anglo-Americans in Texas, almost nine out of every ten came from some frontier section of the United States. Alabama accounted for twenty-one percent, Tennessee for sixteen and one-half percent, Mississippi for fifteen and one-half percent, Arkansas Territory for ten percent, Georgia and Louisiana for nine percent, Missouri for seven percent, and the remainder came primarily from Kentucky, Illinois, Ohio, southern Indiana and the Carolinas.[56]

3

The Colony at Gonzales and "Old Station"

By October of 1825 Green De Witt, with his petition confirmed, was ready to launch his career as an empresario. In January of that year he had appointed James Kerr as his surveyor-general. De Witt had faith in Austin's influence and was confident that through it he would receive the grant. Apparently De Witt was so confident, as Stephen Austin pointed out in a report to the jefe-politico in 1826, that he appointed his surveyor months before the grant was confirmed.[1]

The work that Kerr performed for De Witt and the colony was invaluable. It can safely be said that without Kerr's assistance, De Witt's efforts would have been fruitless. He merits as much credit as De Witt for laying the foundation of the colony, and in some instances more.

James Kerr was the first Anglo-American settler west of the Colorado River. A son of a Baptist preacher, he was born two miles from Danville, Kentucky on September 27, 1790. In 1808 the Kerr family moved to Missouri and settled in Saint Charles County.[2] He participated in the War of 1812, in which he won distinction by his heroic deeds. During a skirmish near Fort Mason, Kerr, alone held a war party of Indians at bay. His action saved the lives of two wounded men.[3] He was commissioned a lieutenant and served with Captain Nathan Boone, the son of the famous Daniel Boone. After the war, he read law under a prominent attorney. However, Kerr never practiced that profession, since he neither had the talent nor the desire. For a time, he was the sheriff of Saint Charles County.[4]

In 1819 he married the daughter of General James Caldwell of Saint Genevieve, the influential Speaker of the Territorial House of Representatives. Kerr then moved to Saint Genevieve where he was twice elected to the legislature. In 1824 he was elected to the Missouri state senate, became interested in the colonizing activities in Texas, and soon resigned his seat.[5] He left Missouri in 1825 with his family and slaves. At this time, his main concern was with the status of slavery in Texas. The only information he received, in regard to this matter, was that previous experience showed that slaves were taken into Texas with no difficulty encountered with the government.[6]

He remained in Brazoria, an Austin colony settlement until June. A month earlier he lost his wife and two of his three children there. After leaving his last child with friends in San Felipe, he took up his duties as De Witt's surveyor-general. In the company of Erastus Deaf Smith, Bazil Durbin, Geron Hinds, John Wightman, James Musick, and a Mr. Strickland, he set out to select the site for the capital of the colony.[7] The group traveled west from Brazoria until they reached the spot where the Guadalupe and San Marcos rivers joined. Kerr selected this site because of the abundant water supply. The group erected a few crude cabins on what came to be known as Kerr's Creek, a mile east of the present town of Gonzales. Kerr then drew up the plan for the proposed town. He named the site Gonzales in honor of the governor of Coahuila-Texas, Don Rafael Gonzales.[8] The Kerr party busied itself surveying the town itself and the four leagues of land assigned to every capital town. Their surveying efforts were continually hampered by the hostility of the Indians.

De Witt arrived at Gonzales by the latter part of October. He remained at the site for three or four weeks. He inspected the work that had already been done and made future plans for a more complete survey. In November, he left Gonzales and returned to Missouri by way of Nacogdoches, but altered his plans at the Trinity River crossing. Instead he decided to go to New Orleans and, from there, ascend the Mississippi.[9] The route by way of New Orleans was safer and, above all, was less time consuming.

Near the Trinity crossing, De Witt encountered Frost Thorn, in the company of Hayden Edwards.[10] De Witt intended to see Thorn on his way to Missouri in order to settle some financial matters. From De Witt's letter to James Kerr, it appears that Thorn had, in some fashion, provided financial aid. De Witt intended to reimburse him by issuing him land scrip.

> I arrived at this place [Trinity] a few days since and after resting two or three days, proceeded on my journey; but after traveling a few miles, was agreeably surprised to meet Colonel Haden [sic] Edwards and Frost Thorn, my partner, which saves me a long trip, as I shall not go by Nacogdoches, as was contemplated when I left you. They are on their way to San Felipe de

Austin, where I hope you will have the pleasure of seeing them. Whether you meet Colonel Thorn or not, should he call on you for one or two hundred dollars in Guadalupe land office money, you will please fill his order . . . It would be well for you to let it be known that all who apply for settlement must produce certificates of good character and industry. You will complete the survey of the town and permit its settlement accordingly. . . .

  I shall proceed on my journey tomorrow [sic] and hope to return in April next.[11]

The land scrip which De Witt issued to Thorn, and, eventually, to others, appears to be the first form of paper money used in Texas. There is much doubt surrounding the speculation that an earlier form of paper money was authorized by the Mexican government. This doubt arises from the fact that no evidence of the notes, supposedly issued by a bank in San Antonio, has ever been discovered. De Witt, in need of funds, resorted to the practice of issuing this handwritten currency in amounts of five, ten, and twenty dollars. These notes, soon became transferable and were used as a mode of exchange.[12] The pioneer-historian John Henry Brown, who was in possession of some of these notes has left a description of them.

Here is a literal copy of his [De Witt's] bills. I have eight such in my possession, the chirography of all equal to the finest copy plate:
'No. 2. This bill will be received as a cash payment for ten dollars on account of fees for land in De Witt's Colony. 'River Guadalupe, district of Gonzales, 15th day of October, 1825. Green De Witt, Empresario.'[13]

Either by the end of 1825 or the first part of 1826, the exact date being unknown, De Witt was back in Missouri. During his trip up the Mississippi, he advertised the unlimited opportunities available in Texas, particularly in his own colony. Frank W. Johnson related that he met his old friend, Green De Witt, in Natchez. It seemed that Johnson had suffered from a recurring case of malaria and the attending physician suggested he seek a healthier climate. When Johnson related this situation to De Witt, the latter intensified his glorifying reports about the colony.[14]

While in Missouri, De Witt spent most of his time advertising the settlement and preparing to organize his colonists. He did find time, however, to deliver some letters to Austin's friends and relatives.[15] By March, De Witt finished his business and was prepared to return to Texas.[16] In April, he and his small party of colonists set out for Texas. The party was composed of four families. The De Witt family consisted of De Witt himself, his wife, his two sons, Christopher Columbus and Clinton, and three of the four daughters, Naomi, Evaline, and Minerva. The youngest child, Eliza, was left in New London, Missouri, to finish school.[17] She did, however, join the family two years later. The three other families from Missouri had accompanied the De Witts were the Stephens, Locklands, and Reynolds.[18]

The small party came down the Mississippi River to New Orleans. There De Witt chartered a schooner to transport them to the mouth of the Lavaca River on the Texas coast. From the coast, the De Witt party would then head inland. The coastal schooner's inability to navigate the waters of the Gulf of Mexico delayed the party almost two months in reaching its destination. By July, De Witt and his colonists lay anchored in Lavaca Bay. He sent word of his arrival to Kerr, who, at that time, was at a site known as "Old Station." He informed Kerr that he was hesitant to land since Indians had been sighted in the vicinity. He requested that Kerr bring assistance at once. Kerr readily complied and in his letter to Austin succintly wrote that ". . . [De Witt] is afraid to land on account of the Indians that are in the neighbor-hood. . . ."[19] Kerr soon found De Witt and the colonists and escorted them to "Old Station," some six miles up the Lavaca River.[20]

The tiny settlement known as "Old Station" was established during the time De Witt was in the United States. As has already been mentioned, James Kerr and his surveying party erected a number of crude cabins on the banks of Kerr's Creek at the Gonzales site. Some weeks after the Kerr party arrived, the first family of Anglo-American immigrants came. Francis Berry and his family, from Missouri, settled near by on Kerr's Creek. In the Berry family were John and Elizabeth Oliver, grown children of Mrs. Berry by a previous marriage.[21] This small gathering of fifteen immigrants and three of Kerr's slaves was the total population of Gonzales from August, 1825 to July, 1826. However a number of individuals visited the small settlement in 1825 and expected to return sometime during the following year.[22]

These early settlers of Gonzales did not, at first, find life too exacting. Despite the settlement's isolation, their larders were never empty. They found subsistence easy since the area abounded in bear, antelope, and deer. Bread was made from Indian corn and honey was always available. The only scarce item was coffee. It was considered by Texan frontiersmen an absolute necessity and not a mere luxury.

The only real danger the settlement faced was the Indian menace. At first relations between the two races were friendly. The various tribes that passed through the area seemed to have tolerated the presence of the colonists. However, by July, 1826, the situation changed. Gonzales was attacked. It was the first of many setbacks that the De Witt colony was to have.

The attack was not a direct attempt to obliterate the settlement; it was merely a horse-stealing raid. If it had been anything more there would have been greater damage inflicted. However, this raid was sufficient to force all the De Witt colonists from the area. They fled for the sanctuary of Austin's colony on the Colorado River, "not knowing what to do."[23]

When the attack occurred a number of the colonists were not at the site. James Kerr was in Brazoria making future plans for the colony.[24] Erastus Deaf Smith and Geron Hinds were on a buffalo hunt. A small party consisting of Bazil Durbin, John Oliver, Betsy Oliver, and Jack, Kerr's Negro slave, left Gonzales on July 2 to attend a Fourth of July celebration at the Atascosita crossing on the Colorado River. James Musick, Mr. Strickland, and Kerr's Negro slaves, Shade and Anise, left to spend the day at Francis Berry's place, a few miles from Gonzales. Only John Wightman remained.[25]

The group that set out for the Atascosita crossing was fourteen miles out of Gonzales when they encamped for the night. Around midnight they were surprised by a party of Indians. Durbin was badly wounded in the shoulder but managed to escape in the nearby thickets. The other members of the party, unharmed but badly shaken, also escaped in the thickets. The Indians soon departed with all of the blankets, horses, and goods. The colonists made their way back to Gonzales and by noon had arrived. Instead of finding the sanctuary they hoped for, they found the body of John Wightman. He had been killed attempting to defend the cabin. The interior of the cabin was disturbed and robbed of important papers, books, and surveying instruments. The exterior of the cabin showed signs of an unsuccessful attempt to burn it. Also all of the horses were taken. The group then went to Francis Berry's cabin. When they arrived there, they found it deserted. On the door of the cabin written with charcoal were the words: "Gone to Burnham's on the Colorado."[26] They quickly followed.

The retreat to the Colorado River took three and a half days. They were delayed by Durbin's condition. There was a fear that his wound might become gangrenous, but this was prevented by the administration of a mud and oak juice poultice. They arrived at Burnham's on July 6 and were joyfully welcomed by the Berrys, Musick, and Strickland. A few days later, the refugees were joined by Erastus Deaf Smith and Hinds.[27] With this incident, the first phase of the establishment of the colony at Gonzales ended on a dismal note.

Through the efforts of James Kerr the colonists did not disband. The De Witt Colony, although small and dislocated, still remained a reality. Kerr realized that the area around Gonzales could not be sustained with the small number of immigrants. Since he was De Witt's unofficial representiave he took it upon himself to procure another site.[28] He decided that a settlement nearer the coast would be beneficial to the colony. He journeyed to San Antonio to obtain permission for his change. He believed that the jefe-politico should allow the colonists to settle at the mouth of the river rather than be required to move into the interior. Kerr's request was in part denied. The Mexican authorities saw nothing objectionable in establishing a port to receive colonists, but the request to settle permanently was denied.[30] It should be recalled that the National Colonization Law and the State Colonization Law prohibited settlement within the ten league coastal reserve.[31] It was not so much Kerr's ignorance of the law but rather a misinterpretation of it by him. He, along with a good number of settlers, thought the ten leagues began with the off shore islands rather than the coast of the bay itself.[32]

When De Witt arrived from the United States Kerr informed him of the events at Gonzales and pointed out the desirability of establishing a site at the Lavaca, or "Old Station." De Witt, however, never intended that the Lavaca site should become an area of permanent settlement, but merely a convenient port of entry for immigrants "destined for the colonies."[33] De Witt realized the danger involved in attempting to settle Gonzales with so few colonists. He decided to locate them at "Old Station" ". . . in order that we may be more secure from the Indians. . . ."[34] He postponed the move into the interior ". . . until we can collect strength enough to venture out on our lands. . . ."[35] The Mexican authorities, sympathetic to the plight of the De Witt colonists, appreciated the utility and advantage of the Lavaca settlement. Although De Witt's action was a direct violation of the law, Jose Antonio Saucedo, the jefe-politico, conditionally sanctioned it.

Kerr had only begun the work at "Old Station" when De Witt returned from the United States, in July of 1826. The small settlement was located on the west bank of the Lavaca River, some six miles from the coast. It was officially referred to as "Station of the Labaca" by Kerr and De Witt, but, after a while, most referred to it as "Old Station." At first the settlement could offer only a few blockhouses which were built by Kerr.[37] By September of 1826 the settlement was well underway. De Witt contracted for a four year period the services of the fifty ton schooner, *Dispatch*, mastered by W. J. Russel. The craft was to convoy immigrants and cargo to the colony. De Witt arranged for the construction of a thirty by twelve foot flat boat. The flat boat was to shuttle immigrants and supplies from the *Dispatch*, to the shore. De Witt also contracted for the building of a warehouse at or near the mouth of the Lavaca River. The warehouse would be of value to both the newly arrived settlers and those who were already established.[38]

The colonists themselves erected cabins and planted a corn crop. However, it should be pointed out, that they were not in legal possession of the lands which they occupied. Since they were located in the prescribed ten league coastal area, no land titles were issued or, for that matter, could be issued.[39] By October the population had grown to some forty persons and a form of governmental organization was necessary. Consequently, the jefe-politico appointed James Norton as temporary alcalde.[40]

The De Witt colony was only a few months old when it received another setback. The problem, at first, only involved Green De Witt and James Kerr, but, before it was over, the entire colony at "Old Station" would feel the effect.

The problem arose from a dispute with the neighboring empresario, Martin De Leon, over land claims and the issue of contraband trade. The difficulty over the land claims began soon after De Witt first obtained his grant. While on his way to inspect the work which had been done at Gonzales by the Kerr party, he noted that a portion of his grant had been already occupied by settlers. These were twelve of the forty-one Mexican families who had been given permission to settle by the empresario, Martin De Leon.

While on a cattle drive from his ranch in Tamaulipas to New Orleans, De Leon passed through southeastern Texas in 1823. Impressed by the fertility of that region, he obtained an informal grant in April, 1824 from the Provincial Deputation of San Fernando de Bexar. De Leon was authorized to settle Mexican families on any unoccupied lands between the lower Lavaca and Guadalupe Rivers. The grant, however, did not specify the exact boundaries or the exact number of families which he was required to introduce. By October of the following year, his grant received sanction under the state colonization law and, acting under the order given him by the commandant of the Interior Provinces, De Leon removed forty-one Mexican families from Tamaulipas to the lower Guadalupe River.

The area in which some of the De Leon colonists had settled was in a portion of De Witt's grant. To make matters worse for De Witt, these colonists already had begun the cultivation of their crops and had organized a flourishing town at Guadalupe Victoria.[42] The problem was one of simple legality. The fact that De Leon's grant predated that of De Witt, strengthened the former's case. But more so the stipulation contained in the colonization laws which provided that any empresario must respect existing land claims, provided De Leon and his colonists with all the security they needed. De Witt could do nothing.

De Witt, however, seemed to press the matter by writing the governor to suggest that De Leon be compensated with lands along the Guadalupe River in exchange for his lands along the Lavaca River. De Leon also wrote the governor and cited the passages of the colonization law as they related to the situation. By October, 1825 the governor ended the dispute by ordering the land commissioner to sanction the titles of the De Leon colonists and to inform De Witt of the decision.[43] In 1826, James Kerr continued the matter, maintaining that granting both banks of the Lavaca River to De Witt would be beneficial to the welfare of the colony.[44] The controversy made De Leon extremely suspicious of De Witt's motives and hindered any cordial relations that could have existed between the two empresarios. The difficulty, as seen in relation to subsequent events, did precipitate De

Leon's lasting emnity for Green De Witt and his entire colony. At least this is the way James Kerr interpreted the situation. He wrote Austin that while he was on his way to assist De Witt in July of 1826, he found a small boat that had been destroyed. The boat, left on Garcitas Creek, was owned by one of the De Witt colonists. Kerr maintained that it could be proven that De Leon or his sons had been responsible for its destruction.[45] Kerr did not elaborate on how the proof was arrived at, but nevertheless, he believed it and found no difficulty in convincing De Witt. When De Witt was later accused of allowing contraband trade, Kerr was convinced that De Leon was responsible.

The question of contraband trade and the trouble it engendered had lasting effects upon both De Witt and his colony. The problem began when Thomas Powell of Missouri landed at the mouth of the Lavaca River in October, 1826. He arrived with a great deal of property and hoped to settle in the area for reasons of health. He claimed to have obtained from De Witt permission to settle in the colony and to land and store his cargo of goods at "Old Station." These goods he intended to sell to the colonists.[46]

On the same schooner which brought Powell was another passenger by the name of Dr. Oliver. He was a Frenchman by birth but was now an officer of the Mexican army. During the voyage he made Powell's acquaintance and offered to assist him in selling the cargo of goods. Among the many items contained in the Powell cargo was a great quantity of tobacco, an item which was emphatically proscribed by Mexican tariff regulations. The presence of the great store of tobacco prompted someone to inform the authorities and soon the entire cargo was seized. Many arrived at the conclusion that it was Dr. Oliver who informed De Leon of the tobacco and that both men informed the authorities and were responsible for having the cargo confiscated.[47]

Within a few days the entire cargo was released, with the exception of the tobacco.[48] For some undetermined reason, the authorities suddenly reversed their position and ordered that the entire cargo be confiscated once more. Martin De Leon, assisted by the garrison at La Bahia, was authorized to take the cargo. Martin De Leon and Rafael Manchola, the military commander of La Bahia, started for "Old Station" determined to carry out the assignment. When the nature of De Leon's task was circulated at "Old Station" the settlers there became alarmed. Distorted reports were circulating that the Mexicans intended to stamp out the settlement and that De Leon boasted he would return with De Witt's head tied to his saddle.[49] The colonists were persuaded by Kerr, who managed to maintain his composure in this very strained situation, not to resort to any drastic action, primarily that of firing upon the garrison. When De Leon and Manchola arrived they convinced the population that no harm would come to them. They only desired the contraband goods. The garrison soon seized the cargo. When De Leon and Manchola departed for La Bahia they took De Witt with them. No reason or explanation, according to Kerr, was given for this action.[50]

What occurred at La Bahia is not absolutely clear, but it is known that Kerr requested the intervention of the jefe-politico. He asked that official to have the individuals involved in the matter appear in San Antonio. Both Kerr and De Witt wrote Austin and asked him to intercede in the matter.[51] The entire proceedings seemed to have been dropped, for by December 13, 1826, De Witt was back at "Old Station" going about his business of running the colony.[52] Probably the jefe-politico, and even the governor, desired that the matter be settled since the evidence implicating De Witt was questionable.

The controversy, however, did do irreparable damage. The authorities, fearing the recurrence of such an incident and the possible conflict between the De Witt and De Leon colonies, began to question the policy of allowing the De Witt colonists to settle, even temporarily, at "Old Station." The incident also convinced Kerr, who never really trusted De Leon, that Dr. Oliver had been bribed by the Mexican empresario. Kerr felt that the entire proceedings, after the first confiscation, had been instigated and designed by De Leon, especially the apprehending of De Witt.[53] James Norton, the temporary alcalde at "Old Station," was also convinced of De Leon's complicity in the matter. Norton claimed that Dr. Oliver approached him with a scheme in mind. Dr. Oliver planned to ruin De Witt's reputation with the government. Once De Witt's reputation became suspect, his empresario contract would soon be nullified. When this occurred, Dr. Oliver would recommend Norton for the vacated contract. Norton for his part was required to do only one thing. In his report to the governor, Norton was to state that Dr. Oliver was responsible for uncovering the contraband goods. Norton, however, refused to be a party to this plan. He claimed that De Witt's actions or intentions were never illegal.[54]

De Witt had been totally unnerved by the whole affair. He admitted that he knew of Powell's entrance into the colony but claimed he never gave him permission to settle or to sell his goods. De Witt, however, admitted that he became very concerned over the large quantity of the prohibited tobacco. However, he came to believe that Powell was merely decoyed and tricked by Dr. Oliver's tactics. He felt that it was through the scheming efforts of Martin De Leon that the cargo was seized. The entire affair, in De Witt's mind, was designed to ruin his colonizing efforts.[55] From that time on De Witt made a conscious effort to inform the government of all unorthodox activities that occurred within his colony. He seemed to have been making a special effort not to become involved in a similar incident.[56]

No sooner did the contraband trade controversy subside, when the outbreak of the Fredonian Rebellion caused De Witt and his colonists some concern. The rebellion stemmed from difficulties over land titles in the empresario colony of Hayden Edwards. Edwards, in 1825, received an empresario grant to a large area of eastern Texas. Within the boundaries of the grant were a number of Mexicans who received lands in that area during the Spanish period. Any titles that were issued and registered were lost during the twenty years of filibustering and revolutionary strife that plagued that area. When the Mexican government was established, it recognized these original rights of ownership even without registered titles. It should be recalled that both the national and state colonization laws stipulated that great care was to be taken by the empresario to respect the land holdings of earlier settlers.

Contrary to the law, Edwards required these settlers to show proof of title or suffer the loss of their holdings. The original land holders protested this action and appealed to the Mexican authorities. Edwards was informed by the authorities to respect the original land holdings. The suggestion went unheeded and, consequently, the grant to Edwards was voided in June, 1826.

Before the revocation of the grant, Edwards left for the United States to interest a number of wealthy men there to invest in the colony. He left his brother, Benjamin, in charge of the colony. Benjamin, and some forty Anglo-Americans, angered by the controversy with the Mexican authorities, rode into Nacogdoches and proclaimed the Republic of Fredonia on December 16, 1826. The Fredonians then issued a call for support from all Anglo-Americans in

Texas, but none answered. At that time a strong Mexican military detachment was on its way to Nacogdoches to enforce the orders of revocation and to restore order. When the Mexican detachment, supplemented by volunteers from Austin's colony, reached Nacogdoches, the Fredonians fled across the Sabine River on January 21, 1827.[57]

The reaction of the De Witt colonists to the rebellion was one of disapproval. As the hostilities were coming to a close, a meeting was held by the De Witt colonists and resolutions were adopted condemning the rebellion.

The resolutions, approved by all of the colonists, declared that ". . . their great objective in leaving their parent Country, and migrating hither, was not for the purpose of unsheating the sword of Insurrection, war, bloodshed, and desolation, but as peaceable and industrious subjects, to cultivate and inhabit the bounteous domain so liberally extended and offered them by the Government of the land of their choice."[58] The resolution suggested that the Mexican government should draw a distinction between those peace-loving citizens (the De Witt colonists) and "those refugees and fugitives of justice who raised the flag of 'Independence' at Nacogdoches, a group worthy only of contempt and disgust."[59] The resolutions expressed faith and confidence in the Mexican government and restated the colonists' pledge of loyalty. The resolutions ended with a statement of gratitude to the government and those forces of arms which were sent to crush the rebellion.[60] The resolutions signed by the chairman, Byrd Lockhart, and the secretary, James Norton, were sent to Austin for translation into Spanish. Austin, in turn forwarded the document to the governor.[61]

James Kerr, no doubt, influenced the position which the De Witt colonists assumed. He was one of the members of the volunteer group of Anglo-Americans sent against the Fredonians.[62] Kerr realized that it was in the best interest of the colony to state its views officially on the matter.[63]

There is no reason to doubt the sincerity of the resolutions. Each statement of the resolutions was what the colonists believed. However, it is questionable if they really convinced some of the Mexican authorities of their loyalty. To some Mexicans, such as General Anastacio Bustamante, who was distrustful of most Anglo-Americans, there was no distinction between the De Witt colonists and those of Hayden Edwards.[64]

By the middle of July, 1827, De Witt still remained at "Old Station" along with all of his colonists. He continued his attempts to place the colony on a firmer footing and supervised the construction of defense works, cabins, and warehouses. By that time it became apparent that the tasks of firmly establishing the colony, performing the various functions required of an empresario, and encouraging immigration were too demanding for De Witt. He informed the jefe-politico in July that he had appointed an attorney for the colony.[65] The need for such an agent had already become clear to many of the colonists a few months earlier. James Kerr, in writing to Austin, stated that "The people are anxious that the Colonel [De Witt] should appoint some person to manage his affairs."[66]

It was understood that James Kerr would act as De Witt's representative whenever a need arose. But his position as attorney for the colony was not officially sanctioned until De Witt found it necessary to return to the United States once again. Because of his abilities, experience, and a general desire among the colonists themselves, Kerr was given greater authority. His power of attorney was officially sanctioned on July 14, 1827.[67]

Know all men by these presents that whereas I, Green De Witt, of the colony of my name, in the department of Texas, in the Mexican United States, did obtain a grant from the supreme government of the state of Coahuila and Texas, bearing date the 15th of April, 1825, to settle four hundred families in the department aforesaid, and within certain described limits as will fully appear by reference being had to said grant. Now know ye that I, the said Green De Witt, have made, constituted and appointed and by these presents to make, constitute and appoint James Kerr, of said department, my true and loyal agent and attorney in fact, for me and in my name as empresario of said grant, to do and perform all and singular the duties imposed on me, the said Green De Witt, by virtue of said grant and the nature of my contract with the state aforesaid, in as complete and full a manner as I myself might or could do, were I doing the same in person; and by my name to use as his own, at his will and pleasure, touching these premises to carry into effect all legal proceedings by me made; to seal, execute and deliver such grants, deeds, any conveyances and other instruments as might be fit and lawful for me to do under the colonization law, the instructions of the commissioner and political chief, and also of the state and general government; hereby ratifying and confirming and by these presents allowing whatsoever my said attorney shall in my name, lawfully do, or cause to be done in and about the premises, by virtue of these presents.

In witness whereunto I set my hand and seal, at the Lavaca Station ["Old Station"], on this 14th day of July, 1827, and the sixth year of Mexican independence.[68]

With the administration of the colony now in competent hands, De Witt was free to pursue other matters. He was absent from "Old Station" for two months, but what he was doing during that time has never been determined. It can only be assumed that he was either at the Gonzales site, supervising the renewed construction effort, or in the United States, attempting to recruit more colonists. More than likely he was in the United States. The colony's population had to be increased to number at least one-hundred families. If it did not, De Witt, would, by 1831, lose his contract and the "premium lands." It was already more than two years since he first obtained his grant and not a great deal had been accomplished. In August of 1826, the settlement had only forty colonists.[69] When the only official census of the colony was taken in 1828, there were seventy-five colonists: eleven families and twenty-seven single men.[70]

When De Witt returned to "Old Station" in September, 1827, he found the colony, as well as himself, confronted with a grave crisis. The government ordered the De Witt colony to move from "Old Station."[71] It is impossible to state just how long the Mexican authorities would have allowed the settlement to remain near the coast. The authorities were always apprehensive about contraband goods. When the prohibited tobacco was uncovered in De Witt's colony, the soundness of allowing the continuance of the settlement in that area was questioned. Also the strained relations between Martin De Leon and De Witt played no small part in prompting the eventual removal of the settlement at "Old Station." The Commandant General of the Eastern Interior Provinces, Anastacio Bustamante, felt that contraband goods were still being introduced through the Lavaca River and Garcitas Creek, "under the shelter of the provisional privilege, extended to the empresario Green De Witt. . . ."[72] By August 18, 1827, it was definitely decided by Bustamante that the settlement must be moved. Bustamante informed the jefe-politico that "the secret introduction of prohibited goods . . . and the disturbances of public tranquility which are still liable to arise there . . . make it necessary for you to order their removal."[73]

On August 29, 1827, Saucedo, the jefe-politico, informed De Witt of the government's decision and ordered him to remove the colony to Gonzales within one month.[74] He also, suggested, but did not order, that any new immigrants should not be introduced by way of the Lavaca River.[75] This was a major setback for the fortune of De Witt and his colony. If this provision were enforced the shorter route to the De Witt colony, i.e., New Orleans to Lavaca Bay via coastal schooner, would not be available to future colonists. They would have to take the longer overland route. Because of the remoteness of the De Witt grant overland immigration to it would be greatly reduced.

De Witt was fully aware that one day he would have to transfer the settlement to Gonzales. But to move there within one month came as an unpleasant surprise. Compliance with the order meant that the colonists would be at a disadvantage. Not only were means of transporting them and their possessions in short supply, but that year's crop had not yet been harvested.[76] De Witt found himself in a dilemma. On one hand he owed obedience to the authorities. He well recalled the contraband trade incident. If he did not comply, grave difficulties might arise which would jeopardize the whole colonizing scheme. On the other hand, he was obligated to his colonists. He had to act in their best interest. Their interest dictated that to move to Gonzales by October would be disastrous. Some of the colonists became unreasonable. They threatened to merely move north into Austin's grant.[77]

De Witt appealed to Saucedo for an extension. In September Kerr was sent to San Antonio with De Witt's appeal and a petition signed by some of the colonists.[78] Saucedo, sympathetic with the plight of De Witt and his colony, granted an extension to December 1.[79] Saucedo, the jefe-politico, interceded on behalf of De Witt and his colony by requesting the governor of Coahuila-Texas to extend the date for removal. Governor Jose Maria Viesca complied with Saucedo's request and extended the date to June, 1828.[80]

General Bustamante suspected De Witt's appeal for an extension. To him, the De Witt colonists' occupation of the prohibited area had already been too long and had caused unpleasant consequences. He felt that De Witt never had any intentions of relocating to the grant.[81]

Bustamante's suspicions and accusations were false. In early January, 1827 De Witt sent a number of men to the Gonzales site to begin construction of a fort.[82] The group, under the supervision of Byrd Lockhart, labored on the fort until February. Baptist Lacount, one of the members of the work party, arrived at "Old Station" that month with a report that all work in the area had ceased. The men there were fearful and were talking of leaving since there was a good possibility of renewed Indian attacks. It seems that a party of Comanche and Waco Indians attacked a party of Lipan and Tonkawa Indians nine miles from Gonzales on the San Marcos River. The Lipans and Tonkawas were badly defeated, losing many men and horses. The surviving Indians retreated down river, hoping to find sanctuary in De Leon's colony, and told De Witt's work party of the presence of the Comanches.[83]

Apparently Lockhart dissuaded the men from abandoning the site, for by April the fort was completed. Probably as important as the good news that the fort was finished was Lockhart's report that all was quiet in the area and no Indians had been seen since that day in February.[84] Obviously De Witt always intended to locate at Gonzales, but was waiting for the most opportune time. Now that the fort was built, De Witt and his colonists abandoned "Old Station" by the end of December, 1827.[85] Quite possibly De Witt removed the colony before the June date so as to avoid any further problems with the Mexican authorities over their fear, or at least Bustamante's fear, of contraband trade. More so, De Witt removed the colony so that he could begin the actual settlement of his grant and hopefully qualify for his "premium lands."

4

The Growth
of the Colony

There were only forty persons in the De Witt
colony when they left "Old Station" in 1827. However, by 1828, the colony almost doubled in population. The first and only census taken in De Witt's colony shows that thirty-two settlers entered that year.

Name	State	Age/Years
Berry, Elizabeth	Missouri	43
Nancy		14
James		11
Rheney		8
Tillman		6
Burns, Arthur	Missouri	45
Salley		35
Squire		18
Synthia		14
Lillah		12

Callahan, Joseph	Tennessee	30
Clark, Samuel	Kentucky	26
Coleman, Young	Tennessee	23
De Witt, Green	Missouri	40
Sarah		38
Eliza		17
Naomi		13
Evaline		11
Christopher C.		8
Clinton		5
De Witt, James	Missouri	45
Durbin, Bazel	Missouri	37
Fulcher, Benjamin	Illinois	23
Gregg, Daring	Kentucky	23
Harvey, Robert	Mississippi	21
Henry, John W.	Louisiana	35
Hibbens, John	New York	37
Jones, John	Kentucky	50
Kent, Joseph	England	25
Lawrence, John	Kentucky	47
Lockhart, Byrd	Missouri	46
Looney, Joseph K.	Kentucky	28
Mc Coy, John	Pennsylvania	33
Mc Coy, John	Missouri	52
Martha		47
Jesse		22
Daniel		14
Louiza		12
Mc Coy, Joseph	Missouri	37
Catharine		32
Prospect		11
Green		9
Elizabeth		7
Christopher		5
Infant		½

Nash, William	Louisiana	25
Polly		25
Thomas		5
Betsey		3
Infant		—
Oliver, John	Missouri	22
Perrey, John	Massachusetts	30
Philips, Alexander	Missouri	50
Porter, Fielding	Alabama	38
Shup, Samuel	Pennsylvania	25
Smeathers, William	Indiana	55
Taylor, Felix	Tennessee	35
Elizabeth		18
John		8 months
Taylor, Josiah	Alabama	45
Hepnebeth		34
William		21
Joannah		13
Crud		11
Josiah		9
Pitean		6
Rufus		5
James		3
White, Wiley B.	Missouri	25
Wightman, Elias R.	New York	30
Williams, John	Pennsylvania	32
Margaret		45[1]

From the official census given above, there were in the colony, thirty-four adult males whose median age was thirty-five years. Of these men seven were between the ages of twenty-one and twenty-four, nine between the ages of twenty-five and thirty, two between the ages of thirty-one and thirty-four, eight between the ages of thirty-five and forty, six between the ages of forty-five and fifty, and two were over fifty years of age. Eight of the men were married and had families, two were widowers with families, and twenty-four were unmarried, widowers without children or married men whose wives were in the United States. Of the married men, the ages ranged from twenty-five years old to fifty-two years old, with the median age being twenty-nine years. In this group, however, men in their mid-twenties constituted the majority.

The women and children in the colony numbered thirty-seven. Of these, nine women were married and had children.[2] Their ages ranged from eighteen years to forty-seven, with the media being thirty-five years of age. The remainder were the twenty-eight children of the colony. Of these, eleven were girls whose ages ranged from seven years to seventeen years, with the median being eleven years of age. There were seventeen boys whose ages ranged from five years to eighteen years, with the median being seven and one-half years of age.[3]

The vast majority of these original colonists came from the socio-economic region of the United States known as the Upper South. The Upper South consisted of the states of Tennessee, Kentucky, Missouri, Arkansas (territory, 1819-1835), portions of western Virginia, and portions of North Carolina. This area was characterized by a predominance of slaveless, yeomen farmers. The Upper Southerners relied primarily upon the raising of corn and wheat, rather than cotton and other semitropical cash crops. The remainder of the original De Witt colonists came from the area of the Lower South or other regions of the United States. The lower South consisted of those states which fronted on the Atlantic and Gulf coasts and characterized by the slave-cotton system.[4]

There were nine families counted among the original settlers of the colony. Six families, or thirty-two persons, were from the Upper South: five families, totaling twenty-nine persons, were from Missouri, and one family, totaling three persons, was from Tennessee. Two of the nine original families, or fourteen persons, were from the Lower South: one family, totaling nine persons, was from Alabama, and one family, totaling five persons, was from Louisiana. One family, the Williams's was from Pennsylvania.

Of those colonists listed as "soltero," thirteen were from the Upper South: six from Missouri, five from Kentucky, and two from Tennessee. The Lower South contributed only three: one from Louisiana, one from Alabama, and one from Mississippi. Seven colonists came from states outside of the Upper and Lower South: two from Pennsylvania, two from New York, one from Indiana, one from Illinois, and one from Massachusetts. One colonist came from England.

Consequently the original population of the De Witt colony consisted chiefly of persons from the Upper South. There were forty-five of them out of the total of seventy-two. Seventeen colonists came from the Lower South and nine came from states outside of the south. This distribution, with its Upper Southern features, was characteristic of the population until the period following Texas independence. After that time the population became more balanced between the Upper and Lower South.[5]

Of the original settlers, however, a number did not receive a land title in the De Witt colony. This indicates that they probably remained at the colony for a while but eventually moved on.[6] Of the original colonists, it has been determined that the following received land titles in Stephen Austin's colony: Young Coleman in 1830, Basil Durbin in 1830, and John Williams in 1834. William Smeathers and Elias Wightman already held land titles, 1824 and 1827, respectively, in Austin's colony, and it is assumed they eventually returned there. James De Witt and William Nash received land grants in 1835 from commissioner Carlos Taylor in the Red River area in northeast Texas. Edward Perry received land in the empresario colony of Powers and Hewetson in 1834.[7] It is of importance to note that except for William Nash and John Williams, all of the above-mentioned were single men.

Among those listed in the De Witt colony census of 1828, seven individuals received no land anywhere in Texas — neither in De Witt's grant nor any other. They appear to be merely itinerant or transient in character. These men, Joseph Callahan, Samuel Clark, Robert Harvey, John Lawrence, Alexander Philips, Fielding Porter, and Wiley B. White, in comparison to the other colonists were not materially prepared for farming operations. With the exception of Lawrence and White, who owned six and eight horses, respectively, these men owned nothing other than one horse each.[8] Lawrence and White might possibly have been engaged in horse trading.

When the De Witt colonists moved from "Old Station" to the Gonzales site, they found a marked difference in the geography of the two areas. "Old Station," located in that region known as the Coastal Prairies, was characterized by vast stretches of flat, wet prairies and many pools and lagoons. The area was slightly above the sea level of the Gulf with the great stretches of grassland being broken occasionally be wooded regions. These wood regions were few and were found only along sand ridges and the banks of streams. During the summer months rain was frequent but soon evaporated because of the heat. In the winter months rain seldom fell. The area did not abound in great quantities of animal life, but the waters of the lagoons, pools, and bays held great amounts of marine life.[9]

As the colonists made their way westward from the Coastal Prairies they found the land continually rising. They emerged finally upon that geographic division known as the Blackland Prairies. Here the land was a continuous series of rolling plains, which were gently undulating in the south and swelled markedly in the north. The various streams that coursed their way through this region were lined with stands of timber. The area as a whole was open, but occasionally was broken by isolated groves of timber. These timbered regions consisted mainly of live, post or Spanish oaks, mesquite, elm, ash, black walnut, cypress and, to a much lesser degree, pine.[10] The nature of the Blackland Prairies did not come as a surprise to the colonists. Many of them had used or knew of the value of the oak openings and fields in the United States. Consequently, they were not repelled from settling upon the prairies. They did however, select sites that offered both prairies and timber land. Timber land, of course, was chosen for its shelter and fuel resources. Also it was hoped, that at some future date, the surplus timber could be harvested and profitably sold to a growing population.

The site of Gonzales itself was situated on the east bank of the Guadalupe River. Some three miles up the Guadalupe River the San Marcos River entered it. (See map page 54)[11] Here the water ran rapidly and could provide the power needed to operate mills. On either side of Gonzales stretched large prairies which were variegated with groves of timber and knolls. Upon the knolls were scattered a good quantity of building stone. The soil was "dark unctuous mellow mould," mixed with white sand. It was superior for the "production of the garden, the orchard, and the farm."[12]

At first the settlers of Gonzales relied upon the fort for shelter. However, by the early part of 1828 they had erected a number of "log pens" for living quarters.[13] The log pen was a crude cabin constructed from unhewn logs. The cracks and joints were filled with clay or mud. The entire structure had only a door and one window with a wooden shutter. The floor of the pen was either clay or "crude wooden planks." Adjacent to these log pens was usually a small plot of corn. Nearby was a corral into which the stock was driven every night after grazing upon the prairie. This small settlement of six or seven such log pens was not far from the safety and security of the fort. However this seems to have been only a temporary situation for they eventually settled in all directions from Gonzales.

No generalization can be made as to when the settlers ventured out onto their respective tracts, however. A few of them never actually lived on the land to which they had title. Instead they lived in Gonzales.[14] No doubt they were holding the land for speculative purposes. A number of those individuals who held town lots, in addition to a quarter or a full league of land seem to fall within this category. The greater majority of the colonists moved to their lands as soon as possible during 1828. (See maps pp. 87 & 88)[15]

By the middle of 1829, the De Witt colony had more than doubled in population for the preceding year. There were thirty families and thirty-four single men now in the colony. This increased the population to 158.[16] The major part of this increase occurred in March of that year. In a letter to Stephen Austin, De Witt briefly mentions that fifty-five new colonists were making their way to Gonzales. According to De Witt, they had been brought into Texas by Byrd Lockhart. The group landed at the Bay of Aransas, near the present-day city of Corpus Christi, and were awaiting transportation to the colony when De Witt

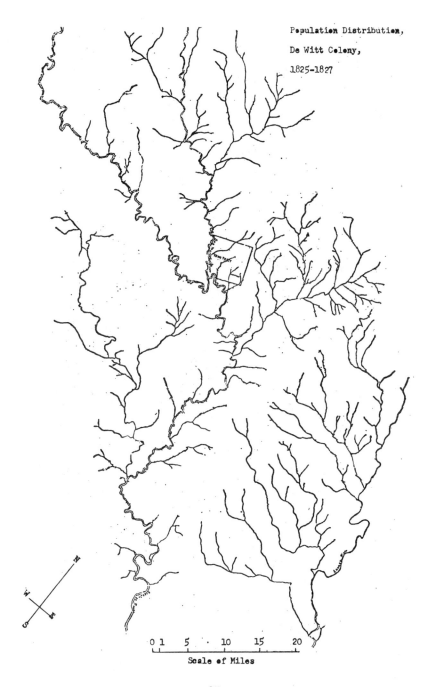

Population Distribution,
De Witt Colony,
1825-1827

N

W

S

E

0 1   5   ·   10   15   20

Scale of Miles

Population Distribution
De Witt Colony,
1828

Scale of Miles

wrote Austin.[17] Unfortunately, information regarding these colonists and Lockhart's role in their introduction to the colony has not been found. The Bay of Aransas or rather the area adjacent to it, was in the grant awarded to the empresarios John Mc Mullen and James Mc Gloin in August, 1828. Throughout the remainder of 1829, immigrants continued to enter the colony. By the end of that year the population increased to 186.[18] (See map, p. 90)[19]

In order to facilitate transportation to the site of Gonzales two roads were constructed during 1829. It has been determined that along these roads were travelling not only incoming colonists and settlers but traders in contraband goods. Just how much contraband was passing Gonzales on its way to San Antonio is not known. According to De Witt, however, there was a substantial amount. Recalling his unfortunate experience with a similar situation in 1826, De Witt's anxiety was understandable. De Witt pointed out to the jefe-politico that the smugglers always avoided Gonzales. Since this was the case and since he had no troops at his command to prevent it, all he could do was inform the authorities. He indicated that his colonists were not taking part in this trade and were fearful of being blamed for encouraging it. "And you will remember the censure which has been thrown on me at the Labaca [sic] on account of contraband of which I never took any part."[20] It is quite possible that De Witt exaggerated the amount of contraband entirely out of proportion. He well knew that the Mexican authorities were sensitive when it came to this issue. This was one way, perhaps, to obtain the long desired garrison for Gonzales. The garrison's presence in or around Gonzales could not help but deter any Indian raids. This was probably how the Mexican authorities assessed the situation, for there is no evidence of any garrison being permanently established.

Population Distribution
De Witt Colony,
1829

0 1 5   10   15   20
Scale of Miles

The authorities, quite logically, were more concerned with a flow of contraband trade along the border and coastal areas than any illegal trade occurring in the interior.

The following year, 1830, saw the greatest influx of settlers into De Witt's colony. (See map p. 92)[21] During that time, twenty-six families, a total of 160 persons, and thirty-one single men arrived. This brought the population of the colony to 377.[22] The trend seems to indicate that the influx of settlers would have continued were it not for the passage of the Law of April 6, 1830 which prohibited further immigration. Although De Witt's colony was exempt from the law, the flow of immigration was affected by it and eventually ended.

The decrease was hardly noticeable in light of the population figures for 1830. The figures for 1831 clearly show the effectiveness of the law. In that year 154 persons, twenty-three families and nine single men, entered the colony, but the interesting fact is that this flow occurred entirely within the first three and one-half months of that year. Had the Law of April 6, not been passed, it seems reasonable to assume that the influx of immigrants during 1831 would have clearly surpassed that of 1830. The first three months of 1831 alone witnessed an influx almost as large as that which occurred during all of 1830. After April 1, there is no evidence which indicates any new arrivals.[23] These last three months of immigration, however, did increase the size of the colony to 531,[24] thereby making it the second most successful empresario colony in Texas.[25] (See map p. 93) Based on population alone, it was a poor second.

From 1828 until 1831, the colonists were in actual possession of their lands. However, they had not yet received titles to them. According to the colonization law, no titles could be issued until a min-

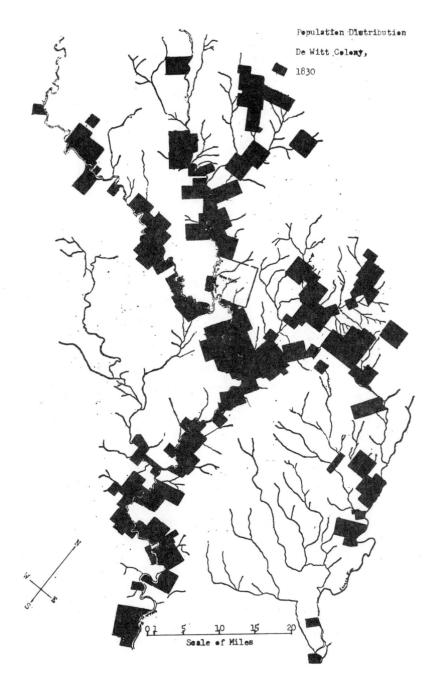

Population Distribution

De Witt Colony,

1830

Scale of Miles

92

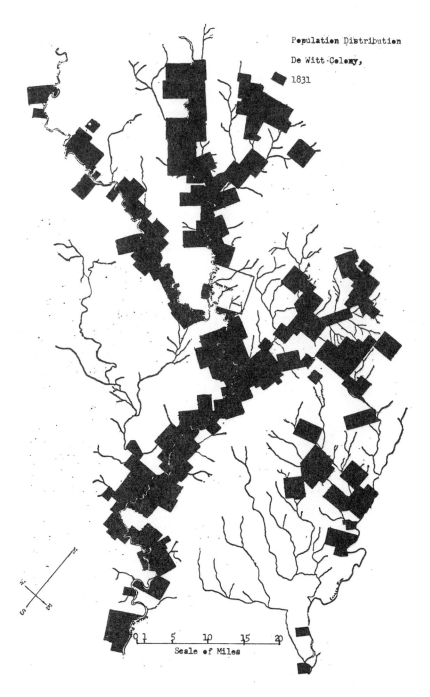

Population Distribution
De Witt Colony,
1831

Scale of Miles
0 1   5   10   15   20

imum of one-hundred families had been introduced. By the end of 1830 the minimum had been exceeded and it remained for the governor to appoint the necessary land commissioner. This was accomplished in January, 1831, when Jose Antonio Navarro[26] was appointed land commissioner for the De Witt colony.[27]

The entire procedure of obtaining a title was handled solely by Navarro. Although his actions required the sanction of Green De Witt, Navarro became one of the most important men in the colony. His duties as land commissioner did not entail the issuance of titles alone. In addition he was to examine the certificates of the settlers to determine that they were of good moral character; to administer the oath of allegiance to them; to select the sites for the founding of a town or towns; to ascertain the location of strategic and important river crossings; to build ferries at the important river crossings; to preside over the popular elections for the ayuntamientos of any new town or towns; to induct into office the newly elected officials; to form and furnish a book of records for any new town or towns; to maintain a bound record of all the land titles that were issued; and to appoint the surveyor.[28]

The most important duty, obviously, was to begin issuing and registering the land titles. Navarro appointed Byrd Lockhart as the surveyor-general of the colony in April, 1831. This had been the position which Green De Witt had given James Kerr in 1825. The confirmation of the position to Kerr was never officially approved by the government. In any event Kerr continued the survey. When the colony was returning to the Gonzales site in 1827, Kerr appointed Lockhart, a trained surveyor himself, as the deputy surveyor for the colony.[29] As for all surveys after 1826, they were performed by Lockhart. James Kerr never returned with the colonists to the Gonzales site in 1827. Instead he remained on the land which he held title to in the Lavaca district.[30]

Lockhart, assisted by Charles Lockhart, immediately took up the surveying assignment. Lockhart for his efforts was, by law, to receive eight dollars for every league of land surveyed, three dollars for every labor, or 177 acres, surveyed, and one and one half dollars for every town lot surveyed.[31] It is doubtful if he ever received much money for his services, since money was scarce. More often then not, he was paid in either goods or services. He obtained four leagues of land for his skills in surveying and building roads.[32]

Surveying was one of the most widespread professions on the frontier. The surveyor was an indispensable functionary within the empresario system. The tasks performed by the frontier surveyor have until recently, been overlooked by historians.[33] In Texas, the assignment of surveying the lands within any given colony was entrusted to some 103 surveyors during the years 1821 to 1836. The various field notes made by these men provide an interesting type of historical literature which is technical, scientifically colloquial, and topographically descriptive. The surveyor's world was not always one of mathematics and geometry. On many occasions they were the first white men into an area and encountered the native tribes which were often hostile. Such an incident, it should be recalled, occurred with the surveying team of James Kerr in 1825.

The surveyors, at least in Texas, were also hindered to some degree by instructions which attempted to avoid a possible monopoly of riparian rights. A riparian[34] right is a water right that an individual possesses if he owns the bank of a stream and has access to it by virtue of possession. Spanish and Mexican law held that water, when present, was an

integral part of an owner's rights in his land.[35] Consequently the Mexican government desired that every
tract of land front on running water, but limited the
frontage to only one bank of a river or creek. This
characteristic of water frontage became common to
all tracts of land during the period.[36]

The land survey itself was one of the final steps
in processing a clear and valid title. The initiation of
the titling process was the sole responsibility of the
settler himself. Anyone who desired to obtain land
was required to present his petition to the land commissioner. The petition was a written statement,
signed by the settler, which indicated the date of his
arrival, where he arrived from, the number of persons in his family, if he were married, a description of
the land which he desired, a statement which attested
that the land was vacant, and a request that he be put
in possession of the area described. Along with this
petition was a statement of his character and a statement attesting the fact that he had taken an oath of allegiance to the Mexican government. If he had not
taken an oath, it was then administered at the time of
petition.[37]

The petition was then approved by the land
commissioner and Green De Witt. The survey of the
area was made and possession was confirmed. All
married colonists were entitled to purchase one league
of land, or 4,428 acres. Those colonists who were
single were allowed to purchase one fourth of that
amount. An interesting provision, obviously designed to populate the area, stated that an unmarried
individual could augment the quarter league to one
full league after marriage. The land given in title was
not a gift from the Mexican government, however.
The settler was obligated to pay for the land. The purchase of the land, was on a credit basis. The payment
for the land was made in installments, each being one-

third of the total purchase price. The first payment fell due four years after the date of the land title. The second and third payments were made after the fifth and sixth years respectively.[38] It should be noted that this method of land purchase was similar to the credit system which the United States abandoned in 1820.

The colonists were required to pay the state thirty dollars for one league of land. Unmarried men who received a quarter league, paid fifteen dollars. There were additional fees which increased the total purchase price. All of the settlers paid fifteen dollars for the clerical services of the land commissioner. Green De Witt was to receive five dollars of this fee. For the services of the surveyor, the fee was eight dollars. The price of the legal stamped paper on which the original title was written, and copies of it, was eight dollars. In all the total purchase price was $46 for a quarter league and $61 for a full league of land. The most land that a non-Mexican could own was eight leagues. Consequently land in Texas was more attractive than land in the United States because of its cost. The price of land in the United States, at this time, was $1.25 per acre if purchased from the public domain. In Texas the price per acre was much cheaper. The purchase of a quarter league of land amounted to four and two-tenths of a cent per acre. The purchase of a full league of land amounted to one and four-tenths cent per acre.

The settlers, once in possession of the land, were required to cultivate or occupy it within a period of six years from the date of title issuance. If this did not occur, the title was forfeited.[39] In reality, this provision was never defined and, consequently, very little improvement was all that was necessary to satisfy this requirement. All the settlers who acquired land, either a quarter league, a full league, or town lots,[40] became naturalized Mexican citizens with all the rights that were accorded to the Mexican nationals. The new settlers were to be free from all duties upon agriculture and industry, and free from all general taxes for a period of ten years.[41]

Commissioner Navarro recorded the first titles, four in number, on April 15, 1831. These were given to Eliza De Witt Hamilton, Stephen Smith, C. Stinnett, and Winslow Turner. During the last two weeks of April, ten more titles were processed. The following month thirty-six titles were issued which was the most during any one given period. On May 1 and May 5 alone, twenty-seven titles were registered. Titles continued to be issued for the remaining seven months of the year, totaling ninety-five titles and averaging about one title every two days. During the first four months of 1832, no titles were recorded. From May to September of that year Commissioner Navarro registered forty more titles. The last title was issued to William B. Lockhart on September 17, 1832.[42] This title, as it applied to the De Witt colony, was the last such official title given under the empresario system. When De Witt's contract expired on April 15, 1831, and was not renewed, anyone who entered the colony after that date could not legally procure land from him.[43] Although all of the titles were dated after the expiration date of the contract, none of those who received titles entered later than April 1. The last arrival who was able to qualify for a land title was Valentine Bennet. He arrived on April 1, 1831.[44]

In all there were eighty-two leagues and eighty quarter leagues deeded.[45] This amounted to a total of 451,656 acres, or 705 square miles of land. However, a greater portion of the De Witt grant had not been deeded. When the De Witt contract expired, almost two million acres, or 3,000 square miles, reverted to the Mexican domain.

Since the land office in the De Witt colony did not begin operating until 1831, the issuance of the titles to the early settlers was delayed. However, this was in a way advantageous to those settlers. The colonists who arrived in 1828 and 1829 had virtually free use of the land without any obligations until three years after the title was issued. If the colonists obtained the title in 1831, then those having arrived in 1828 or 1829, had free use of the land for seven and six years, respectively. They even had a year longer if the title was not obtained until 1832. As a rule most of the colonists obtained their titles as soon as possible.[46] (See charts, pp. 100 & 101)

Regardless of when they obtained their titles, many had, by 1830, distributed themselves throughout the colony. At first, they erected the temporary log pens or even lean-tos. These soon gave way to more permanent structures. The types of dwellings varied. The traditional hewn timber variety was the most common.[47] It was a one-story house which usually measured twenty-five feet long by eighteen feet wide. However the dimensions always varied, depending on the length of the available timber in a given area. When timber of suitable length could be obtained, then two rooms were constructed within the cabin. For the most part, the cabins were one-room structures. Where necessity required the use of two rooms, then two one room cabins were built and placed under the same roof.[48]

The timber was cut and hauled by oxen, or at times, dragged by the colonists, to the site. There they were hewed with a hoe like instrument known as a foot adze. This instrument was used to scrape the timber into a shape having four flat surfaces. After the preparation had been done, the "house raising" was accomplished by as many persons as could be obtained. The house raising usually took only one day.

Number of Colonists Receiving Titles, Per Month, Per Period of Immigration

Date of Title: Apr. May June July Aug. Sept. Oct. Nov. Dec. Jan. Feb. Mar. Apr. May June July Aug. Sept.

1831   1832

........1825-1828
— —1829   Periods of Immigration (Arrival Dates)
———1830
— · —1831

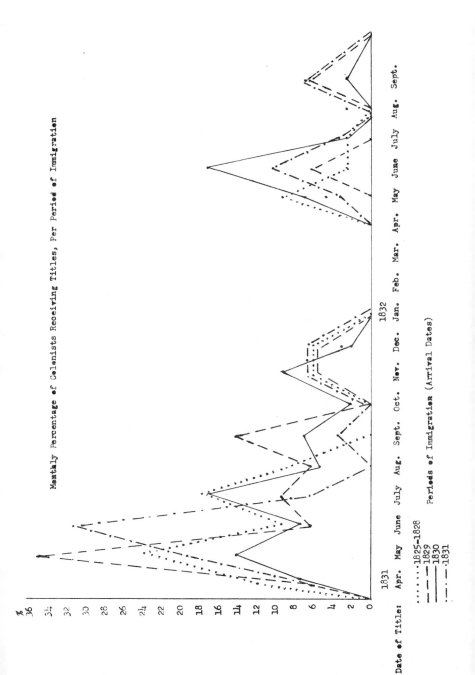

Monthly Percentage of Colonists Receiving Titles, Per Period of Immigration

Date of Title: Apr. May June July Aug. Sept. Oct. Nov. Dec. Jan. Feb. Mar. Apr. May June July Aug. Sept.

1831   1832

..... 1825-1828   Periods of Immigration (Arrival Dates)
——— 1829
——— 1830
—·—· 1831

The finer finsihing work was completed later by the individual colonists. When the main structure was completed, one window, twelve inches square, was cut out. Since glass was not available, the opening was covered with a hide curtain. A thick wooden shutter was added for protection against man or the elements. When they could be obtained, iron bars were placed in the window opening. One door way was made and provided with a heavy door. Once again, when it could be obtained, sheet iron was used to cover both the inside and outside of the door.[49]

The roofs of these structures were made of either prairie sod or shakes. The sod roof had the advantage of offering easy and rapid construction. It was, however, not waterproof while, at times, cattle came to feed on it. The shake roof, enduring longer, was more common. It was constructed from splitting oak logs into two and one half foot lengths. The shakes were fastened like shingles to purlins. The purlins, with twelve to twenty-four inch centers, parallel to the ridgepole, were fastened to the end framework of the cabin. The fastening of the purlins to the frame and the fastening of the shakes to the purlins was accomplished by tying, pegging, or nailing.[50]

Two other types of structures were also used, but were not as wide spread as the log cabins. These were the cedar-picket house and the "dug-outs." The cedar-picket was used in areas where cedar trees were abundant. This structure was made of poles of cedar which were planted upright in the ground. The basic form resembled a small stockade. Over the cedar pickets were fastened thin boards. The dugout was prevalent in areas where very little timber was available. It was a durable and simple structure. It was constructed by simply digging a pit. The pit was then covered with logs. The logs, in turn, were covered with either prairie sod or clay. The structure, unattractive as it was, had an advantage of offering warmth in the winter and cool relief in the summer.

The colonists found no difficulty in obtaining the necessities of life. Game in the colony was in great abundance. When deer, bear, turkey, and antelopes could not be had, there were always the wild mustangs. The soil of the colony was rich. The ground was cleared by burning and superficial plowing. The plowing was strenuous work at first, but with each succeeding year it became easier. Indian corn or the larger, soft, white Mexican variety was planted.[51] It was merely dropped into the shallow furrow and covered with a hoe. Even if the most primitive method of cultivation was used, a substantial crop was yielded. This primitive method of cultivation consisted of puncturing the soil with a sharpened stick and dropping the grains of corn into the holes.[52]

For the most part, the ripened corn was allowed to stand in the fields and was harvested as the need arose. When the corn was in "roasting ear" it was either boiled, fried, or roasted. Roasting the corn was the most popular. Husked corn was placed before a fire and rotated until all sides of it were roasted. Sometimes the corn, unhusked, was buried in hot ashes for roasting.

Corn was the basic grain of the colony. Aside from being consumed while on the cob, it provided meal for bread. When the corn was hardening, it was grated over tinware. The tinware, primarily old coffee pots, was flattened and punched full of small holes. This crude instrument was then shaped into an oval and nailed to a board. After this rough grating process, the corn was placed into a mortar to be pulverized. The mortar was made from a stump of a tree, some three to four feet high. The stump was hollowed out by burning and scraping it. The eventual depth of the mortar was enough to hold a peck of grated corn. The corn was ground into meal by the force of the pestle which was fastened to a long pole. The pole, in turn, was swung in an up-and-down motion while resting in the fork of a nearby tree. The corn meal that was produced from this process was then baked into bread in a skillet. Needless to say it was a bit heavy.[53]

The cultivation of wheat was not absent from the De Witt colony, but was not very extensive.[54] Consequently flour was scarce and considered a luxury item. When it could be obtained the absence of any leavening agent produced a hard bread and some humorous incidents. One such incident was related to Noah Smithwick during his stay in De Witt's colony. A settler told the story of his son's first experience with biscuits made of unleavened flour. A batch of freshly made biscuits was laying on the table and the son helped himself to one of them. He went out of the cabin and immediately returned for another biscuit. The father, who doubted that his son could have consumed the biscuit so rapidly, followed him outside. There to the father's amazement he saw what the son had done with the biscuits. The youngster had punched holes in the center of the biscuits and inserted an axle through them. He had fabricated a miniature Mexican ox cart.[55]

Overall, great variations in agricultural products in the De Witt colony did not exist. As has been mentioned corn was primarily raised. Other items, however, were found scattered throughout the colony, but not in great quantities. Wheat, barley, and rye were raised only in small amounts. Sweet potatoes and sugar cane, in the extreme southeast portion of the colony, were also raised.[56] With the exception of sugar cane, all of these crops could have been grown easily in the De Witt colony but were not. One possible explanation for the absence of these crops was due to the upper-southern character of the majority of the colonists. As upper-southerners they were traditionally tied to the corn economy. However, a contemporary observer in the De Witt colony explained it differently. Since the cultivation of other grain products required more work and effort than corn did, they were not grown because of the indolent nature of the colonists. In his critical manner he pointed out that life was too easy because of the abundance of game and the high fertility of the soil.[57]

Cotton, like these other crops, was not grown in any great quantities and cannot be considered of major consequence. Even in the extreme eastern and coastal portions of Stephen Austin's colony, the exportation of cotton was minimal.[58] It can be safely assumed that in the De Witt colony the production of cotton was even less. One single, great prerequisite for the growth of cotton was the existence of a profitable route of shipment to a market. Aside from the Old San Antonio Road, a portion of which formed the northwestern boundary of De Witt's grant, the "roads" in Texas were mere paths. Even the Old San Antonio Road was subject to great limitations which were caused by the season, the weather, and the mood of the Indians. Particularly in the area between the Sabine and Colorado rivers, the Road became a sea of mud when the streams overflowed. Also neither any of the trails nor the Road had bridges at important river crossings. Because of these circumstances, an overland route to market such crops as cotton was not possible.[59] Water transportation was even less encouraging. All the principle rivers of Texas, including the Lavaca and Guadalupe, were shallow and plagued by shifting sand bars.[60] Consequently the De Witt colony did not possess a route to profitably transport goods to a market.

Stock raising also provided the De Witt colonists with sustenance. The raising of beef cattle was predominant, but was followed closely by the raising of hogs. Little effort was required of the colonists to provide for the cattle. They were allowed to range freely and fed off of the prairies and bottom lands. Hogs were not confined to pens or corrals but were allowed to roam.[61] An interesting departure from the upper southern characteristics, was that the De Witt colonists did not feed the excess corn to their hogs. The hogs simply fed on the unlimited quantities of mast found in the timber bottoms and roots on the prairies. It has been stated that a two-year-old hog, feeding on mast alone, weighed well over 350 pounds.[62]

Milch cows, as a rule, were not found in the colony. Consequently such diary products of butter, cheese, or milk were not available. No doubt a few of the De Witt colonists brought such cows with them, but these were not sufficient in number to provide a general feature in the colony. The milk that was available was obtained from goats. However, this milk was produced on goat ranches, near Laredo some distance south of the De Witt colony.[63]

The ratio of more cattle to hogs continued throughout the existence of the De Witt colony. Cattle, however, were raised for marketing purposes.[61] Hogs were raised because of a dietary preference. The colonists' normal bill of fare consisted mainly of corn bread, fried pork, and coffee without milk or sugar. This menu, of course, was always supplemented with wild game and honey. With the exception of wild turkey, there were no poultry products. Any garden products were uncommon.[65]

Since a great majority of the De Witt colonists came from the upper south, the practice of slavery was not prevalent. As a group, the De Witt colonists owned few slaves when they immigrated to Texas. Because of the economic pattern that developed there, the colonists were never required, or, for that matter, capable of procuring any slaves. Some colonists, however, did bring their slaves with them. Of the first colonists, only James Kerr possessed any slaves. He owned a total of seven. The others held none.[66] Since Kerr no longer resided in the colony after 1828, there were no slaves in the colony during the first two years of its existence. By 1831-1832 there were a few slaves in the colony. However since census figures do not exist, the exact number of slaves can only be approximated by the use of other evidence. In the "Titles" of De Witt's colony, each colonist, receiving land, indicated the number of persons in his family. All of the colonists, with the exception of three, gave the size of their families as some number between one and ten. It is reasonable to believe that these figures only reflected the kindred members of the family, and did not include slaves. The size of the families given by three of the De Witt colonists indicates that they must have included the number of slaves in their families. Caleb P. Alexander, Si Bateman, and Caleb Brock indicated the size of their families as twenty-five, thirty-eight, and fifteen respectively.[67]

In 1834 Colonel Juan Nepomuseno Almonte was dispatched by the Mexican government to make a general inspection of Texas. He estimated that the Anglo-American population was 10,000 and the number of Negro slaves was no more than 1,000. The greatest majority of these slaves were held in the Austin colony.[68] The Austin colony already had some 500 slaves as early as 1825. It appears that the number of Negro slaves was in decline during the last remaining years of colonial Texas. A strong impediment was the hostile position adopted by the Mexican government to slavery.

Nature did not demand much from the De Witt colonists, but gave bountifully. Consequently only a minimum of effort was required by the colonists to exist. This characteristic evoked comments by contemporary observers, but two in particular are of interest. In 1828, at the time that the De Witt colony was just forming, Jose Maria Sanchez described the colony in images of pastoral simplicity. "On seeing the tranquility which these peaceful inhabitants enjoy in contrast to the passions that wreck our soul in the populous cities, an involuntary sigh escaped by breast . . ."[69] David B. Edward, who resided in the colony, looked upon the settlers as being indolent, filthy, and intemperate.[70] Edward ascribed the indolent nature of the De Witt colonists to the fertility of the land and the abundance of game. In describing their filthiness, Edward quoted a De Witt colonist as having said, "I am well enough, for my neighbor is no better; and what does if signify in this new country how I dress? A leather hunting shirt, and a pair of buckskin breeches, are good enough for the mud and briers; besides I believe I'll just go and hunt a little to day, which will make me dirty enough before I return. . . ."[71] Edward blamed intemperance on the lack of literary amusement, lack of "religious excitement" and few and limited enjoyments. The people spent much time in meeting their friends in "one of those petty stores, which should rather, if they had the right cognomen, be termed grog shops!"[72]

Of course these two opinions represent the extremes. The De Witt colony was certainly not as utopian as Sanchez described. But it was not as depraved as Edward pointed out. The colony was simply in its early stage of development. The conveniences of life and many creature comforts were not available in the De Witt colony. For that matter they were not available anywhere in Texas, but for a few exceptions. A more sophisticated economy did not exist because of the absence of money, credit and banking facilities, good roads, and other means of transportation. To be sure, there were individuals who desired to "promote" a more active economy. But by and large the average colonists' outlook was limited. Basically agrarian, they thought in terms of land, land ownership, and the eventual sale of some or all of their holdings for a profit. The conveniences, as well as the demands, of a market economy were not established in the De Witt colony.

These farmers and stock raisers broke the monotony of their so-called "indolent" lives with social gatherings. The pursuit of pastimes and hunting was paramount in their lives.[73] There were parties, house-raisings, hunting and fishing parties, horse racing, rifle shooting matches, various athletic exercises, mustang catching and simple social gatherings. The one social institution that did not exist in the colony was the church.

By law the colonists were to be Roman Catholic, or become so. A church was to be built and a priest was to be obtained for the colony. The entrance of Protestant ministers or the erection of any Protestant churches was prohibited by law. In the De Witt colony there was no church, no priest, and few of the colonists were Catholic.[74] None ever bothered to become Catholic. There was little interest in a formal religion. Only a few of the colonists, mostly women and children, observed the Sabbath. Religion was practiced only within the family circle where there were readings, prayers, and singing. The Sabbath was always a day of visiting. A journey of five to ten miles for Sunday dinner was not unusual. Some of the colonists spent the day by driving stock and breaking mustangs. One of the De Witt colonists remarked, "There is no such thing as attending church, since no religion except the Roman Catholic is tolerated, and we have no priest among us. Indeed I have not heard a sermon since I left Kentucky, except at a camp-meeting in Arkansas."[75]

The De Witt colony was visited from time to time by the Protestant missionary, or circuit riding preacher, Sumner Bacon. He received permission from the Cumberland Presbytery of Tennessee to go to Texas as a colporteur. By 1832 he was holding prayer meetings and camp meetings. He distributed many Bibles, both in English and Spanish, at his own expense.[76] The Mexican authorities never fully enforced the prohibition against Bacon and others like him. The state legislature at Monclava, in an attempt to promote land sales, decreed in 1834 that "No person shall be molested for political and religious opinions, provided he shall not disturb the public order."[77] Interestingly, during the Revolution, Bacon joined Sam Houston's army and aided it by purchasing and transporting ammunition.

The absence of any church in the De Witt colony created an awkward situation in some cases. A problem arose when some of the colonists decided to marry. Since there was no civil authority stationed within the colony until 1832 and never any priest, what agency could legalize a marriage? No matter how much in love a couple might have been, it was simply too far to travel to either San Felipe de Austin or San Antonio just to wed. It would have been a great inconvenience as well as a hazard for the colonists to make the trip. The problem was solved by bestowing upon Green De Witt the authority to perform the marriages. The marriages performed by De Witt were fully binding. The first marriage in the colony was between John Oliver and Nancy Curtis.

> Know all Men by these Presents:
> That we, John Oliver . . . and Nancy Curtis
> . . . are held and firmly bound one to the other
> in the penal sum of ten thousand dollars, well

and truly to be paid, sued for and recovered of either of our lands, tenements, goods, chattels on the following conditions to-wit:

Whereas the said John Oliver and Nancy Curtis have mutually agreed to enter in the solemn bonds of matrimony; and there being as yet no church erected in this colony, or ecclesiastical authority established in said colony, and it being a great distance to San Antonio de Bexar, and no Alcalde yet appointed before whom this bond should have been taken, as is the custom in Austin's colony in such cases;

Now, therefore, it is fully understood by and between the said parties, that if they do faithfully appear before some priest or person legally authorized to solemnize marriage as soon as circumstances will permit, and be married as the laws of this government may require, why, then this bond to be forever void.

And it is further to be understood by and between the said parties, that if either of the said parties shall fail or refuse to comply with the conditions of this bond . . . the party so failing or refusing shall forfeit and pay the penalty in the said bond mentioned. . . .

Done before me, Green De Witt, Empresario of De Witt's Colony, there being yet no Alcalde election for said Colony. . . .[78]

The manner in which the marriage problem was solved demonstrated frontier expediency. It also was a prudent measure in maintaining the social and moral decorum within the colony.

The absence of any ecclesiastical agency also deprived the colony of any educational opportunity. The De Witt colony had no educational establishment until the arrival of David B. Edward. Edward was a Scotchman who had been a principal in the academy at Alexandria, Iowa. He came to the De Witt colony in 1831 and there established a "seminary." In his work, *The History of Texas*, he styled himself as the preceptor of "Gonzales Seminary." Unfortunately this is all the information he related concerning the status of education in the colony. No doubt he found it difficult to obtain pupils because of the economic situation in the colony.

Despite the relatively small population, the absence of an active economy, and the absence of any cultural and social niceties, the De Witt colony was a fact. Where only a few short years before their arrival stretched a vast emptiness, now the river areas of the Guadalupe and the San Marcos were dotted with crude cabins and plowed fields. These colonists, aided by no one and encouraged only by the Mexican offer of land, accomplished much in a few short years. They accomplished the long-desired Spanish goal. They accomplished the desired Mexican goal. They, along with a few other Anglo-American colonies, were settling Texas.

5

The Colony and the Indians of Texas

The De Witt colony never witnessed an Indian attack of any major proportion. Severe depredations did not actually occur in that portion of the Texas frontier until the Revolution had ended. However, the De Witt colony was subjected to many scattered raids. The colony sustained more raids than any other Anglo-American settlement in Texas. Although the raids were not extremely devastating, they were sufficient to deter other less courageous colonists from settling in that area. Because the raids continued, the colony did not grow rapidly.

The first contact that the De Witt colonists had with any Indian tribe of Texas was at "Old Station." The tribe which inhabited this region of Texas was known as the Karankawas or, as the colonists referred to them, "Cronks."[1] They were one of the most primitive tribes of Texas. The first European to encounter them was that intrepid Spaniard, Cabeza de Vaca. It was the Karankawas who destroyed the ill-fated La Salle expedition. This tribe, like most of the Texas Indians, had strenuously resisted all missionary civilizing efforts of the Spaniards. By the end of the Spanish period, the Karankawas had been greatly reduced in numbers due to diseases and vices introduced with the European invasion.

The Karankawas had a nomadic-maritime form of culture. Their principal possession was the dugout canoe which was fabricated from a trunk of a tree with the bark yet intact. This unstable craft, however, allowed the Karankawas greater mobility in their constant search for food. The craft allowed them to easily escape an enemy, but also gave them an advantage during an attack. The craft was able to be poled silently across the lagoons and inlets of the area, thereby giving them the element of surprise. As suddenly as the Karankawas appeared, they could disappear. The canoe left no trail an enemy could follow. The Karankawas, relying on the swiftness of their dugouts and their long bows, were formidable adversaries when they chose to be.

Some of their habits and their appearance, as described by some contemporary observers, is of interest. During an inspection of the Spanish missions in Texas in 1767, Friar Gaspar Jose De Solis commented on the Karankawas eating habits.

> [they] are unique in their gluttony. They eagerly eat locust, lice and even human flesh. They eat raw meat, tallow, bear fat, and when they have them are thankful. . . . With all of this they show a great passion for spoiled food. There arises from their bodies such a stench that it causes one who is little accustomed to them to become sick at the stomach.[2]

The young French scientist, Jean Louis Berlandier, commented in 1828, that the Karankawas "have a musky odor about them, which the Spanish call *amizle*, which they acquire from eating alligator." Noah Smithwick in 1828 was awestruck by their appearance. "They were the most savage looking human beings I ever saw. Many of the bucks were six feet in height, with bows and arrows in proportion. Their ugly faces were rendered hideous by the alligator grease and dirt with which they were besmeared from head to foot as a defense against mosquitoes."[4]

Of all the Indians of North America, only those that inhabited the Coastal Prairies of Texas, particularly the Karankawas, have been classified as cannibals. Recent research has determined the origin of this erroneous classification and has properly explained this Karankawa practice. The concept of considering the Karankawas as cannibalistic most likely originated with Friar De Solis. His statements were, a short while later, incorporated into the comments made by Friar Juan Agustin Morfi. It should be mentioned that neither of these two men ever witnessed any cannibalistic acts on the part of the Karankawas, or, for that matter, any other tribe of the Coastal Prairie. However, the concept remained unchallenged and provided a convenient rationalization for the eventual extermination of these unfortunate people.

Noah Smithwick recorded that ". . . the Karankawa Indians, a fierce tribe, . . . were against every man. They lived mostly on fish and alligator, with a man for fete [sic] days when they could catch one."[5] Friar De Solis, the probable author of this concept, gave a more vivid account, in spite of the fact he did not witness it.

> . . . they set a nailed stake in the ground . . ., they light a big fire, tying the victim . . . to that stake. All assemble and . . . begin to dance . . .

with well sharpened knives in their hands. As
they jump around they approach the victim and
cut a piece of flesh off of his body, going to the
fire and half roasting it in sight of the victim,
they eat it with great relish, and so they go on
cutting off pieces and quartering him until they
take off all of the flesh and he dies. . . . They do
not throw the bones away but distribute them,
and each one whose turn it is to get one walks
along sucking it until he is thus finished . . . For
others they do not use a knife to cut them to
pieces but tear them to pieces with their teeth
and eat them raw.[6]

Undoubtedly the Karankawas did consume
human flesh. This consumption was not for feeding
purposes. It was performed out of supernatural or
spiritual belief. Behind this practice lay the belief that
if one were to eat certain portions of an enemy's body,
the latter's power or courage would be transferred. Of
course, most Europeans, Mexicans, and Anglo-Americans hardly looked upon this practice in this light.[7]

It was probably most unfortunate for the tribes
of the Coastal Prairies, particularly the Karankawas,
that Anglo-Americans had come to Texas. Although
the tribes were not always on the best terms with
either Spaniard or Mexican, there was a place for
them within the overall scheme of Hispanic civilization. The civilization of the Anglo-Americans was not
as accommodating. With them the Karankawas faced
either removal or extermination.

Diffciulties between the Karankawas and the
Anglo-American settlers occurred as early as 1821.
The Indians' continued thieving and harrassment of
colonists brought about a resounding reaction. The
Austin colonists, who were the first to be plagued by
the Karankawas, eagerly began the policy of chastise-
ment. Once the hostilities had begun it spread to the
colonies of Green De Witt and Martin De Leon. By
1827 a general campaign against the Karankawas was

begun. Perhaps Stephen Austin's comments best reflect the tenor of this campaign and demonstrate the attitude which pervaded Anglo-American thinking throughout the period. ". . . the Karankawas may be called universal enemies of man — they killed all nations that came in their power, and frequently feast on the bodies of their victims — the [approach of] an American population will be the signal of their extinction for there will be no way of subduing them but extermination."[8]

The anxiety of the De Witt colonists, at "Old Station," was as great, or possibly greater, than that of the Austin colonists, regarding the presence of the Karankawas. For one, the population of "Old Station" was small. Also the ability of the De Witt colonists to properly defend themselves was questioned. During the contraband controversy in 1826, many of the De Witt settlers had been disarmed.[9] These weapons had been confiscated by the Mexican commandant, Rafeal Manchola. By January, 1827, only a few of the weapons had been returned but were in poor condition. They were practically useless.[10] The remainder of the confiscated weapons were never returned.[11] Consequently the colonists were hard pressed to provide themselves with game, let alone defend themselves against the Indians.[12]

Green De Witt was uneasy about the proximity of the Karankawas and was distrustful of them. He noted that the station was visited on many occasions by small groups of Karankawas, numbering as many as twelve at one time. For the most part, they were friendly. Whenever they approached the settlement, they always had a number of opportunities to attack those colonists, laboring a few miles from it. Interestingly, this never occurred. However, De Witt did not trust their peaceful appearance and felt they were merely awaiting a better opportunity to attack the entire settlement.[13]

During the first eight or nine months of the life of the colony, De Witt hesitated to lend any effectual aid in the campaign against the Karankawas. De Witt promised that as soon as the corn crop was planted he would send a number of men to the expedition that was forming in Austin's colony. Until such time he would attempt to keep on peaceful terms with the Karankawas and report any of their activities.[14] Considering the status of the De Witt colony, this was the most prudent policy to follow.

In the campaign against the Karankawas a majority of the forces were from Austin's colony. However a number of colonists from Martin De Leon's colony also participated. The exact number of De Witt colonists that participated in the campaign is unknown, but there obviously could not have been many. Aside from those forces of Anglo-Americans, there was in Texas, at this time, a large force of Mexican troops under the command of General Anastacio Bustamante. The Mexican force was in Texas because of the hostilities stemming from the Fredonian Rebellion.[15] When the rebellion was suppressed, it was decided that these troops would be employed to assist the colonists in the campaign.

The outcome of the campaign was probably never in doubt. The Anglo-Americans and Mexicans did eventually triumph, in spite of themselves. In some instances, it remains a wonder that they were so successful. One such instance occurred when a segment of the forces of the colonists obtained a four pound swivel gun to use on the Karankawas. The swivel gun was mounted on a jackass and the column set out in search of the Indians. When the Karankawas were discovered they were driven into cover by small arms fire. The artillery-bearing jackass was brought up. The weapon was aimed and fired. Fortunately for the Karankawas, no one ever took the precaution of bracing the jackass. When the swivel gun was touched off, the recoil sent the animal into a somersault. The poor beast landed on top of the gun with his feet in the air and there he remained. Efforts were made to right the animal, but it declined to co-operate. Frantically the swivel gun was removed from its uncooperative carrier, and reprimed for another volley. By that time the Karankawas had made their retreat deeper into the thicket and could not be pursued.[16] It was doubtful any Karankawas died during this skirmish. If any deaths resulted, it was due to laughter, not marksmanship.

Unfortunately, from the standpoint of the Karankawas, the overall campaign was not that humorous. When the colonists became more organized and the Mexican regulars deployed, the campaign became ruthless. The Karankawas were defeated soundly and driven into Matagorda Bay. There approximately half of the Karankawas were killed or drowned. The survivors had no other alternative but to sue for peace.[17] On May 13, 1827 a peace treaty was concluded at the town of Goliad. It was signed by General Bustamante, Green De Witt, James Kerr, Martin De Leon, Fernando De Leon, and Jacob Betts, who represented Stephen Austin. Father Miguel Miro and Antonito, one of their chiefs, signed for the Karankawas.[18]

After this campaign the Karankawas no longer figured as a factor in the history of Indian-white relations in Texas. No more than a hundred Karankawas survived.[19] However, efforts went on to complete the extermination of these few survivors. Killing Indians became a favorite sport. Some of the De Witt colonists even contrived schemes whereby they could hasten the fate of the Indians by having them annihilate each other more effectively. One such scheme was related by Noah Smithwick. One of the early Anglo-American colonists attempted to rid the area of both Karankawas and Tonkawas, simultaneously. These two tribes had been at war for some time. This colonist, an owner of a trading post, was informed that the tribes agreed to meet at a certain designated place and settle the matter once and for all. This colonist then gave arms and ammunition to the Karankawas. When the Tonkawas found out, they requested arms and ammunition which they quickly received. When the day of the battle arrived the colonist went to the pre-arranged site to watch the tribes destroy each other. As he peered through his field glass one can only imagine the astonished and chagrined look on his face. The Karankawas emerged from a stand of timber at the edge of a broad prairie. At first both groups looked at each other and then opened fire. However the distance between both groups was too great and no damage was done. Neither Karankawas nor Tonkawa were hurt. After the exchange of only one volley, both sides retired claiming a total victory.[20]

Not only did the colonists continue to harass the Karankawas, but the Mexican authorities persecuted them relentlessly. Because of this pressure exerted upon them, many of the remaining Karankawas fled north across the Lavaca River. There they, ironically, sought refuge among the De Witt and Austin colonists. They were given sanctuary as servants, forming the lowest class and performing menial tasks.[21] They were depraved, scorned by almost all the colonists, and had lost all self-respect. The Karankawas were reluctantly assimilated into the Anglo-American civilization as individuals. When this occurred all semblance of tribal or group affiliation ended. When this affiliation ended the Karankawas slid into oblivion.

Those few Karankawas that chose to remain in the tribal state disappeared from Texas after the Revolution. The common belief, as Noah Smithwick related it, was that Philip Dimmit developed a good relationship with the remnants of the Karankawas tribe. Dimmit had a ranch near "Old Station" and followed a policy of giving the Karankawas some beef whenever they came there. He found that this pacified them. When the Revolution broke out Dimmit left his ranch and joined the Texan army. The Karankawas, unaware of the struggle in Texas, came to the ranch and found it deserted. In need of food, they proceeded to help themselves to the beef. While the Karankawas were slaughtering a steer, a detachment of Mexican soldiers approached the ranch and asked them what they were doing. The Karankawas replied that they were not stealing the beef but obtaining food from the ranch of an old friend. When the soldiers heard this, they assumed that these Karankawas were in sympathy with the Texas cause. The Mexicans then charged them, killing some and causing the rest to flee. While making their escape from the Mexicans, the surviving Karankawas came across a party of Texans. The Indians, fearful of another attack, saw the Texans and shouted "Viva Mexico." When the Texans heard this they charged the unfortunate Karankawas, killing some and chasing the remainder into the canebrakes.[22]

Although their final destruction may not have occurred exactly in the manner described above, the unstable and hostile situation in Texas only hastened their demise. In 1843, the Karankawas received permission from the Mexican government to settle across the Nueces River. Later some of them moved further south and crossed the Rio Grande. There were also a few found living on Padre Island.[23] In the initial struggle for Texas, the Karankawas and similar tribes of the Coastal Prairie were the only losers.

The discussion of the relations between the white men and the Karankawas was necessary in order to demonstrate the marked difference in relations that occurred when more advanced Indians were encountered. This is especially true when the De Witt colonists encountered the Plains Indians. The Plains Indians were culturally more advanced than the Coastal Tribes. Moreover, in the methods of warfare, the main factor in the contest of civilization in Texas, the Plains Indians' techniques far outdistanced those of the Coastal Prairie Indians. The Plains Indians which the De Witt colonists had to contend with were the Wichita, Kiowa, Kiowa-Apache, and the Comanche. Of these the Comanche were the most formidable and truly deserve the title "Lords of the Southern Plains."

The first encounter that the De Witt colonists had with the Plains Indians occurred in July, 1826. As has already been mentioned, those few colonists who were in the area of the colony in that year, fled the vicinity when an Indian raiding party came through. More than likely they did not know the tribal identity of this raiding party, and probably could care less. When they found sanctuary in Austin's colony on the Colorado and related the circumstances, it was determined that the raiding party had been Comanches and their allies, the Wichitas.[24] The upper areas of Austin's colony, those on the Colorado and Brazos Rivers had been troubled by Wichitas since the previous year. A campaign against the Wichitas' villages was subsequently planned, but then cancelled when it was determined that Comanches were also at the village.[25] By February, 1827, it had been established that there were Comanches in the area of the De Witt grant. They were not only passing through to conduct raids on San Antonio and Goliad, but were pressuring their bitter enemies, the Tonkawas. A good portion of the Tonkawa's range lay within the limits of De Witt's grant.[26] It should be recalled that in the early part of 1827 a number of De Witt colonists, under the direction of Byrd Lockhart, were sent up the Guadalupe River to begin construction of a fort at the site of Gonzales. They witnessed first hand the sound defeat that the Tonkawas and Lipan Apaches had suffered at the hands of the Comanches and Wichitas. As the Tonkawas and Lipans were making a hasty retreat they informed the De Witt colonists of the misfortune that had befallen them, only some nine miles from Gonzales.[27]

Already at this early date, De Witt and Kerr had heightened anxieties over the relative safety of the area of the grant. They realized full well that some added effort must be made in order to insure the safety of the colonists. Consequently Kerr requested Austin to assist in obtaining a heavy caliber weapon from the government arsenal. "Could a small piece of arteary [sic] be obtained from the Government. It would no doubt be of great utility to that place."[28] It is not definitely known if Austin complied with the request. However in light of his previous assistance and his desire to see the De Witt colony succeed, there is no reason to doubt that he attempted to procure such a weapon. The success of the De Witt colony might establish a buffer zone to protect the western flank of his own colony.

The request was not complied with by the government. The De Witt colonists did not receive a cannon. Instead they received a promise. At the time the colony was ordered to be moved from "Old Station," the Mexican authorities promised that as soon as all the families from "Old Station" were in and around Gonzales, a Mexican garrison would be ordered to that town and stationed there.[29] By the first part of 1828 all of the families were at Gonzales, but no Mexican garrison arrived. Fortunately, during that year no dangerous situations developed. From the evidence, it appears that the colony was relatively free from any depredations that first year. Limited contact with the Indians was probably due to the limited population of the De Witt colony at that time. The colonists avoided any contact because most stayed near Gonzales for at least the first months. For the most part, the Indians avoided Gonzales. However, the situation could not remain static for long. More settlers were coming into the colony and were moving out upon their farmsteads.[30]

The first known instance of difficulty between the colonists and the Indians occurred in December of 1828. A party of Indians had stolen a number of horses from Henry Stevenson Brown[31] while he was on the road between San Antonio and Gonzales. Brown came to Texas as early as 1824. Between the years 1826 and 1832 he was engaged in trading activities between the Anglo-American colonies and Mexico. He established his trading headquarters in the towns of Brazoria, Gonzales, and San Antonio.

John Henry Brown has indicated that some 500 horses were stolen from his father during that incident in December. However he does not indicate the tribal identity of the Indians who were responsible for the raid. When Henry Brown arrived at Gonzales he quickly organized an "expedition" there to assist him in recovering the horses. He already had earned a reputation as an "Indian fighter," a recognition that had become "a sort of title of nobility."[32] In 1825 he had been in command of a party of Austin colonists who attacked and destroyed a war party of Wichitas, near present-day Waco, Texas. The 1828-1829 expedition out of Gonzales lasted thirty-two days and took Brown and some of the De Witt colonists as far northwest as present-day Brown County, Texas, a distance of nearly two hundred miles in one direction. Little or nothing was accomplished by the expedition.[33] The direction taken by the expedition seems to argue strongly against the horse thieves being Tonkawas. If the Tonkawas had committed the raid, the expedition would have pursued in a north or northeasterly direction. The direction which the expedition took was toward Comanche territory.

In March of 1829 a number of raids occurred near Gonzales. In one such raid, the Indians "committed an outrage" by taking one horse and killing a few hogs some three miles from Gonzales. According to De Witt and the settlers who were victimized, the Tonkawas carried out the raid. Some miles away four more Tonkawas robbed a milling camp of some wooden planks and about one-hundred dollars worth of goods. In these instances not one of the De Witt colonists was harmed. They were, however, unnerved by the raids. After the initial shock and fear dissipated, the colonists were enraged. These Indians had to be chastised and dissuaded from committing any such future acts.[34]

It was determined that the various Tonkawa groups that had committed the raids had joined together and were moving toward Goliad. It was estimated there were, in total, about thirty Tonkawas. Green De Witt quickly assembled a party of seventeen of his colonists and pursued the Indians. When the De Witt colonists were about twenty-five miles from Goliad, it was determined a larger party of Indians, numbering about forty, had joined that group which the colonists were pursuing. This larger party had just completed a successful raid on Goliad and were in the possession of some fifty stolen horses. The Tonkawas now numbered about seventy.[35]

Since this was the case, De Witt decided not to pursue the Indians. Because of the Indian's superiority in number, he decided any engagement with them would be disadvantageous for the colonists. De Witt then sent out a scout to determine the exact position of the Indians and in what direction they were moving. The scout did not travel far when he sighted one of the Indians. The scout fired his weapon, missed and then gave chase. With this, four of De Witt's colonist went out to assist the scout. Then the remaining colonists, including De Witt, went after the preceding four. When De Witt and his group finally overtook the four colonists, they found a skirmish in progress.

The scout and the four colonists were being fired upon by the Indians. The Tonkawas were entrenched in a thicket and had good cover. De Witt ordered his group to fire upon the Indians so that the scout and the four colonists could escape from the precarious situation they had gotten themselves into. De Witt then decided against a frontal attack on the Indian's position, since it would have been suicidal for the colonists. A flanking movement was not attempted since the colonists would become separated in the thicket. If that occurred many of them would perish. De Witt decided to hold the group intact and attempt to entice the Indians from their cover. The Indians, probably realizing the advantage of their position, did not leave the thicket. It is of interest to note that the Indians, at first, did not attempt to charge De Witt and his men. When De Witt finally ordered a slow retreat, the Tonkawas charged. After the charge had been repelled, it was estimated that two Indians were slain.[36]

Both groups now realized they had worked themselves into a standoff. De Witt then decided to do nothing but hold his men together and wait. When darkness arrived the De Witt colonists slowly withdrew and went home.[37] The Indians probably withdrew sometime earlier. The colonists were fortunate that the Tonakwas were only interested in escaping.[38] Had it been a party of Wichitas or Comanches, they would never have dismounted. If they chose to flee the large group would have segmented into small groups difficult to follow. If they had chosen to fight, their abilities and superiority in numbers would have probably annihilated the colonists.[39]

With the expedition De Witt realized the fruitlessness of chasing the Indians after every raid. He then suggested that the only way to curb these raids was to station troops in the area. These troops would patrol an area from the Colorado to the Guadalupe River and down to San Antonio. He pointed out that these troops would not only be used for defense, but would also act as sentinels. They would be able to alert the colonists who would then be ready and waiting. De Witt suggested that if regular or militia troops could not be had, then "public troops" should be organized. These troops could be drawn from the ranks of the settlers themselves. This "Company of Rangers" would be responsible for patroling the area.[40]

It does not appear that either of the De Witt suggestions were acted upon. At that time no troops were sent to patrol the designated area and no permission was given to organize a select body solely for the purpose of Indian fighting. For one the Mexican government did not have a sufficient number of troops in all of Texas. Those few troops that were in Texas in 1829 could not be spared; they were needed to protect the more populous area of Texas and to guard against contraband trade. No action was taken on the part of the government regarding the creation of a company of rangers since Mexican law, as it applied to the colonization program, charged De Witt with the responsibility of creating and maintaining a body of militia within the colony. No doubt the Mexican authorities saw no need in creating such a military group when one, supposedly, already existed in the colony. There is no evidence which indicates that De Witt organized a formal militia. The fighting forces that were organized to chase and guard against the Indians were spontaneous. They were impulsively formed.

In April of 1829 the Tonkawas conducted more raids on the De Witt colony. During one of these raids, De Witt, with a group of his colonists, gave chase once more. Only this time when De Witt and his group finally overtook the Indians, no battle took place. De Witt used diplomacy. In a discussion with the Tonkawas, De Witt attempted to learn why they had been raiding the settlement. They obligingly informed him that they were being hard pressed by the Comanches from the north. Because of the Comanche menace the Tonkawas found it next to impossible to hunt. Therefore in order to keep from starving, they found it necessary to raid the white settlements. They pointed out to De Witt that, as far as they knew, they had harmed no one. They took only corn that was laying in the fields and some cattle and hogs which they butchered.[41]

For some time the Mexican government attempted to reduce the Plains Indians from their nomadic way of life. If they could be settled in a definite area, they could be more easily controlled. The colonization and land laws of Mexico made special provisions regarding the Indians. With this in mind, and acting under the orders of the jefe-politico, Green De Witt suggested to the Tonkawas a possible solution to their problems.

> I then laid before them the great benefits of them going to work, and embracing the privileges of the laws of the land . . . and informed them at the same time that I was sent by you [jefe-politico] to make them the offer of land where on to settle themselves, and that you had a great regard for them, and wished them to become a great and good people.[42]

De Witt tried to convince the Tonkawas of the benefits they could derive by becoming farmers. He even suggested that not only would the Mexican government assist them in any way, but also the colonists would do their part. He promised the Tonkawas he would send out a request to his colony, to Austin's colony and to the Mexicans for a donation so that the Indians might buy corn.

> I would send a paper into Austin's Colony and throughout this colony and request all the Americans to give them a Small Sum to buy . . . corn. . . . If a Small Sum of money can be raised and sent to New Orleans, they can be furnished with as many hoes and axes as will do things; and then an industrious man should be placed among them to labour [sic] with them and instruct them.[43]

The Tonkawas were also told the Mexicans would either donate horses outright, or enough money to buy them. Also the government would assign them four leagues of land for a town. If the Tonkawas showed they were sincere in settling down, then the government would give them more land.[44] Obviously the Tonkawas were pleased with these proposals, especially the one which involved the donation of horses. However, it is doubtful if they even were aware of what De Witt was talking about when he made reference to the donation of land. This well-intentioned plan was never put into effect. Nonetheless, the Tonkawas seemed to have been impressed with the force and vigor the colonists displayed. From that time on, the De Witt colony seemingly was never bothered by the Tonkawas.

Although the understanding with the Tonkawas was an achievement, the anxiety of the colonists was not eased. There were still the activities of the Comanches. The Comanches had been hardened and tested by a century-long conflict with the Spaniards and other tribes of Texas. They emerged as the undisputed victors. Every Comanche was a warrior, highly skilled in his art, cunning, intelligent, and courageous. They never asked for quarter, nor did they ever give it. Their abilities with a bow and war lance were unsurpassed. It has been said that a Comanche would loose a dozen or more arrows to every shot fired from a cap-and-ball rifle by a white man. Their most noted ability, however, was in their skill at horsemanship.[45] They were probably the finest light cavalry of the day. In addition to their excellent abilities and skills, they were most familiar with their lands. They had a distinct advantage over their adversaries in that they could choose when and where to fight.[46] Above all the Comanche were a proud people. They were morally superior to all of the Texas Indians. Of all the Texas Indians only the Comanches scorned the use of whiskey.[47] Unlike the tribes of the Coastal Prairie, the Comanche and their Wichita and Kiowa allies exacted a high price for their land and independence. In the final analysis, they were defeated economically. When food diminished they were forced to surrender.

By the middle of the eighteenth century the Comanche nation had extended its power from the upper reaches of the Arkansas River, to the edge of the South Plains. A number of decades later, advanced bands of Comanches were migrating deeper into Texas and the South Plains. They drove the supposedly invincible Lipan Apaches from the upper stretches of the San Saba River. By the early part of the nineteenth century, their country had reached as far east as the Cross Timbers and as far south as the valleys of the Colorado and Brazos Rivers.[48] When the Spanish period ended in Texas, the Comanches were reaching the height of their power and had virtually pushed back the Spanish Frontier.[49] Because of the geographic barrier posed by the Cross Timbers, the Comanche movement took a more southernly course.

The Cross Timbers of Texas were a unique geographic feature. They consisted of two long and narrow strips of forest region which ran parallel from present-day Oklahoma to the central portion of Texas, between the 96th and 99th meridians. The two distinct strips of forests were known as the Western, or upper Cross Timbers, and the Eastern, or Lower Cross Timbers.[50] Of importance to the present discussion are the Eastern Cross Timbers since they extend further south into Texas and were more of a barrier than the Western Cross Timbers.

The Eastern Cross Timbers, consisting of post and blackjack oak, spanned the ninety-seventh meridian in varying widths of five to fifteen miles. It ran southward for four hundred miles, from the Red River to the Brazos River.[51] At the Brazos, or near present-day Waco, Texas, the Cross Timbers began to diminish and to blend into the prairie terrain. The complexion of the Eastern Cross Timbers is more imposing because of the density of the timber. It was not only a formidable barrier to travelers, but also the Comanches who never penetrated it. The Comanches, with habits formed and dictated by the Plains environment, were wary of all forest regions, especially such an area as the Cross Timbers.

Geography and their mental composition determined that the Comanches, in their movement eastward, had to skirt this barrier. Because of these circumstances the development of the De Witt colony was, in turn effected. The northern portion of the De Witt grant was only a little more than eighty miles from where the Cross Timbers began to diminish. Consequently the Comanches and the De Witt colonists were brought into direct contact with each other. The Anglo-American colonists found that the Comanches were different than the relatively weak and docile tribes encountered on the Coastal Prairie. It was most fortunate for the De Witt colonists, however, that Comanche power was limited. The Comanches were limited in their capability to unite to prosecute a national war. Instead the Comanches were divided into small war bands, a situation dictated by the subsistence economy of the Plains Indians. The Plains environment simply could not sustain a larger tribal division for any great length of time. The De Witt colonists were also most fortunate in that the full force of the Comanche movement had not reached that far east yet. The De Witt colonists were encountering only the first wave of small war bands. The greater majority of 10,000 Comanches had not reached that sector of Texas.[52] What the De Witt colonists encountered was only the leading edge of the Comanche frontier. Had they encountered the full force of the Comanche movement, this discussion of the De Witt colony might well have ended much sooner.

Although the Comanche, or their allies, the Wichitas, did not make it a practice to raid the colony, their presence disturbed the settlers. The position of the De Witt colony, in a military sense, was strategically ideal. The position proved to be a vantage point from which much of the Indians activities could be detected, especially Comanche and Wichita raiding parties heading for the Mexican settlements of San Antonio and/or Goliad.[53] For the De Witt colonists this vantage point was disturbing. On can only imagine the deep concern in the minds of the colonists as they viewed the procession of raiding parties going and coming. The colonists could only relate their activities and nothing more. Their numbers were too small to follow and deter the raiding parties. It is of interest to note that the colonists did not have this attitude with regard to the Karankawas or Tonkawas. In a report to the jefe-politico, Green De Witt summed up the situation when he wrote ". . . I am only able to keep out spies and to watch them [Indians], least they should make an attack on this place. . . ."[54]

In that same report, De Witt wrote that it was only a matter of time before his colony would suffer raids similar to those experienced by San Antonio and Goliad. He pointed out that it was only the Comanche's desire for peaceful relations with all Anglo-Americans that spared his colony from any attacks. De Witt informed the jefe-politico that one of his colonists, Jesse Mc Coy, had returned from a several weeks stay with the Comanches.[55] De Witt mentioned that when Mc Coy was at the Comanche camp, he noted that a number of Wichita war chiefs were also there. They were there to invite the Comanches to assist them in waging war against the Mexicans and all of the Anglo-Americans. Mc Coy reported that many of the Comanches refused to aid their allies. A majority of the Comanches were at peace with the Anglo-Americans and desired to remain so.[56] No doubt their desire for peace was inspired to some extent by the trading relations that the Comanches and Anglo-Americans had established with each other.[57]

Green De Witt was convinced that the growth of the settlement was retarded by the nearness of the Indians. In his mind the problem could be alleviated by having a Mexican garrison at hand.[58] Even if the garrison were limited in capability, their presence would be comforting to the colonists. It should be recalled that De Witt's suggestion, made in March, 1829, of having Mexican regulars or a company of Anglo-American rangers patrol the district was not acted upon at that time. However, his request on May 8, 1829 was granted. A small detachment of Mexican

133

soldiers was sent to Gonzales. This action on the part of the government may have been prompted by De Witt's mention of contraband goods passing near Gonzales.[59] However, as has been previously mentioned, De Witt probably exaggerated the issue of contraband in order to obtain the troops.[60] Whether contraband trade existed, or whether De Witt merely used it as a pretext, is of no consequence. Within a few days the Mexican soldiers were withdrawn from Gonzales and returned to San Antonio.[61] No reason can be found for this action. When the Mexican detachment left Gonzales, De Witt immediately wrote the jefe-politico and requested another garrison.[62]

For the remaining months of 1829 and all of 1830 the Mexican government neither gave material assistance or sent any troops. There were not that many Mexican troops available in Texas. Those few troops that were in Texas were needed to protect San Antonio and Goliad. These two areas, more populous and more important than Gonzales, suffered the most from Indian depredations. Because the young Mexican Republic was suffering from internal probblems, the national resources and revenues were drained. Those few soldiers in Texas were unpaid and unsupported. Most had to work at occupations other than soldiering in order to support themselves. Consequently the Mexican soldier could offer only limited protection.[63] There is a good possibility that the Mexican troops that were in Gonzales for only a few days in May of 1829, were removed because they could not find work there to support themselves.

During 1830 the De Witt colony experienced more Indians raids than it ever had before.[64] It is of interest to note that this was the same year that the greatest influx of Anglo-American immigrants arrived at the De Witt colony.[65] The increase in population, as it encroached upon Comanche and Wichita territory, precipitated these raids. A larger population increased the material wealth in the colony. This increased material wealth, primarily in horses and cattle, did not escape the attention of the Comanches and Wichitas. The expression of friendship and aid which De Witt proposed to the Tonkawas, bitter enemies of the Comanches and Wichitas, also was no small factor in the increase of Indian depredations on the colony. De Witt lamented that the situation had gone from bad to worse. To him, the colony seemed to be surrounded by the Indians. At first their raids only amounted to killing and stealing cattle. Soon thereafter the Indians not only stole cattle, but were taking a good number of horses, an item which occupied a place of importance in the Plains Indians' system of values.[66] To make matters worse, the raids were occurring near the town. One such instance was a raid at the mill, located on the Guadalupe River, three miles from Gonzales. The raid on the mill was bad enough, but during it a De Witt colonist, George Singleton, was killed.[67]

There exists no positive indication that the Indians ever attacked Gonzales itself. In writing to the jefe-politico, De Witt stated that the Indians ". . . have made every attempt *from appearances*, to have made an attack upon the town."[68] What probably occurred was that someone had misinterpreted the movement of a large raiding party, or even a war band, as a general attack. If the Wichitas and the Comanches had ever decided upon a general attack, there certainly would be more evidence attesting to it. David B. Edwards, in his *History of Texas*, mentions, only in passing, an attack upon the town. If an attack of major consequences occurred the colonists would probably have not returned to their homes as soon as they did. They returned to their homesteads the next morning, according to Edwards.[69] Lastly, if such a major attack had transpired, De Witt certainly would have gone to great lengths in describing it to the jefe-politico, if for no other reason than to obtain the desired troops.

De Witt continued to request troops, but now he would even be satisfied if they were only assigned for a few months. He offered a somber prediction if aid were not given. Without some form of military assistance the settlement would break up, according to De Witt's views. If the settlement were to disband, not only would the crops and mills be lost, but the public good, in general, would be affected. The vantage point for detecting impending raids on San Antonio and Goliad would not exist.[70] Despite De Witt's use of logic and pleas, the troops could not be sent. In January, 1831 he made another request for troops and added this time, a request for an artillery piece. If, at least, this type of weapon could be lent to the colony, it might be of great benefit. The weapon of course would be returned, De Witt promised, whenever the authorities requested it.[71]

Suddenly De Witt's fortunes changed. It appears reports had reached the jefe-politico that some contraband trade was occurring between San Antonio and San Felipe de Austin. In response to this, the jefe-politico ordered a detachment of Mexican regulars to patrol the road between those two towns and prevent contraband trade. The detachment was also ordered to prevent any Indian hostility.[72] This might not have been entirely what De Witt had been requesting for so many months, but it was better than nothing. Then, In March, De Witt was informed by the jefe-politico that the artillery piece he had requested was available for his colony. De Witt immediately dispatched a wagon to bring the weapon, a six-pounder, unmounted cannon, back to Gonzales.[73]

It appears these efforts on the part of government, already overtaxed, did not fully please De Witt or alleviate the problem for the colony. In official correspondence to the jefe-politico, Commissioner Jose Navarro enclosed a description of the state of affairs in the colony as De Witt had written to him.

> As to the small number of actual settlers, I must observe for your information that a great many were discouraged by the actual condition of the country, the want of security for their families and property against the excesses of the Indians, . . . all of which induces them to settle in other Colonies. Several men after having taken the oath returned to the U.S. of the North, to dispose of their property and return with their families. . . . This Colony must remain with its small population in the very center of the incursions of the Indians. . . .[74]

Commissioner Navarro saw a possible solution to the problem that De Witt and his colony faced. He suggested that the government authorize the introduction of all of the foreigners in the Department of Bexar into the De Witt colony. These foreigners were individuals who were scattered through the Department and did not belong to any colonization contractor. Since it would have been difficult to expel them anyway, they might be of value in the De Witt colony. ". . . when being compelled to take up arms for their own protection, they would assist in bringing to an end the plundering and bloody war carried on by the Indians."[75] As excellent as this plan was, it does not appear that it was ever put into effect.

By June of 1831, the detachment sent to patrol the area between San Antonio and San Felipe was in the field. With a complement of fifteen men the detachment incurred no difficulty until August 18, 1831. On that day, near Gonzales, the Mexican detachment was attacked by a party of nine Comanches. The attack was swift and devastating. The Mexicans lost two men and thirteen horses.[76] On September 22, the detachment of Mexicans was removed from the area and returned to San Antonio.[77]

During the years 1832 to 1836 the De Witt Colony continued to sustain attacks by the Indians. However, in spite of De Witt's prediction, the colony did not break up. On a number of occasions the colonists mounted an offense campaign against the Comanches and Wichitas. One such expedition, led by Doctor James H. C. Miller, attempted to overtake an Indian raiding party who had attacked a group of French and Mexican traders only fifteen miles from Gonzales.[78]

By and large though, the period from 1825 to 1836 was relatively peaceful. As one Mexican official noted, only ninety-seven persons were killed by the Indians in San Antonio, Goliad and the De Witt colony during that period.[79] Intense hostility occurred between Texans and Indians, particularly Comanches, only after the Revolution. By that time, however, the Anglo-American frontier was hurling back the Indian frontier.

Texas, then, was a two stage contest of civilization: the Indian against the Anglo-American and the Mexican against the Anglo-American. The De Witt colony, in a way, symbolized this struggle. The colony represented the westernmost advance of the Anglo-American frontier. West and north of the De Witt colony was the Indian frontier. South and southwest of the De Witt colony was the furthest extension of the Mexican frontier.

Although the Indian menace was always of deep concern to the De Witt colonists, by 1832 Indian raids were, to a degree, being over-shadowed by events of greater consequence. Anglo-Americans, primarily those in Austin's colony, were becoming restless under Mexican rule. The De Witt colonists were to play a major role in the second stage of the struggle for Texas.

6

Town
and
Government

Both the agricultural frontier and the urban
frontier developed at the same time in the De Witt
colony. The only town of the colony, Gonzales, did
not develop from the needs and services of the agricultural frontier. In one respect the town was there
before the main body of settlers arrived. This is true if
the crude cabins, constructed on Kerr's Creek in 1826,
are considered as the first site of Gonzales. It is also
true when the fort, constructed near the Guadalupe
River in 1827, is considered the first site. At first the
town, or rather the fort, provided safety for the colonists. Later, as the town grew, it not only afforded
safety when needed, but provided a center for the
social and limited economic life of the De Witt
colony.

Mexico looked upon the town as having a vital function to perform and encouraged town development. The Mexican colonization laws made specific reference to the establishment of towns and set aside four leagues of land for urban use. Consequently, one of the first duties of an empresario was to survey an area of his grant for a town site. As has been mentioned, James Kerr performed this task for the De Witt colony in 1825. However his was only a preliminary survey. His survey, moreover, was incomplete since it was not fully in accord with Mexican law. It appears the Kerr survey did not make provisions for public squares. In April, 1831 Commissioner Navarro was instructed by the jefe-politico to re-survey the town tract.[1]

Commissioner Navarro, assisted by Byrd Lockhart, laid out the town on a grid pattern, with approximately the same number of lines running east and west as running north and south. The center of this grid was set aside for a square or plaza. It measured 333⅓ feet on each side. Another plaza, east of this main square was designated for the church and its necessary buildings. A third plaza, west of the main square, was to contain the administration buildings. A fourth plaza, north of the main square, was set aside for the market. A fifth plaza, south of the main square, was to be called military square. Two other plazas were also established. The jail plaza and the cemetery were to be established at the extreme western and eastern edges of the town, respectively. A huge cross was shaped with the town laid out in this form. The streets, all at right angles to the plazas, were to be 55½ feet wide.[2] The distance between all streets was 333⅓ feet. The areas formed by the intersecting streets were the town blocks. There were forty-two such blocks, each measuring 333⅓ feet square and each containing six lots. Each lot measured approximately fifty-five feet wide by 166 feet long.[3] This area was known as the "inner town."

The "inner town," located in the extreme southwestern portion of the town tract, occupied only a small fraction of the four square leagues. The "outer town" consisted of the remaining portion of the town tract. The outer town was divided into lots of two distinct size categories. Water Street which formed the western boundary of the inner town was extended so as to provide the dividing line between the two types of lots in the outer town. Those lots that lay west of this street measured approximately 1400 feet square. These lots were, in turn, divided into four smaller lots, each measuring 700 feet square. The entire section was divided by streets, seventy feet wide, running north to south and east to west.[4] A number of the lots fronted on the banks of the San Marcos and Guadalupe Rivers. Their delineations did not extend across to the opposite bank since the river was designated as the western boundary of the outer town. Consequently a number of irregularly shaped lots were created by the winding courses of the rivers. The area east of Water Street was divided into fifteen ranges. Each range, running north to south, contained fifty-eight lots. These lots, measuring 433 feet by 110 feet, were divided by streets seventy feet wide. The streets in this section, however, only ran from north to south.[5]

All town lots were disposed of by a public auction, after they had been appraised. The payments, collected by the ayuntamiento when established, were made on an installment basis of six, twelve, and eighteen months. As an incentive for immediate payment, a discount of six percent was customary. The payments for town lots were used for the building of the church and municipal needs. A tax of one dollar per year was levied on all inner town lots. The lots of the outer town were tax exempt.[6] Aside from the purchase price there were a few additional fees involved with purchasing a town lot. The fee to record the deed was three dollars. The fee for the legal paper, on which the deed was written, was one dollar.[7] The surveyor's fee amounted to one dollar for an inner town lot and two dollars for an outer town lot.[8] Any mechanics and all empresarios were given lots outright, free of purchase price.[9]

By March of 1836 the inner town of Gonzales had thirty-two structures. Of these, twenty had been built prior to 1831 and the other thirteen structures after that date.[10] It is impossible to state the exact order of construction of these buildings since the records reveal only the date of title issuance. The first title to an inner town lot was recorded on December 7, 1833.[11] However, it is known that of the original twenty structures, the fort was built first.[12] The fort, located some sixty yards from the Guadalupe River, was constructed on what was later one of Green De Witt's two "premium lots" in the town. It was directly across from the jail plaza and adjacent to Water Street. South of the fort by some one-hundred yards and on Water Street was Thomas R. Miller's store. Some thirty yards from the river were the Almeron Dickinson and George Kimble hat factory and the home of James Hinds.[13] These two structures, completing the row of buildings on Water Street, were respectively 150 and 200 yards, south of the fort. Across from the jail plaza and some 130 yards north of the fort was the home of James Tumlinson on Water Street. One hundred yards north of Tumlinson's was the residence of Lewis D. Sewell.[14] Directly across, but still on the east side of Water Street, was the home of John Sowell. The home of James B. Patrick, an alcalde, and John Saddler's shop completed the series of structures on Water Street north of the fort.[15] Saddler's shop was over 300 yards from the fort. All of these structures were on the extreme western edge of the inner town, i.e., the east side of Water Street.

Some one hundred yards east of Saddler's shop was the home of Umphries Branch. South of Branch's, by some 250 yards, was a structure called "Luna." Exactly what was meant by the word is not clear, but the property was deeded to Benjamin Fuqua. Fuqua, a mechanic, left Austin's colony in 1830 and came to Gonzales. There he established a mercantile business.[16] Thirty yards south of "Luna" was Winslow Turner's hotel. Both "Luna" and the hotel were directly east of the jail plaza. East of the hotel by one hundred yards were Adam Zumwalt's residence and "kitchen."[17] Across from the jail plaza and fifty yards east of the fort was the Stephen Smith home. Fifty yards from Smith's was the home of George Davis. Directly south of Davis's by one hundred yards were Best's home and smoke house. The last and southernmost home in Gonzales, prior to 1831, was that of Geron Hinds.[18]

Of the thirteen structures added after 1831, nine of them were located south of the jail plaza. Of these only one was located on Water Street, that was the home of John Castleman. East of the Castleman home was the resident of Joseph Lawler. To the north of Castleman's was the residence of Thomas R. Miller who built it adjacent to his store. Eli Mitchell's home was seventy-five yards east of Miller's. One hundred yards from the fort was Stephen Smith's store which was adjacent to his home built earlier. Across from Smith's store was the store of Horace Eggleston. Over three hundred and twenty-five yards southeast of the fort was the home of William Arrington. East of Arrington's by one hundred yards was the home of Joseph Martin and, beyond the southern limits of the town was Martin's mill. These three structures were the most remote buildings in Gonzales until 1838. Only three structures were erected north of the jail plaza after 1831. These were Jacob C. Darst's home which was near "Luna," Dr. J. H. C. Miller's home, one hundred yards north of Darst, and James B. Patrick's new residence, one hundred yards east of his old home.[19]

Of the 252 lots contained in the inner town of Gonzales, 92 of them had been deeded by 1835. Of the 92 deeded lots, twenty-six had structures erected upon them. The owners of the remaining sixty-six lots either eventually intended to build on them or meant to hold them for speculative purposes. The lots which were deeded by 1835 were all west of the main plaza. Only eighteen lots in the western portion of Gonzales remained unsold. These were the sixteen lots north of the municipal square and two lots on Water Street. All of the northeast and southeast portions of the town were available for purchase.[20]

In appraisals the lots varied in value from as high as seventeen dollars to as low as five dollars. The lots with the highest appraisal value were those which comprised the blocks nearest the jail plaza. The lots with the lowest appraisals were those contained in the blocks at the northern and southern limits of the town, those farthest removed from the plaza. Those lots on which the above mentioned structures were built were appraised as follows: "Luna," and Turner's hotel at $17; Tumlinson's home at $16; Zumwalt's residence and kitchen at $15; Darst's home at $14; Castleman's home at $13; Smith's home and store at $12; Mitchell's home at $12; Best's home and smoke house at $12; Hind's home at $11; Miller's home and store at $11; Mrs. Brown's home at $11; Dickinson and Kimble's Hat factory at $10; Saddler's shop at $10; L. D. Sewell's home at $9; John Sewell's home at

$9; and Branch's home at $7.[21] The determining factor in appraisal was a lot's location. Whether or not a lot had a structure upon it had no effect on the overall appraisal. Many lots without structures had a higher appraised value than those with structures.

The greater majority of lots disposed of in the outer town were in the area west of Water Street. In this area which contained 450 lots, 123 were sold. Many of these lots were along the banks of the San Marcos River to the west and the banks of the Guadalupe River to the south. In the area of the outer town east of Water Street there were 940 lots. Here, only 22 lots were sold. Most of them were directly east of the inner town. Large portions of land remained unsold in the western outer town and even larger portions in the eastern outer town.[22]

In appraisals the lots on the outer town, like those of the inner town varied in value. The outer town's average appraisal was much less than the average appraisal of lots in the inner town. In the outer town the average appraisal was greater for those lots east of Water Street than those west of it. In the western outer town the appraisals were as high as four dollars and as low as thirty-one cents, while in the eastern outer town the highest appraisal was eight dollars and the lowest was two dollars.

Of the sixty individuals who purchased town lots, both inner and outer, thirty-nine of them were residents of the De Witt colony, the remaining twenty-one owners were non-residents.[23] Those individuals, both resident and non-resident, who purchased unimproved lots in the inner and outer town were engaged in town land speculation.

Once set into motion a town, in this case Gonzales, developed independently from the empresario. After the basic designation the surveyor, land commissioner and purchasers were responsible for the town's future. Aside from the two lots which he received as his "premium" Green De Witt did not rank above others in promoting the growth of the town. In some respects it appears he did little or nothing in taking a direct hand in guiding the development.

It should be recalled that De Witt's empresario contract expired in April, 1831. Consequently, it seems that he took no further interest in either town development or in the town government. This is not to say he was politically inactive, but merely that he was just another citizen. High ranking offices did not come to him automatically because of his position as empresario. Green De Witt never held an elected, political office in the government of the colony.[24]

The political life of the De Witt colonists was reflected in the institution known as the *ayuntamiento* located in Gonzales. Although the ayuntamiento was the governing body of the town, its jurisdiction extended beyond the limits of the town. The creation and establishment of any ayuntamiento was contingent upon the degree of population. Any municipality which had attained a population of more than 200 inhabitants was required by law to form its own ayuntamiento.[25] The ayuntamiento was composed of *alcaldes*, *regidores*, and *sindico procuradores*, who were chosen by electors. The electors were chosen by voters at popular convention held every December.[26]

The principal official of the ayuntamiento was the alcalde. To merely define the function of an alcalde as that of a mayor is not totally accurate, since Mexican law, as the Spanish law earlier, made no provision for the office of mayor.[27] The alcalde's role consisted of a multiplicity of functions. In addition to being councilman, legislating measures for local affairs, he acted as a judge in cases involving minor crimes. He administered the political and economic functions for the town, and, at times, even acted as a policeman. Overall, his position carried with it prestige and authority superior to that of the other members of the ayuntamiento. The regidor shared with the alcalde the function of legislating measures for the town.[28] The sindico procurado acted as a city attorney and from time to time as treasurer.[29]

The term of office for all the members of the ayuntamiento was one year while no member could be re-elected until two years after his term of office had ended. No man could be elected to any office of the ayuntamiento unless he were twenty-five years of age. The age requirement was reduced to twenty-one years of age if a candidate were married. Any candidate had to reside for four years within the jurisdiction of the ayuntamiento and had to have a means of income. Any candidate had to be capable of reading and writing.[30]

The size of the ayuntamiento was dependent upon the population within its jurisdiction. Basically an ayuntamiento whose jurisdiction included two hundred persons was to elect one alcalde, two regidores, and a sindico procurador. As the population became larger the number of alcaldes and regidores was increased.[31]

When the De Witt colonists were at "Old Station" the population was much too small to qualify for the creation of its own ayuntamiento. The colony was therefore under the direct supervision of the Mexican authorities in San Antonio. This arrangement, however, failed since no one in the De Witt colony was very proficient in writing Spanish. The imposing amount of correspondence required to be written in Spanish soon prompted the government to place the colony under another authority. From October, 1828, to November, 1832, the De Witt colony was subject to the ayuntamiento of San Felipe de Austin and its civil and criminal code.[32]

The civil code, drawing heavily upon Anglo-American experience, fixed the alcalde's jurisdiction and outlined a judicial procedure. The alcalde had final jurisdiction in cases amounting to less than ten dollars. In cases involving $200 or more the alcalde still maintained jurisdiction, but the right of appeal was guaranteed. To assist the machinery of justice a fee bill was instituted, the first of its kind in Anglo-American Texas. The criminal code covered murder, robbery, theft, gambling, profanity, seduction, drunkeness, and counterfeiting. The alcalde was to investigate matters falling under the code and the cases were to be tried by a jury of six. Capital offenses were to be referred to the Commandant General at Monterey. Penalties such as whipping, banishment, and fines were imposed for minor offenses.[33]

When the De Witt colony was placed under the jurisdiction of the ayuntamiento at San Felipe, it became known as the District of Gonzales.[34] It was represented in the ayuntamiento by a regidor who, however, was a resident of San Felipe. The only governmental official who was present in the De Witt colony itself was the *comisario* of police. His function must have been to maintain law and order. It appears a De Witt colonist by the name of Fielding Porter held this position until June, 1830. Unfortunately the "minutes" of the ayuntamiento do not reveal if Porter was elected on this position, or was appointed to it.[35]

The De Witt colony did not merit the attention of the ayuntamiento at San Felipe again until July, 1830. At that time the ayuntamiento ordered the district of Gonzales to "elect another comisario of police."[36] Sometime during the preceding month Porter was murdered by a man named Hirman Friley. The murderer, knowing that he could not get a fair treatment in Gonzales, fled. He concealed himself in the wooded river bottoms and managed to get word to

Gonzales that he would surrender only to Captain Henry S. Brown.[37] Friley agreed to surrender only if Brown would accompany him to San Felipe where he would stand trial. Brown and most of the De Witt colonists agreed to this proposal.[38] Friley would have to go to San Felipe anyway since that was the seat of the ayuntamiento and had primary jurisdiction with reference to custody in such matters. From there he would be taken to Saltillo to stand trial. Friley's desire not to return to Gonzales, even in the custody of Brown, stemmed from his fear of mob violence there.[39]

During the trip to San Felipe, Brown and Friley encountered five De Witt colonists. These men, unaware of the agreement, drew their weapons and vowed to kill Friley then and there. At first Brown attempted to explain that he was taking Friley to San Felipe to stand trial, but the colonists paid no attention to him. At that point Brown vowed that he would kill the first man who fired at Friley. Reason returned to the colonists who then allowed the two men to pass unmolested.[40] No doubt these De Witt colonists respected Brown's marksmanship more than the law.

Since there was no jail in San Felipe and no official, at that time, was going to Saltillo, Friley was put in chains until such time that a trip was made. While Friley was awaiting his fate, a friend of his, Noah Smithwick, took matters into his own hands. Incensed at the treatment accorded to the prisoner, Smithwick gave him a file to cut the irons. He also gave him a weapon and other items with which to leave Texas.[41] Friley made his escape on August 24, 1830, but it was not until some two weeks later that the ayuntamiento placed a one-hundred dollar reward for his capture.[42] Friley, however, did not leave the area, but he, as Smithwick pointed out, "lay around in the hills, stealing in to [sic] the house of his brother-in-law at intervals to learn if his case had been decided."[43] On one such occasion Friley was seen by someone who reported it to the ayuntamiento. The authorities then managed to extract a confession from Friley's brother-in-law and went to the place where he was hiding. In his attempt to escape, Friley was killed.[44]

Noah Smithwick was implicated in the entire matter since the weapon which Friley had was traced to him. As Smithcwick, commenting on the situation, pointed out, "The gun I had given him was rather a noted weapon, being all of my own make and the first rifled gun made in the colonies; hence the charge against me."[45] For his part in facilitating Friley's escape, Smithwick was banished from the jurisdiction of San Felipe. The ayuntamicnto then had Smithwick escorted from Texas when he threatened to have satisfaction on them.[46] He did not return there until 1835.

The murder of Porter seemed to be the only problem that occupied the attention of the San Felipe ayuntamiento with reference to the Gonzales District. As has been mentioned earlier, the ayuntamiento ordered the Gonzales District to elect another comisario in July, 1830. Almost a month later this special election was held with only fifty-six colonists voting. James B. Patrick received a total of thirty-eight votes to Silas Fuqua's eighteen.[47] Patrick merely completed the term which Porter vacated. In the general election in December, Patrick was re-elected to the position.[48] Also in this election, one of the De Witt colonists, Thomas T. Miller, was elected to the position of sindico procurador to the San Felipe ayuntamiento.[49]

No further reference to the Gonzales District was made in the "minutes" of the ayuntamiento after the elections in 1830. This does not mean that the De Witt colony was unimportant, since the colony was large enough by this time to qualify for its own ayuntamiento. The most plausible explanation why the ayuntamiento of San Felipe did not deliberate any matter concerning the De Witt colony was that no major problems occurred. Also those problems which were particular to the colony were, by the first part of 1831, probably handled by the Mexican land commissioner, Jose Navarro, then in the De Witt colony.

The issuing of land titles and supervising the surveys kept Commissioner Navarro from forming the Gonzales ayuntamiento until the latter part of 1832. However, by November of that year he called for a convention of citizens of the De Witt colony to elect their ayuntamiento.[50] The colonists elected Ezekiel Williams as alcalde, Winslow Turner as first regidor, Silas Fuqua as second regidor and Stephen Smith as sindico procurador.[51] It should be noted that the election of the first ayuntamiento occurred a month earlier than the time prescribed by the Constitution of Coahuila-Texas. According to the constitution, notices of elections were to be posted on the first Sunday in December and the elections were to take place on the second Sunday and Monday of that month.[52] Consequently when the first Sunday of December arrived, notices for another election were posted, a little more than three weeks after the installation of the first Gonzales ayuntamiento.[53] There exists no explanation for Navarro's action in calling another election. If he were so eager to comply with the strict letter of the law, there appears no reason why he could not have waited until December. More than likely he wanted the colonists to become accustomed to electing their own ayuntamiento. Perhaps he was attempting to demonstrate to the authorities in San Antonio that he was properly fulfilling the duties of his office. It appears that according to the law, the ayuntamiento at Gonzales should have been established much earlier, but was not. The colonists, for their part, were not forcefully demanding its creation. They seem to have been entirely satisfied with the arrangement existing since 1828.

Once again, as in the preceding month, the De Witt colonists cast their votes. James B. Patrick was elected alcalde, Charles Lockhart was elected second regidor and Almond Cottle was elected sindico procurador. In accordance with the law only one of the two regidors was to be elected every year. So the situation in Gonzales only required the election of one regidor. The office of first regidor was therefore automatically filled by Silas Fuqua who had been elected second regidor in November. The position of second regidor, now vacated by Fuqua, was filled by Charles Lockhart.[54]

The ayuntamiento began its sessions in January, 1833 but established no regularly scheduled meeting dates. Meetings were held as the need arose.

One of the first acts passed by the Gonzales ayuntamiento was to limit the number of town lots that an individual could hold. The ayuntamiento resolved that ". . . all persons may have two in lots [inner town] and four out lots [outer town] deeded to them and no more."[55] Any non-residents who purchased town lots were required to locate all of them in the same block. Also, any owners of town lots, either residents or non-residents, who held four or more lots were required to improve the property.[56] These measures were designed to prevent a few speculators from obtaining a disproportionate share of important lot locations.

When the ayuntamiento convened for its February session, it dealt with a circumstance that posed a problem for the future growth of the town. The town was situated nowhere near a suitable place to ford the Guadalupe River. Obviously, a ferry would solve the problem and the ayuntamiento authorized the construction of one.[57]

The ayuntamiento contracted Stephen Smith and John Mc Coy to build the ferry at a cost of ninety-five dollars and seventy-five cents.[58] When Smith and Mc Coy finished the ferry in July, 1833, the ayuntamiento then enacted a schedule of rates. The rate for a wagon which was loaded was one dollar and fifty cents. The rate for an unloaded wagon was one dollar. The rates for the smaller Mexican-style ox cart were only slightly reduced. For a loaded cart the charge was one dollar and twenty-five cents and for an unloaded cart it was seventy-five cents. A man on horse back was charged twelve cents. Any individual who was driving a herd of cattle or horses and had need of the ferry, was charged six cents per head. During periods of high water or at night, the rates were usually doubled.

Considering the economic condition of the colony and the scarcity of money, these rates seem excessive. It was quite possible, however, that the ayuntamiento was looking forward to the day when commerical traffic would greatly increase between San Antonio and the Anglo-American colonies in East Texas or, for that matter between East Texas and the Mexican towns further to the south. Because of the town's location, between San Antonio and the East Texas settlements, Gonzales stood to gain if commercial traffic increased.

This optimistic outlook regarding future commercial activity was also seen in the ayuntamiento's concern for the condition of the "roads and highways" in the colony. The roads, at least the two main ones,[60] had to be kept in a state of repair. The Gonzales ayuntamiento required not only the few residents of the town, but all of the colonists under its jurisdiction to assist in maintaining the roads. Any abled bodied male of the De Witt colony was to contribute a maximum of six days per year to "opening and keeping said high-ways in order . . ."[61] If the colonists were unable or unwilling to work on the roads, they were fined by the ayuntamiento, one dollar for every day of road work duty missed. A maximum fine for one year was six dollars.[62]

There is no record of whether or not any fines were ever imposed. More than likely the law was never rigidly or effectively enforced since the quality of the roads remained poor during this period. This was true not only of the De Witt colony, but all of Texas for that matter.[63] Even in the United States, an area economically and technologically more advanced than Texas, the roads, in general, remained poor.[64]

The Gonzales ayuntamiento of 1833 ended its term of office by enacting an ordinance which imposed a fine on anyone found guilty of removing or defacing boundary markers. At times boundary stakes were removed outright. Other markers, such as "corner trees," were cut or defaced. Landmarks, such as a stone pile, were disturbed or even removed. The fine which the ayuntamiento imposed was one dollar for each offense.[65] It does not appear that boundary defacing remained a grave problem after the passage of this ordinance since the "minutes" of the ayuntamiento made no further reference to it. Other sources, such as the Bexar and Nacogdoches Archives make no references to the problem of defaced boundaries. Probably boundary defacing was perpetrated by mere pranksters. Consequently the ayuntamiento's ordinance was sufficient to deal with the problem.

The last official action of the Gonzales ayuntamiento of 1833 was to supervise the election of the ayuntamiento of 1834. With the exception of the second regidor, Charles Lockhart, none of the officials of the 1833 ayuntamiento could stand for re-election. According to the Mexican law no official could be re-elected until two years after the expiration date of his last elected position. In one way this policy was beneficial since it guaranteed the concept of rotation in office. On the other hand it would deprive the colony of the services of a competent official for at least two years.

During the election in December, 1833, James C. Davis was elected alcalde, Charles Lockhart became first regidor, Eli Mitchell was elected second regidor, and Thomas R. Miller was elected sindico procurador. Charles Lockhart, by law, was automatically elevated to the position of first regidor.[66] The newly elected ayuntamiento of 1834, like its predecessor met only occasionally. Unlike its predecessor, however, it did have a definite meeting place. Since none of the municipal buildings had as yet been constructed the home of the sindico procurador, Thomas R. Miller, was rented for the municipal office. It was rented for a period of one year at a rate of eighteen dollars.[67]

The ayuntamiento of 1834 chose a permanent site for the municipal office because it was more convenient and probably necessary to do so. The rent which was paid to Thomas R. Miller indicated that the ayuntamiento was deriving a revenue. What further substantiates this fact was that the ayuntamiento of 1834 found it necessary to create the position of a public treasurer.[68] The previous ayuntamiento did not officially have such an administrative office. The office of the public treasurer was not elective, but appointive. The ayuntamiento decided that the alcalde, James C. Davis, should fill that position.[69]

Whereas the ayuntamiento of 1833 was concerned about the condition of the roads throughout the entire colony,[70] the new ayuntamiento was primarily concerned with the streets and roads within the town tract. The ayuntamiento of 1834 required that only those colonists who had interest in the town were obliged to contribute some of their time to work on those streets or roads. The ordinance provided that, after having received one warning, an individual who did not perform his scheduled road work duty, was to be fined one dollar per day.[71] It is of interest to note that this ordinance, unlike that of 1833, did not provide for a maximum number of days that an individual was required to perform road work duty. It also made no provision as to a maximum amount that an individual would have to pay in fines.[72] It was possible that the maximum number of days and maximum amount in fines were understood to be the same as the earlier ordinance. On the other hand, the omission of maximum days and maximum fines may have been deliberate so as to ensure compliance with the law.

It appears that by 1834 commerce was increasing in Gonzales. This trade was primarily in dry goods and groceries which were brough in to meet the limited consumer demand of the hinterland population of the colony.[73] At this time three men, Horace Eggleston,[74] Thomas R. Miller, and Stephen Smith, were primarily engaged in the retail trade.[75] Although the retailing trade was not overwhelming, it was sufficient to create a source of revenue for the ayuntamiento. Any retailer, resident or non-resident, was required to obtain a license from the ayuntamiento. The retail license fee was ten dollars and was issued on a yearly basis.[76]

The wholesaling trade also existed in Gonzales. The three retail merchants mentioned above may very well have engaged in the wholesale trade also. It does appear that James B. Patrick also was engaged in this form of trade. On one occasion he obtained permission from the ayuntamiento to use the Gonzales ferry to bring goods up the Guadalupe River.[77]

The ayuntamiento required that resident or non-resident engaged in the wholesale trade to obtain a license also. The wholesale license fee, however, was set at two cents.[78] Apparently the ayuntamiento was attempting to attract wholesaling trade to the town. If Gonzales could become a dominant distribution point for trade with the Mexican towns to the south and southwest of it, then an increase in property and land values must necessarily follow. It should be recalled that Green De Witt earlier, while at "Old Station," thought in such terms.[78]

The presence of merchants in the De Witt colony provided the foundation for credit and lending institutions. By the nature of their business, only the merchants were in a position to establish any lending facilities, and thereby stimulate the economic activity of the colony.[80] Although lending and credit procedures were, at this time, in a crude and rudimentary phase, the ayuntamiento attempted to regulate the practice. The faint outline that a more active economy was emerging in the De Witt colony was apparent when the ayuntamiento deliberated and set a ceiling on interest rates. The ayuntamiento resolved that the interest rate would be ten percent.[81] It should be noted that the percentage of interest was no different in the De Witt colony than it was in the western portions of the United States, where it ranged from eight to ten percent.[82] Probably more important than the rate of interest itself was the fact that a credit economy was beginning to develop.

The ayuntamiento, in its attempt to promote Gonzales, dealt harshly with certain transgressions that might make the town less attractive to merchants, investors, and speculators. The ayuntamiento of 1834 established an ordinance which prohibited the shooting of guns or pistols within the boundary of the inner town. Anyone who violated this ordinance was fined a sum of twenty-five dollars. Also the ayuntamiento prohibited the running of horses through the streets of the town. The fine for this violation was also set at twenty-five dollars.[83]

In order to stimulate interest in the town, and hopefully to promote its growth, the ayuntamiento of 1834 repealed the ordinance which regulated the maximum number of outer town lots an individual could purchase.[84] It should be recalled that in January of 1833, the ayuntamiento for that year stated that an individual could own only four outer town lots. The ayuntamiento of 1834, after it had repealed part of this ordinance, substituted one which was more attractive to investors. The ordinance provided that "any person wishing to take out lots will be intitled [sic] to as many as he will improve and pay for at the valueation [sic]."[85] Also the ayuntamiento reduced the cost of surveying an inner town from one dollar to fifty cents and an outer town lot from two dollars to one dollar.[86]

The Gonzales ayuntamiento of 1833 and especially that of 1834 did much to encourage the economic advancement of the town as well as that of the entire colony. In December of 1834 the ayuntamiento for 1835 was elected with Andrew Ponton as alcalde, Joseph D. Clements as second regidor, and Matthew Caldwell as sindico procurador. Eli Mitchell was maintained by law in the ayuntamiento, but as first regidor.[87] The role which the ayuntamiento of 1835 played in promoting the town is not absolutely clear. Since the "minutes" of that ayuntamiento are not available, it can only be assumed that it continued its predecessors' policy of town promotion whenever possible. However the ayuntamiento of 1835 was faced with a problem that was more urgent than merely governing the colony or promoting the town. It was this ayuntamiento, the last that the De Witt colony would have, which was called upon to guide the colony during those crucial months when relations became strained between all of Texas and the Mexican central government. This was the ayuntamiento which, through its particular action, precipitated the Texas Revolution.

7

The Demise
of the Colony

The cause, as well as the events of the Texas
Revolution have received their fair share of historical
treatment.[1] It is, of course, beyond the scope of this
discussion to go into great depth and detail concerning those events which culminated in the rupture between Texas and the Republic of Mexico. However, it
is necessary to give a brief explanation of the causes
which led to this rupture in order to describe the role
which the De Witt colony played in the overall development. Of all the Anglo-American settlements,
the De Witt colony, because of its geographic position, was the least hostile, the least troublesome, and
the most conciliatory toward the Mexican government. It was with a touch of historical irony that the
first phase of the Revolution began there.

Aside from the differences in language, religion, and customs, the break with Mexico was accelerated by a series of developments. None of these developments, taken by themselves, would have been sufficient to cause difficulty, but taken collectively, they produced the events which led to Texan independence. The empresario system, the essence of which was to populate Texas in order to protect the northeastern frontier and integrity of Mexico, came under criticism. This became especially true after the Fredonian Rebellion when many of the Mexican officials began to distrust the basic motives of all the Anglo-American immigrants. Suspicions were compounded by the attempts of the United States government to purchase portions or all of Texas.[2] In response to the growing concern over Texas, the Mexican government dispatched a scientific commission, under the leadership of General Manuel Mier y Teran, in 1828. His report confirmed the suspicion that the Anglo-American colonists were not being assimilated as well as the colonization policy intended. The report emphasized that the Mexican government should exert its authority. The transition of Mexican policy, in regard to Texas, was consequently embodied in the Law of April 6, 1830. This law, embodying the Teran proposals, was the turning point in the relations between Mexico and the Anglo-Americans in Texas. The law not only prohibited colonization from the united States, but also provided for customs duties and the garrisoning of more Mexican troops in Texas.[3] The colonists, used to tariff exemptions and accustomed to governing their own affairs, looked upon the Mexican policy as a threat to their interest. The law interjected doubt and mutual distrust into the relations between the colonists and the Mexican government. Until this time, it was only the Mexican government that questioned the intentions and sincerity of the colonists. Now the colonists, for the first time, began to question the intentions and sincerity of the Mexican government. In such a situation, the actions of either one of the parties was viewed by the other with suspicion, anxiety, or doubt.

The Mexican garrisons at Nacogdoches, Goliad, and San Antonio were increased and other, smaller garrisons were placed on the Brazos River, Galveston Bay, Neches, and the Lavaca rivers, and near the mouth of the Nueces River. Interestingly, in an attempt to thoroughly Mexicanize the province, those new posts which were established were given Aztec names. The post on the Brazos was Tenoxtitlan, the post on Galveston Bay was Anahuac, and the post on the Nueces was Lipantitlan. (See map, p. 163)[4] The garrisons at these posts were to be used to curb contraband traffic, to prevent the evasion of paying custom duties, and to prevent any unlawful immigration. The new posts, as well as those older ones, were strategically placed around the then-existing Anglo-American colonies in order to prevent their spread and forestall any external invasion of Texas. Nacogdoches, Teran, Anahuac, and Velasco would defend the frontier and coast of East Texas. Tenoxtitlan would defend the western flank, while San Antonio, Goliad, Lavaca, and Lipantitlan would guard the south.[5]

With the establishment of these posts, it was expected that a Mexican settlement would evolve around each of them. Ironically, Mexico was attempting to return to the mission system concept. In effect it would have been the mission system, less the mission, by establishing presidios and pueblos, peopled with Mexicans rather than Indians. This attempt, probably coming too late, never succeeded simply because a sufficient number of Mexican colonists could not be drawn into Texas.

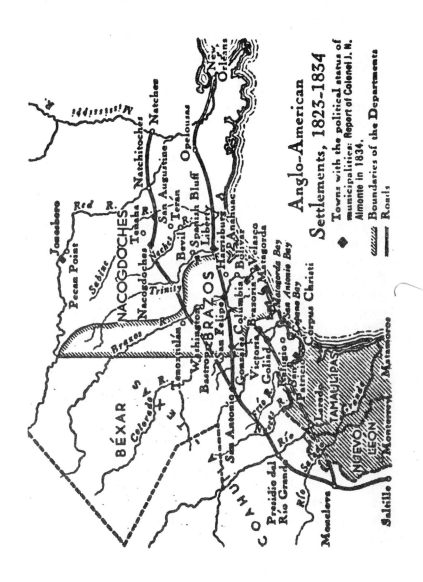

Anglo-American
Settlements, 1823-1834

◆ Towns with the political status of
   municipalities: Report of Colonel J. N.
   Almonte in 1834.
● Boundaries of the Departments
///// Roads
——— Roads

By May of 1830 customs collectors and contingents of Mexican troops began arriving in East Texas. However, no friction developed over the collection of customs duties until November, 1831. Due to abuse of his office, a port collector was removed by the government, in September of 1832, only after much correspondence and remonstance on the part of the colonists. No hostilities resulted.

Unfortunately a similar result did not occur when the use of the military was abused. This event occurred at the port of Anahuac, a site where the Trinity River enters Galveston Bay. The military commander of this post, who was a Kentuckian in the Mexican service, had arbitrarily arrested a number of colonists and generally alienated the rest. When the commander refused to release the prisoners and threatened to try them in a military court, the colonists reacted. Anahuac came under siege and a contingent of the colonists was sent to Brazoria for cannons. On returning from Brazoria the colonists were challenged by the Mexican garrison at the fort of Velasco. The ensuing engagement resulted in a Mexican defeat. The commander of the post, in surrendering, was accorded the honors of war and was allowed to depart for Mexico. Meanwhile at Anahuac, word reached the colonists that Antonio Lopez de Santa Anna was leading a rebellion against the regime of Bustamante. The Anglo-Americans, in turn, issued their Turtle Bayou Resolution in which they declared their support of Santa Anna and Federalism. Further bloodshed was averted at Anahuac with the appearance of Colonel Piedras of Nacogdoches. This astute Mexican officer secured the release of the prisoners, forced the commander of Anahuac to resign, and generally restored peace to the area. The new commander of Anahuac soon declared for Santa Anna and departed for Mexico with the entire Mexican garrison. Soon other military garrisons declared for Santa Anna and left Texas. By the end of the summer of 1832 all of Texas, except for San Antonio, was devoid of Mexican troops.[6]

It is of importance to point out that during these events the De Witt colonists remained aloof, not because of choice but because of position. The activities during the period of 1830 and 1832 occurred far to the east of the De Witt colony. The attitude of the De Witt colonists, as expressed by their ayuntamiento was one of caution. While the other Anglo-American ayuntamientos had declared for Santa Anna, the ayuntamiento at Gonzales issued a statement which indicated the reasons for their neutrality.

> As we have never been officially informed, either by the present reigning Government, headed by Vice President Bustamante, or by his opponents, headed by General Santa Anna, of the nature of these differences which exist between them; and as Citizens of a polity amenable only to our Federal head, we are as yet perfectly satisfied with measures heretofore pursued by that head in relation to us; and, were it otherwise, we feel our insufficiency to step between them and their explanations of the Constitution and laws of our adopted country! Moreover, having never had laid before us in a tangible shape, the difficulties existing between the Colonists of Austin and the Commandants of the Forts of Anahuac and Velasco: we are therefore, at this time, equally unable to decide as to the merits or demerits of either of the contending beligerents!
>
> Therefore, to you, Sir, as our organ of Governmental correspondence, we would have it made fully known, and by them perfectly understood, that we, the colonists of Colonel Green De Witt, are by our present unprotected situation, liable to be cut off by the savage foe! consequently, unable to render any physical assistance, if so required, to our brethren of Mexico, of Vera Cruz, or of Texas.

> Humbly trusting, that our precarious
> condition will be a sufficient excuse for our
> neutrality — not only to you, Sir, who know
> our state experimentally, and who have more
> than once expressed a fatherly solicitude for our
> preservation — but to that Government you re-
> present, on whose paternal care and munificent
> generosity we implicitly rely![7]

However, events were moving in a direction that
would eventually involve the De Witt colonists.

The Anglo-American colonists, particularly
those in the area near San Felipe de Austin, were
flushed with a sense of accomplishment when the
colonists decided to attempt to rectify certain griev-
ances. The ayuntamiento of San Felipe, hoping that
the new Mexican government under Santa Anna
would be sympathetic, issued a call for a convention
in August of 1832. The ayuntamiento requested that
all of the towns or ayuntamientos of Texas send delegates to the meeting scheduled for October 1. When
the convention met, there were fifty-eight delegates
representing sixteen towns or ayuntamientos; San
Antonio was not represented. The absence of a dele-
gation from San Antonio demonstrated that the Mexican population was not committed to the movement.
The De Witt colony sent Henry S. Brown and Cali-
borne Stinnet. Brown and Stinnet were popularly
elected with the Gonzales ayuntamiento conducting
and sanctioning the election.[8]

Working within the framework of the Mexican
Constitution, the convention suggested that "ranging
companies" be created to protect the frontiers of Austin's and De Witt's colony; suggested an extension of
the tariff exemption; repeal of the immigration exclusion of the law of April 6; denied any designs for
independence; and requested that Texas should be
made a separate state. The convention also provided
for a committee of safety and correspondence which

would attempt to circulate important information concerning Indian activities and events in Mexico. Before it adjourned the convention empowered the central committee to call a convention whenever it was needed.[9] The convention adjourned on October 6.

This unprecedented action on the part of the colonists brought severe disapproval from the governor and the jefe-politico. The De Witt colonists for their part, were informed that such action was illegal and were asked to what extent they participated in the activities of the convention.[10] The De Witt colonists, or rather their ayuntamiento, replied to the communication in apolgetic and disavowing terms.

> We acknowledge the receipt of your Lordship's communication . . . in which you request this body to say how far they have taken part in the convention held in Austin's colony, for the purpose, it is said, of making representations to the government. They answer that in no manner have they been officially concerned in said convention, and that the colonists of this jurisdiction have taken officially no part in it. God and Liberty.[11]

The central committee did not wait long before it called for another convention. In January of 1833 it requested that all the districts of Texas send delegates to San Felipe on April 1. The reasons given for the calling of a second convention were that the civil war in Mexico still continued, that the petitions of the previous convention were never presented to the authorities, and that the previous convention was not given sanction by the Mexican government.[12] The De Witt Colony chose once again Henry S. Brown and Claiborn Stinnet.[13] The De Witt colony was one of the few districts to return the same delegates or even individuals of the same frame of mind as those of the first convention. The convention was attended by fifty-six delegates, and of these, only fourteen had served in the convention of 1832.[14] The tempo of this convention had swung toward the more active elements in Texas society. Whereas in the convention of 1832, the delegates were content with petitions, memorials, and resolutions, the convention of 1833 accomplished this but went one step further.

The convention of 1833 dealt with the same problems of extended tariff exemptions, repeal of the anti-immigration law and separation of Texas from its union with the state of Coahuila. However, this convention actually drew up and approved a state constitution. The tentative constitution, modeled on that of the 1780 constitution of Massachusetts, was then taken by Stephen Austin to present to the Mexican government.[15] Clearly the moderates were in minority. The radical party was, for the first time, beginning to exert itself.[16]

The position of the De Witt colonists in relation to the outcome of the convention of 1833 was one of agreement. The De Witt colonists, still essentially moderate in their views, did desire separate statehood for Texas. One primary reason was that the Indian problem and judicial-legal functions could be performed more efficiently if separate statehood were granted. Their attitude was expressed in correspondence to the jefe-politico by the alcalde James B. Patrick. Two weeks after the convention adjourned Patrick stated that the colony concurred in the action taken by the convention regarding statehood for Texas.[17] In light of the previous stand made by the De Witt colonists after the convention of 1832, this firm statement seemed a departure on their part. However, this was not so.

When the outcome of the convention was made known to the Mexican authorities, a response, similar to that of 1832 occurred. The government sternly disapproved and attempts were made by the jefe-politico to have the various ayuntamientos repudiate the convention and its work. When the De Witt colonists, or rather its alcalde, issued the statement approving the action taken by the convention, they did not know how the government would react. Apparently they thought the government might condone any actions taken to remedy the problem of Texas. They were totally in error. By May they were officially informed of the government's attitude toward the convention. The acting jefe-politico informed the Gonzales ayuntamiento that the government condemned the attempted separation. He went on to point out that the convention was an illegal assembly. He suggested that the De Witt colonists refrain from participating in any such future affairs. He pointed out to them it would be better for all concerned that they remain aloof from all political affairs.[18]

Once again, as they had done in December of 1832, the ayuntamiento of Gonzales attempted to conciliate, explain, and apologize. The ayuntamiento, in replaying to the letter of censure, pointed out to the acting jefe-politico that there was no intention of disobeying the government. The ayuntamiento went on to state that since the authorities did not sanction the activities of the convention, the De Witt colony would revoke its previous support of the resolutions of the convention. In the future only those measures, the ayuntamiento promised, which were sanctioned and approved by the Mexican authorities, would be considered valid. The ayuntamiento would adopt no further resolutions without first determining if the authorities recognized their legal status.[19] The reversed position taken by the De Witt colonists was prompted by their respect for the government, but more so, by their faith in Stephen Austin's mission to Mexico. There was still the utmost hope that with the liberals in power in Mexico, the ills of Texas could be cured. Their faith in Austin did seem justified. When Austin saw Santa Anna he extracted promises from the president that the prohibition on immigration would be removed; that a modification of the tariff would be referred to the treasury department; and that the state government of Coahuila-Texas would be urged to create in Texas a more efficient legal system.[20]

By the end of 1833 political agitation and ardor had cooled considerably. The Anglo-Americans in Texas, particularly those in east Texas and the settlements along the coast, the main areas of discontent, were more concerned with the cholera epidemic than any grievance against the Mexican government. Interestingly, the situation in Texas was in direct contrast to what it had been a few months earlier. To Colonel Juan Almonte, Texas was not a seeting hotbed of revolution. Almonte was sent by the Mexican government to observe the situation in Texas, and also as an agent of good will. He found the colonists had legitimate grounds for requesting reforms in many instances. Almonte even went so far as to recommend concessions to the colonists. He took up many portions of their cause. However, in his report, he noted the great increase of Anglo-American immigrants and the decreasing influence of Mexican civilization and culture, almost none of which existed in eastern Texas. To counteract this indirect threat, Almonte suggested Mexican families be encouraged to migrate to Texas and that Texas should be, once more, re-garrisoned with troops.[21] Obviously, Almonte journeyed through those areas of Texas which were considered to be the most troublesome and most volatile. In applying this axiom to the De Witt colony, it appears that the Mexican official considered that area the least likely trouble spot. The De Witt colony was only given passing reference as Almonte made his way to

San Antonio.[22] The De Witt colony never really gave the authorities cause for concern. For that matter they had been one of the most amiable.

During the months after the convention of 1833, relations between the Anglo-American colonists and the government were cordial. The colonists did receive a number of concessions which they had earlier requested: the restriction on immigration was lifted; Texas received three representatives in the state congress composed of twelve members; the English language was recognized for official purposes; religious toleration was granted; a superior court was created in Texas; and a system of trial by jury was established. As far as separate statehood was concerned, this did not occur. Instead, Texas was divided into three political departments of Bexar, Brazos, and Nacogdoches. The De Witt colony was, after 1834, under the jurisdiction of the department of the Brazos.[23] This fact becomes important in the fateful relations between the De Witt colony and the Mexican government during the crucial year of 1835.

Relations between the government and the Anglo-American colonists probably would have remained stable for a number of years if two sets of circumstances had not provided the necessary catalysts which precipitated hostilities. One set of events resulted from an unfortunate rivalry and hostility between two cities of the state of Coahuila-Texas over the site of the state capital and the disposition of that state's public domain. The other set of events stemmed directly from the Texas policy advocated by Santa Anna. It at first may appear that these circumstances do not bear even the slightest relationship to each other. However, they were to interrelate in such a way as to bring about armed rebellion.

The difficulty between the two cities, Saltillo and Monclava, over the location of the state capital began in 1833. In that year the capital was moved, by act of the state legislature, from Saltillo to Monclava. At first Saltillo did nothing. When political events erupted in Mexico City in 1834, Saltillo established a rival state government and declared for Santa Anna, with the hope of gaining his support in the controversy. The matter of the two state governments was then presented to Santa Anna for arbitration. He supported the government at Monclava. However, the Monclava legislature, far from being servile, went so far as to criticize Santa Anna for attempting to destroy the Mexican federal system. There the situation remained until certain action on the part of the Monclava legislature provided a convenient excuse for Santa Anna to rid himself of an area that might possibly form the nucleus of power against him.[24]

The circumstances which provided Santa Anna with a rationale to take action against Monclava stemmed from a series of land laws passed by that legislature. By laws passed in March and April of 1834 thousands of acres of Texas land were squandered by unscrupulous sales to a small number of speculators, many of whom were Anglo-Americans from Texas. Another great land sale, authorized by the law passed on March 14, 1835, brought about action from the central government. The deputation from Saltillo censured this action and withdrew from the state legislature. After their departure, they called upon the central government to nullify these laws and dissolve the legislature at Monclava since the land laws it passed were in conflict with the National Colonization Law. The central government, under the influence of Santa Anna, acted by annulling the March 14 legislation. The legislature at Monclava ignored the decree of the central government. Whereupon General Martin Perfecto de Cos was ordered to march to Monclava to enforce the federal decree. With federal troops marching on them, the legislature at Monclava passed its last land law. This law of April 7, empowered the governor to take appropriate action in face of the impending situation. The governor did take action by selling more Texas land to speculators in order to obtain funds with which to meet this threat. The legislature disbanded and the governor attempted to flee to San Antonio to re-establish the state government. When the federal troops arrived, the governor was captured and the land speculators fled to Texas with the news.[25]

Among the leading land speculators that were found in Monclava in the early part of 1835 was Green De Witt. The policies then being followed by the state legislature afforded him an excellent opportunity to acquire vast holdings of Texas land, not only within the confines of his previous grant, but also in the more populous region of east Texas. His plans were interrupted when the news circulated that the central government had voided the state law and that General Cos was marching toward Monclava to enforce the decision. Green De Witt, along with a number of other land speculators, decided to remain in Monclava and assist in the impending civil war.[26] When the other speculators finally fled from Monclava, Green De Witt was not among them. During his stay there he had contracted a fatal illness, probably cholera, and died on May 18, 1835. He was buried in an unmarked grave in Monclava.[27]

When the land speculators arrived in Texas they brought the alarming news of what had transpired in Monclava. They pointed out that the central government, under the dictatorial direction of Santa Anna, was determined to destroy the federal system, any opposition to his regime, and to re-establish military control in Texas. The general response to these reports, at first, was one of skepticism and doubt. The colonists were under the impression that these land speculators were exaggerating the incident as to protect their own vested interests and to diminish the degree of their own complicity in the nefarious land scheme. The attitude on the part of the colonists was demonstrated by their reaction to the governor's request for militia assistance from Texas. No response came from Texas.[28]

If the affair in Monclava did anything, it destroyed any confidence which the Anglo-American colonists had in the state government. One of the colonists appriased the entire situation by pointing out that to take any action would only assist ". . . a few unprincipled land speculators, and rescue one of the most depraved State Legislatures that ever assembled on the continent of North America."[29] The affair at Monclava also tended to diminish the centralizing efforts of the Santa Anna government. When by June of 1835 news circulated of how Santa Anna had ruthlessly suppressed his opposition in Zacatecas, most Anglo-American colonists began to look differently at the military expedition against Monclava. The affairs at Zacatecas and Monclava began to appear to the colonists as an attempt to abolish the federal system. Their concern was heightened when Santa Anna began to implement his policy for Texas.

Briefly, the Texas policy of Santa Anna was to reopen the customs houses and to distribute Mexican garrisons throughout Texas. The first of these measures was begun in January of 1835 when the customs house at Anahuac was reopened. This action caused some disturbance with the resulting arrest of some colonists. By June news of this incident reached San Felipe de Austin. Almost at the same time a military courier was dispossessed of his official dispatches. Among the letters was one from General Cos to the commander of the post at Anahuac. This communication informed the commander that the troops that had been used in Zacatecas and Monclava were on their way to Texas.[30] From this juncture, events in Texas moved almost parallel to those events in 1832. However the outcome was to be quite different.

Since the legislature of Coahuila-Texas had been dissolved, the Anglo-American colonists now found it necessary to create committees of safety in their various districts. In the De Witt colony one such committee was selected by the colonists. The committee, headquartered in Gonzales, consisted of James B. Patrick, William Arrington, John Fisher, George Davis, Andrew Ponton, Bartlett McClure, and James Hodges.[31] While committees such as this were forming, other, more radical minded colonists from east Texas were taking more extreme action. William. B. Travis and twenty-five men beseiged the Mexican garrison at Anahuac. The following day, June 30, the Mexican commander surrendered the post and left. If the Anglo-Americans desired revolution, this was the time to have begun it. However, the action by Travis was criticized by most colonists. The De Witt colonists were one of the first to denounce this action.[32]

At the behest of Edward Gritten, the ayuntamiento of Gonzales proclaimed its loyalty to the Mexican government, once again, and condemned the extreme action that had been taken. Gritten had been Juan Almonte's secretary during the latter's inspection tour of Texas. Gritten, at the time of his presence in the De Witt colony, was a special representative of Colonel Domingo Ugartechea who had commissioned him to report on the state of public opinion in the settlements. As a representative of Ugartechea, Gritten made an effort to convince the De Witt colonists that no troops were coming to Texas. Apparently he was successful in placating the anxieties of the colonists.[33]

By July the moderates in Texas were asserting themselves. As a result of a general meeting of the committees of safety held in San Felipe, two representatives, Edward Gritten and Don Carlos Barrett, were sent to meet with General Cos. They were to present to him letters of conciliation and loyalty. Gritten always worked to maintain harmony between the government and the colonists. While on his way to Matamoras to see General Cos, Gritten received orders from Colonel Ugartechea which informed him that the general would not treat with the peace commission until those individuals responsible for the disturbance at Anahuac were arrested. It appears the order for the arrest was suggested by a prominent member of the De Witt colony, Dr. J. H. C. Miller.[34]

Dr. Miller was by no means a pacifist. He was, however, an intense loyalist. He was convinced the country would never be quiet until the agitators were removed. Dr. Miller took his oath of allegiance and Mexican citizenship seriously. Dr. Miller felt that the hositilities were engendered by the "war and speculating parties."[35] He held his views to the bitter end, but finally declared his loyalty to the Texas Republic in 1836. He, however, soon left Texas, no doubt, because of the persecution which followed in the wake of his earlier beliefs. John Henry Brown writes of him in the following manner: ". . . there was a spy in the camp at San Felipe, one who had in a residence at Gonzales, made a favorable impression, but who now developed the loathsome attribute of a tory and a traitor. This disgrace to our race was known as Dr. James H. C. Miller. . . . This creature was doing the foul work of a spy for Ugartechea."[36]

The moderates in Texas must have had some strength for they evoked comment by a prominent member of the radical faction, William B. Travis. "The peace party, as they style themselves, I believe are the strongest and make much noise. Unless we could be united, had we not better be quiet and settle down for a while."[37] The moderate, or peace, element in Texas was merely following a policy set down by such men as Stephen Austin years earlier, namely to remain aloof from Mexican affairs.[38] However circumstances were developing whereby the Texans were no longer afforded this luxury. The re-establishment of garrisons in Texas and the possible destruction of the federal system by Santa Anna's measures brought the Anglo-Americans into Mexican affairs.

The situation was reaching an impasse. Mutual distrust, rather than calm discussion, was becoming the order of the day. When it was determined General Cos was marching with a large body of reinforcements to San Antonio, a general consultation of all the committees was called. Not withstanding Gritten's assurances, more Mexican troops were on their way to Texas. However, there was still hope among a number of the colonists that differences could be solved without resorting to force of arms. Those who were hesitant soon altered their position as events developed in the De Witt colony.

When Ugartechea, headquartered at San Antonio, heard of the disturbance at Anahuac in June of 1835, he was concerned over the possibility of armed rebellion. He became unnecessarily disturbed over the six-pound cannon which the De Witt colonists had in their possession. As a sophisticated weapon, the cannon fell far below standard requirements. Its only redeeming qualities were its awesome appearance and the terrible noise it made when touched off.[39] Despite the cannon's low military value, Ugartechea, conscientious soldier that he was, decided the weapon must be recovered and returned to San Antonio. In order to prevent any difficulties, the colonists must be disarmed. Ugartechea then ordered Corporal Casimiro De Leon, with a company of five men, to the De Witt colony to recover the weapon.[40]

When the De Witt colonists, or rather the ayuntamiento, were confronted with the demand for the cannon, they were puzzled. They wondered what need the army had for this obsolete weapon when there were some eighteen superior pieces already in San Antonio. They arrived at only one answer; the military forces were determined to disarm them and leave them helpless. The colonists voted in favor of withholding the weapon. They well realized that to disobey the order to surrender the cannon would bring more troops to the colony.[41] By the end of September many of the De Witt colonists, who resided near Gonzales, decided to move into the town for added protection in the event of hostilities. Others moved from their farmsteads and then east of Gonzales. Still other colonists moved their families as far as the east side of the Colorado River.[42]

One of the De Witt colonists, D. S. H. Darst, recalled that during this exodus he was only a boy of twelve years of age. He stated that he, his mother and sister left Gonzales by river and stopped at a place called Tumlinson's Bend. They did not remain there long for they had observed a group of Mexican soldiers encamped nearby. The refugees then continued up the river, in a northwesterly direction, till they came to Bolin's Bend. There they found the George Davis and Green De Witt families. Darst pointed out that the colonists were so busy moving their families to safety that at certain times there were no more than eleven men in Gonzales.[43]

Those colonists who remained and those that returned after seeing to the safety of their families then proceeded to bury the cannon. Also, the alcalde, Andrew Ponton, requested assistance from the other Anglo-American settlements to the east.[44] While all this activity was going on in the De Witt colony, and primarily in Gonzales, Corporal De Leon patiently waited across the Guadalupe River for the cannon to be delivered to him. Obviously the De Witt colonists had prepared for such a situation. Perhaps this, in a way, explains their conciliatory behavior in the past. In the event of hostilities, they knew full well that because of their geographic position any invasion would have to come through the colony. But, on the other hand, they may have reacted in such a way because of confusion, fear, and primarily, distrust.

On September 26, Andrew Ponton explained to Colonel Ugartechea why the cannon would not be given up. The alcalde of the De Witt colony apologized for the delay in answering the request. He went on to state that he was under the impression the weapon had been given to the colony in perpetuity, in order to protect itself against possible Indian raids.[45] Ponton pointed out that since the possibility of Indian hostility still existed, it would be hazardous for the colony to surrender the weapon. Also Ponton maintained he had not been directed to surrender the cannon by the jefe-politico of the Department of Brazos.[46] Here, Ponton was on firmer technical grounds. It should be recalled that in 1834 Texas was divided into three departments and the De Witt colony was placed under the jurisdiction of the Department of Brazos. With James B. Miller as the jefe-politico of the Department of Brazos, Ponton knew that he never would receive such an order. However, Ponton stated to Ugartechea that he would surrender the weapon only after he had received orders to do so by the jefe-politico.[47]

The De Witt colonists suspected that if they did not comply with the order, more troops might be sent to Gonzales. Their suspicions were confirmed when Ugartechea received Ponton's explanation.

Ugartechea immediately dispatched Lieutenant Francisco Castaneda, with one hundred men, to retrieve the cannon by force if necessary. Castaneda was not to ask for the weapon, but to demand it. Castaneda was not to be put off by the excuse of the absence of any such orders from the jefe-politico of the Department of Brazos. If the order was not immediately complied with, Castaneda was to use force, punish all those who resisted, and arrest Ponton.[48]

Corporal De Leon was still encamped across the river and patiently awaited the delivery of the cannon and the re-inforcements under Lieutenant Castaneda. During the late afternoon of September 28th, the De Witt colonists precipitated the first action of the Revolution. Some twelve of the colonists had secretly crossed the river and surprised the small Mexican detachment. Corporal De Leon and his men, surprised and outnumbered, had no choice but to surrender. The small Mexican detachment was then disarmed and taken as prisoners into Gonzales.[49] The colonists then allowed one of De Leon's men to bring the Mexicans' horses. This soldier managed his escape, at this time, since the colonists had sent no guard with him. The soldier began to make his way back to San Antonio when he came upon Lieutenant Castaneda and his detachment. He informed Castaneda of what had happened. Castaneda continued to make his way toward Gonzales.[50] It must have become apparent to him by now, that he would have to take the cannon by force.

When Castaneda came within a distance of a half mile from Gonzales he met another Mexican soldier coming from the town. The soldier, who, for some unknown reason, had been released by the colonists, informed Castaneda that for the past two days reinforcements of Anglo-Americans had been coming into Gonzales.[51] Many of these reinforcements were the De Witt colonists who returned to the town after they found safety for their families. Other were De Witt colonists from the outlying regions of the colony. Still others were the first wave of Anglo-Americans from other settlements who answered Ponton's call. The number of men now in Gonzales was estimated by this soldier as being more than two hundred and continuing to increase.[52] What originally began as a simple, routine mission was becoming a difficult and grave situation.

The De Witt colonists, now aware of the approach of Castaneda's column, deployed themselves along the left bank of the Guadalupe River. The colonists prevented the possibility of Castaneda fording the Guadalupe by removing the ferry and all boats to their side of the river. The crafts were then concealed and a heavy guard was placed over them.[53] Graves Fulcher and W. W. Arrington, both De Witt colonists, had to resist the great temptation of opening fire on the Mexican detachment as it approached the opposite bank.[54] In the meantime, Lieutenant Castaneda unaware of the presence of the concealed Anglo-Americans and seeing that he could not cross the river then and there, decided to withdraw from the exposed position on the river bank.[55] Castaneda then sent word to Gonzales that he desired an interview with the alcalde. He was informed that Ponton was not at Gonzales, at the time, but would return the next morning. Castaneda decided to wait for the alcalde's return and attempt to persuade him to surrender the cannon.[56]

The following day, September 30th, Castaneda came to the river crossing for the scheduled meeting with Ponton. There he was informed by Joseph C. Clements, the regidor of the Gonzales ayuntamiento, that the alcalde had not returned but was expected shortly. Clements told Castaneda that in the event Ponton had not returned he would assume the responsibility to discuss the matter. Later that day, Castaneda returned to the place for the meeting, but again found Clements waiting. Clements informed him that Ponton was not available and it was decided by the ayuntamiento that he should deal with the matter.[57] Castaneda requested Clements to surrender the weapon. Clements replied, with a prepared communication, that since the ayuntamiento received no explicit instructions from the jefe-politico at San Felipe, he and the Gonzales ayuntamiento assumed the responsibility for the final disposition of the weapon in question. He informed Castaneda that it had been decided that they would not surrender it. Clements stated emphatically that only through the use of force would the cannon be given up. Clements ended the communication by stating, "We are weak and few in number, nevertheless we are contending for what we believe to be just principles."[58]

Castaneda was now faced with a perplexing problem. When he first began the mission, it was merely a question of marching into Gonzales and obtaining the cannon. He, more or less, had this commanding position over the colonists by virtue of the size of his detachment. Within the course of twenty-four hours, however, the situation was reversed. From the reports Castaneda received, it appeared he was outnumbered. However, he himself was not absolutely certain of this. He reported the existence of this supposedly superior force to Colonel Ugratechea in his communication on September 29th. Ugartechea, after receiving the communication, ordered Castaneda not to engage if it were determined that the forces of the opposition were actually superior.[59] Castaneda, on September 30th, received another report from an Indian who came from Gonzales, that many men were coming into the town.[60]

Castaneda, and only Castaneda, had to make the decision. His orders from Ugartechea were explicit. The situation, in the manner in which it developed, dictated that he should comply with his orders and withdraw. He decided to stay. In his communication to Ugartechea, on September 30th he stated that he would move the detachment further up the river and, hopefully, would find a place to ford it.[61] Lieutenant Castaneda was not convinced that such a large force could be in Gonzales and go undetected. In his mind the size of the force had actually never been verified. What if the reports had been exaggerated? Knowing his soldiers as he did, Castaneda probably felt this is what happened. He ordered the detachment to encamp that night about three hundred yards from the river on the De Witt property. The next day, October 1, Castaneda moved his detachment up the river for about seven miles and encamped again. The Mexicans, encamped this time on Ezekiel Williams's land, feasted on watermelons the owner had never gotten around to picking.[62]

Castaneda's doubts concerning the large force in Gonzales were correct only in regard to one day, September 29. On that day there were only eighteen men in the entire town. These eighteen men, or, as they came to be called, the "Old Eighteen," consisted of W. W. Arrington, Valentine Bennet, Simeon Bateman, Joseph D. Clements, Almond Cottle, Jacob Darst, George W. Davis, Almeron Dickinson, Grave Fulcher, Benjamin Fuqua, James Hinds, Thomas Jackson, Albert Martin, Thomas Miller, Charles Mason, John Sowell, Winslow Turner, and Ezekiel Williams.[63] No doubt the Mexican soldier who informed Castaneda of the existence of a large force was exaggerating. The soldier probably had been told by his captors that a large amount of reinforcements were expected. However the Indian, who reported to Castaneda on the 30th of September, was not exaggerating about the presence of a large amount of men. During the night of the 29th and throughout the entire day, Anglo-Americans continued to enter Gonzales. By late afternoon of the 30th it was estimated that there were about one hundred and fifty men under arms in the town.[64] It should be recalled that on the 30th, the Gonzales ayuntamiento, represented by Joseph D. Clements, took its defiant stand and officially refused to surrender the cannon.

In the light of Ugartechea's order and the doubts in his own mind concerning the actual size of the opposition, Castaneda was prompted to manuever his forces so as to obtain a vantage point. If he found this point, he probably could determine once and for all if he should continue his assignment or retreat. The colonists, on the other side of the river, unaware of Castaneda's dilemma, interpreted his movements in only one manner: the Mexican officer intended to attack the town as soon as he could find a place to ford the river.[65] It was then decided that the Mexican column must be attacked and prevented from gaining entrance into the town.

Until Castaneda began his manueverings, there was not even the slightest resemblance of any organization among the colonists. Men came and went as they pleased and the only recognizable form of authority was the Gonzales ayuntamiento. When the activities of the Mexicans became known, the colonists immediately began to organize. The chain of command was established by means of elections. John H. Moore was elected colonel and commander of the group, while Joseph Washington Wallace was elected lieutenant colonel.[66] Moore was a resident of La Grange, in Austin's colony, and had much experience in organizing and leading volunteer forces against the Wichitas and Comanches. He was one of the most outspoken proponents of not only Texas separation, but Texas independence. At the time of his presence in Gonzales his arrest had been ordered by General Cos.[67] Wallace was a resident of Gonzales. He lived in the De Witt colony since 1831 but records reveal that he owned a league of land in Austin's colony.[68]

Once the military organization was created it was decided to unearth the cannon which had been buried in a peach orchard. Jacob Darst, one of the Sowells, (there were three of them in De Witt's colony), and Richard Chisholm dug up the cannon, cleaned it and mounted it on a wagon donated by Jo Martin. All available powder was gathered and pieces of chain and any metal scraps that were found were forged into iron balls. On the evening of October 1, fifty mounted colonists crossed the river with the cannon. There they waited for the remainder of the colonists who were coming on foot.[69]

After all the colonists had assembled on the other side of the river an address was delivered by an itinerant Methodist preacher, W. P. Smith.[70] The colonists did not encamp that night but moved along the river in search of Castaneda's detachment. It was hoped and planned that by daybreak the Mexicans could be engaged. Consequently before they reached the place where the Mexicans were thought to be, the colonists formed for an attack. The cannon was placed in the center and on either side of it unmounted colonists were deployed. The fifty mounted men were placed in front of the cannon. A small group of men, on foot, were ordered to act as a rear guard. A number of men were sent on foot to form a thin skirmish line. With the colonists deployed in this manner, the order was given to move forward. The entire group moved forward for some time. Then the silence was broken when a Mexican picket fired upon one of the skirmishers. The colonist was wounded and the entire Mexican camp was alerted. The Anglo-Americans, on hearing the shot formed a line. The cannon was in the center with the mounted colonists taking up a position at the far right end of the line.[71]

Neither side could see the other, but the noises from both indicated the general direction where they were forming. To make the problem of visibility worse, a dense fog came up. Both sides could do nothing except wait for daybreak. A short while after five o'clock on the morning of October 2, the fog lifted. Both sides were about three hundred yards apart with the Mexicans holding a prominent position on higher ground. The colonists opened fire as soon as the Mexicans became visible. With this, Castaneda tightened his lines, withdrew out of range and proposed a conference with Colonel Moore.[72]

Lieutenant Castaneda and Colonel Moore advanced toward each other and met in the open prairie. The Mexican officer asked why his detachment had been attacked. Moore answered that the attack was decided upon so the colonists would not lose possession of their cannon. However, Moore stated the colonists were merely acting in self defense since the Mexicans intended to use force if the weapon were not surrendered. Moore added that the colonists were resisting Santa Anna's attempts to destroy the system of government as established by the Constitution of 1824. The colonists, Moore concluded, were fighting to uphold the Constitution. To these answers, Castaneda commented that he, as well as most Mexicans, believed in republican principles and that the nation still possessed a federal government. He agreed that certain changes in the government had been made, but these changes were endorsed by the states of the republic. He went on to state that since he was an officer of the republic, he was duty bound to respect and uphold its laws. He stated that Texas also must obey the laws. Castaneda ended by informing Moore he had no intention of fighting or killing any colonists; he simply desired the cannon. Colonel Moore then asked Castaneda to surrender or join the colonists in their struggle to preserve the Constitution. Moore informed the Mexican officer that if he joined in the cause he would maintain the rank he held. Moore stated that Castaneda must accept either one of these proposals or fight. The Mexican officer ended the entire discussion by pointing out that he must obey his orders.[73]

Both commanders returned to their ranks. The relative superiority of the opposition was at last verified in Castaneda's mind. He now could obey Ugartechea's orders; he would neither surrender nor fight. He would simply attempt to withdraw. However before he could order the retreat the Anglo-Americans opened fire. The cannon was fired and its effect was negligible against the Mexicans, but totally disturbing to everyone's hearing. The Mexican detachment then made a rapid retreat toward San Antonio. Castaneda lost but one man, while none of the colonists were injured.[74]

While the "Battle of Gonzales" was going on, colonists from other Anglo-American settlements were coming into the town. The reinforcements continued well into the next day till a total of 250 to 300 men were situated in the small town of De Witt's colony. James Fannin was there with his "Brazos Guards," along with a company from Bastrop and a small company from the Colorado district. William B. Travis was on hand, but not in any position of command. All of the colonists were jubilant at the outcome of the engagement, but there was no general agreement as to what attitude to assume toward the Mexican authorities. Noah Smithwick, one of the soldiers of the volunteer army, observed "some were for independence; some for the constitution of 1824; and some for anything; just so it was a row. But we were all ready to fight."[75]

As yet no plans were made with regard to future action, except that of maintaining the volunteer army intact. In reality the colonists who gathered at Gonzales were yet to be organized into an effective fighting force. They were only small groups of men, from various areas of the colonies, whose leaders were merely elected representatives. These representatives, however, saw the necessity for unity and proceeded to organize a war board. The war board, in turn, saw the necessity of establishing a single, overall commander-in-chief. Consequently they requested that Stephen Austin should come to Gonzales and take over command of the army. By October 11, however, the volunteer army pressured the war board into calling an election for a commander. Each volunteer group put forth its own candidate, none of whom could obtain a clear majority. No compromise candidate could be agreed upon and many of the companies threatened to leave if their representative were not elected. The army was on the verge of disbanding when agreement was reached among the ranks to select Austin.[76] The new commander reorganized the army as best he could and, with his subordinate officers concurring, decided to attack San Antonio.[77]

The army of Anglo-Americans departed for San Antonio the next day. They took with them the De Witt colony's cannon. Since the battle, the weapon had been mounted on a pair of old wooden wheels which had been formed from traverse sections of a tree. The entire affair was christened "the flying artillery." Also some of the colonists were formed into a company of lancers. The lance heads were obtained by converting files, found in and around Gonzales.

The lance heads were then fastened to reeds or poles found along the river bank. The remainder of the army was equipped with Bowie knives and the long, single barrel, muzzle-loading flintlock rifles. The entire army marched out under the flag that had been made for the occasion. Who initiated the idea of having a battle flag is unknown. However, it is known that Sarah Seely De Witt, the wife of Green De Witt, and her daughter, Naomi, designed and made the flag for this first Texas army. The flag, made from Naomi's wedding dress, was six feet long of white cotton cloth. In the center of the flag was painted in black a picture of a cannon. A single star was sewed above the cannon. Below the cannon were written the words: "Come and Take It."[78]

On December 9, 1835 San Antonio fell to the Anglo-American army. After the expedition it appeared to many of the colonists that their safety was secured. However by the first part of 1836 Santa Anna's forces invaded Texas. Santa Anna himself led any army of 6,000 men from Laredo to San Antonio. By February 23, 1836 he took the town and began the siege of the Alamo, where a handful of Anglo-American defenders took refuge. The Anglo-Americans, under the command of Lieutenant Colonel William B. Travis and Lieutenant Colonel James Bowie, were determined to hold the mission as long as possible.[79] Travis immediately dispatched word of Santa Anna's presence and requested aid. One of his first requests was made to the De Witt colonists. On February 23, Travis wrote Andrew Ponton and informed him of the situation. He requested Ponton to send men and supplies. He also requested that Ponton immediately inform San Felipe de Austin of the situation.[80]

Travis continued to hold the mission and continued to send out appeals for assistance. The only effective response to his appeals came from the De Witt colony. Upon the request of the provisional government in San Felipe, the De Witt colonists, like the other Anglo-American settlements in Texas, had earlier organized a voluntary home guard unit. The unit of the De Witt colony was called "The Gonzales Ranging Company of Mounted Volunteers." It should be pointed out that this was the first formal organization of a militia unit in the area of the De Witt colony. Its commander, elected to the position, was George Kimball who held the rank of captain. When Travis's appeal reached Gonzales the unit prepared to come to his aid. Originally, the volunteer force consisted of twenty-two men, but by the time it reached the limits of De Witt's grant, ten more men joined the force. The Gonzales volunteers were led by captains Albert Martin and George Kimball and were guided by John W. Smith of San Antonio. Under the cover of darkness, on the morning of March 1, the group managed to break through the surprised Mexican lines and entered the Alamo. When these De Witt colonists entered, the Alamo was already considered, by most, to be a death trap.[81]

After the tragic fall of the Alamo, the company from the De Witt colony, were memorialized as the "Immortal Thirty-Two."[82]

Isaac Baker	Thomas Jackson
John Cane	Johnny Kellogg
George Cottle	Andrew Kent
David Cummings	George C. Kimball
Squire Damon	John G. King
Jacob Darst	William P. King
John Davis	Johathan Lindley
William Dearduff	Albert Martin
Charles Despallier	Jessee Mc Coy
William Fishbaugh	Thomas Miller
John Flanders	Isaac Milsap
Dolphin W. Floyd	George Neggan
Galba Fuqua	William Summers
John E. Garvin	George Tumlinson
John E. Gaston	Robert White
James George	Caliborne Wright

In addition to these thirty-two men, there were in the Alamo eight others from the De Witt colony. These men were with J. C. Neill, commander at San Antonio, since January of 1836. Consequently they were in the Alamo when Santa Anna's forces began the siege on February 23. This group of De Witt colony volunteers consisted of Daniel Bourne, George Brown, Almeron Dickinson, Andrew Duvalt, John Harris, William Lightfoot, Amos Pollard, and Marcus L. Sewell.[83]

While the defenders of the Alamo were holding off a good portion of Santa Anna's army, other Anglo-Americans were gathering at Gonzales. The colonists that gathered there soon elected Mosely Baker as their commander. He was determined to make a stand against the Mexican invaders and ordered that arrangement be made for the defense of Gonzales.[84] In the meantime, the government of the New Republic of Texas had selected Sam Houston as Commander-in-chief of the army. Houston arrived in Gonzales on March 11, 1836. There he found an army of 374 men without any organization, supplies, or weapons.[85] He immediately began organizing the group and created a chain of command. He still cherished a slight hope of giving assistance to the Alamo defenders.[86]

However, within a matter of hours after his arrival, news was brought to Gonzales by two Mexicans that the Alamo had fallen on the morning of March 6. The news of that tragedy was totally demoralizing. Houston, attempting to calm both the army and the De Witt colonists, refused to believe that the Alamo had fallen. He then sent two of his own scouts to verify the tragedy. The awful truth was verified by eight o'clock on the evening of March 13 when Mrs. Almeron Dickinson arrived at Gonzales.

Mrs. Dickinson was the wife of Captain Dickinson of the De Witt colony. She, her infant daughter, and a number of other non-combatants were the only survivors after Santa Anna had ordered the *dequello*.[87]

The unfortunate widow verified that not only had the Alamo fallen, but advanced detachments of Santa Anna's army were, at that moment, on their way to Gonzales. Citizens as well as soldiers panicked. However Houston was able to control his army and announced to them that they would retreat eastward to the more populous areas of Texas. To remain at Gonzales, now, Houston pointed out, would only result in catastrophe. Houston then ordered every light extinguished.[88]

Military articles that would hinder a general retreat were burnt and the artillery pieces that the army had, were thrown into the river. The few wagons which the army possessed were given up to the civilian population of Gonzales. By eleven that night the order to retreat was issued. When the town was completely evacuated, the rear guard detachment began setting the town on fire. The group, commanded by Captain Sharp, consisted of ten men. They were divided into two groups, one group began burning the buildings at one end of the town while the other performed a similar operation at the other end. Within a few minutes Gonzales was an inferno. The structures, all frame and covered with the thin oak boards, burnt easily. By dawn most of the structures were only heaps of ashes.[89] Only Adam Zumwalt's kitchen and Andrew Ponton's smokehouse were standing, though damaged severely.[90]

By daybreak of March 14th both the retreating army and the fleeing De Witt colonists could see a red glow in the western sky. They were soon under the impression that the Mexicans were burning the town. This impression was strengthened when they heard a series of explosions. These explosions were interpreted as being the sound of the Mexican artillery. However this impression was soon dispelled when it became known that the town was intentionally burnt so as to be of no value of Santa Anna's forces. The noises were merely some kegs of gun powder and whiskey exploding.[91] Houston indicated he was relieved to hear that the whiskey exploded since it had been poisoned. Someone, hoping the Mexicans would drink it, had mixed arsenic into a few barrels of whiskey in one of the stores in Gonzales.[92]

As soon as the significance of the victory at San Jacinto was realized, many of the De Witt colonists returned to their homes.[93] By the end of 1836 that area, which comprised a good portion of what was once the De Witt colony, was organized by the Republic of Texas into Gonzales County.[94] The remaining portions of the colony were later organized into De Witt, Guadalupe, and Lavaca counties in 1846 and Caldwell County in 1848.[95] By that time the actual frontier caught up with the area that was once the De Witt colony.

8

Conclusion

The policy for Texas, which Spain established and Mexico carried out under the empresario system, resulted in a unique method of disposing of the public domain. The sole aim of the policy was to populate Texas in order to hold and protect it. However, this policy was limited at the onset since it was defensive in nature. The policy, as implemented under the empresario system, introduced large numbers of Anglo-Americans into Texas and this proved to be disastrous for Mexico. Perhaps the policy of admitting Anglo-Americans was naive, but it was the only course available. Mexico took the calculated risk and lost. It should be pointed out that the limitation of the empresario system cannot be found in what it did achieve, for it certainly populated Texas. The limitation or the failure of the empresario system lay in what it did not accomplish. It did not satisfy the economic optimism of the Anglo-American colonists. When the De Witt colonists came to Texas, they did not come with the expressed intention of divesting that region from Mexico. From external appearances, the empresario system, which provided the foundation for the organization and growth of the colony, was a beacon of economic advancement for every colonist. However, as seen in the history of the De Witt colony, the empresario system had a number of shortcomings. The system initially encouraged only a subsistence form of economy. It provided no inducements to stimulate the economy, namely credit and banking facilities and internal improvements sponsored by the government. Because of the lack of economic stimulants, the economic optimism of the town of Gonzales, as well as the entire De Witt colony, as well as the other towns in Texas that developed during the period, was established only for administrative purposes. The town was first an area where the procedure of title clearance was accomplished, and second a political administrative unit.

When economic prosperity began returning to the United States in 1830 and 1831, and thereby allowing more individuals to migrate to Texas, a corresponding rise in the population of the De Witt colony occurred. However, Mexico abandoned the empresario system in 1830. After that date, and particularly after the expiration and non-renewal of the De Witt grant in 1831, a prime ingredient for an active economy was removed — a sizable population. What value was there in holding a large supply of land if there were no demand, in terms of an expanding population, for it? What sort of opportunity was there in providing necessary economic services if the population were not large enough to demand it?

The empresario system, in the interest of expediency, fostered a random distribution of grants. A number of these grants to the respective empresarios were, at that time, in poor locations. The De Witt grant was one of these. The De Witt colony was not only the westernmost settlement in Texas, but the westernmost settlement on the entire line of the Anglo-American frontier. For that matter, it was well beyond that frontier.

The empresario system, in the interest of expediency again, could not afford the luxury of taking geographic and environmental circumstances into consideration. Because of this the potential growth of the De Witt colony was restricted. Primarily, Austin's colony lay directly athwart the main avenues of entrance into Texas. One of the main ways of reaching Texas was by coastal schooner out of New Orleans, then landing at any one of the rivers which emptied into the Gulf of Mexico. From the mouths, the immigrants would ascend the rivers to the interior. The Trinity, Brazos, and Colorado rivers, located close to New Orleans were navigable. The courses of these three rivers ran through the Austin grant, and, consequently, directed the major flow of immigration there. The Lavaca and Guadalupe rivers, which flowed through De Witt's grant, were far from New Orleans and were not as navigable.[1] Those immigrants coming to Texas by way of the all land route, traveled along the Spanish built *Camino Real*, or Old San Antonio Road. Since Austin's colony was encountered first along this route many immigrants located in his colony.

The De Witt colony was a fair distance from any other Anglo-American settlement in Texas. Its extreme position on the dangerous Texas plains and in the midst of the Indian menace made the colony uninviting to many prospective settlers. Whether the threat was real or imagined, the colony, because of its problem with the Plains Indians was characterized as unsafe. Needless to say that acted as a deterrent. Also, many of the immigrants desired the companionship of other Anglo-Americans. This companionship not only provided safety by virtue of numbers, it also provided a homogeneous environment for the settlers. The nearest neighbors of the De Witt colony were the predominantly Mexican settlers of the Martin de Leon colony. The nearest town to the De Witt colony was San Antonio with its predominantly Mexican poulation. Interestingly many of the Anglo-American immigrants looked upon the Mexicans as "foreigners."[2]

Because of the limitations of the empresario system, even the empresario himself did not achieve all he anticipated. Green De Witt is considered to rank second only to Stephen Austin in importance, as an empresario. However, De Witt introduced nowhere near the number of colonists and obtained only a fraction of the "premium land" which Austin had.[3] However De Witt does merit attention since he, more than Austin, was typical of the many individuals who aspired to greater heights but failed.[4] He failed because of his own limitations and partly because circumstances contrived against him, circumstances inherent in the empresario system.

The degree of success of an empresario's colony depended upon the ability of the empresario. It appears Green De Witt was not as good a salesman as Austin. He did not possess the organizational abilities which Austin demonstrated so often.[5] Unlike Austin, he did not carry out his duties with great zeal and fervor. J. C. Clopper wrote ". . . — this Colony contains but few settlers nor can it be expected to flourish under its present Empresario — Col. De Witt. . . ."[6] But then Austin was much more experienced than De

Witt in such matters. It should be recalled that by 1822, Austin had already laid the foundation for his colony. Green De Witt, on the other hand, did not receive his grant until some three years later. Austin, too, did not experience the boundary difficulties with Martin de Leon, nor incur that empresario's emnity as De Witt had. By 1828 the Austin colony offered stability. The De Witt colony was only beginning.

Even if the circumstances had been more conducive, it is doubtful if De Witt would have obtained a greater stature and significance than he had. His personality simply did not enable him to fully meet the requirements of the position he held. J. C. Clopper wrote:

> . . . Yet has the Col. [De Witt] been much in refined society — his education is considerable and his natural powers of intellect strong and vigorous — sufficiently so to render him well qualified for his station — but alas dissipation [and] neglectful indolence have destroyed his energies and are rendering, in a great measure, abortive the efforts of his colonizing assistants — he is tho' much of a gentleman and like his most excellent Lady is very kind and hospitable to Strangers. . . ."[7]

Green De Witt located his family in a cabin just a few miles southwest of where the town site was being laid out.[8] He busied himself with the needs of the colony since the next three years witnessed the influx of the majority of settlers. However, he, as well as his colony, was plagued by one continuous problem, the incursions of hostile Indians. De Witt attributed their hostility as being the major factor in his failure to introduce the stipulated number of settlers. As De Witt lamented to Navarro:

> . . . I must observe for your information that a great many [settlers] were discouraged by the actual condition of the Country, the want of se-

curity for their families and property against the excesses of the Indians, and the death of many of their friends, all of which induced them to settle in other Colonies. Several men after having taken the oath returned to the U.S. of the North, to dispose of their property and return with their families. Under such circumstances, I anticipate with deep sorrow the impending and even unavoidable loss of my 'Premiums' [premium land] if the Supreme Government, regardless of the hardships and difficulties under which I have labored these last six years, decides that this colony must remain with its small population in the very centre [sic] of the incursions of the Indians. . . .[9]

De Witt never realized the total fulfillment of his contract. The passage of the Law of April 6, 1830 and the expiration of his contract also prevented him from building a sizable population. The law excluded the further entrance of any Anglo-Americans, but through the efforts of Stephen Austin the decree was not made applicable to either his colony or that of De Witt.[10] However, once the news of the change in Mexican policy circulated in the United States, the flow of immigration subsided. Those few who did come obviously preferred to settle in Austin's colony.

On April 15, 1831, the De Witt contract expired. He petitioned for an extension but the request was denied. Legally he, or rather his land commissioner, could no longer issue land titles. In all there were 189 titles issued and the land that still was vacant had reverted to the government. But, in any event, De Witt was eligible for that "premium land" reflecting the introduction of 189 families. By 1835 he had only received that amount of "premium land" for having introduced one-hundred families. The government still owed him a pro-rated portion of premium land.[11] De Witt, no doubt anticipated obtaining much more, if not all, of the "premium land." Now he had lost more than half of it. Probably in anticipation of a loss, or perhaps also to diversify his financial interest, he made a business arrangement with Joseph D. Clements. In April, 1830 De Witt and Clements contracted to build a saw mill and a grist mill. The mills were to be located twenty miles above Gonzales, on the Guadalupe River. It was hoped these mills would provide the settlers with lumber, so desperately needed, and a convenient place where grain could be efficiently ground into flour.[12] It does not appear the lumbering mill was ever established, but De Witt does make repeated references to the grist mill. Because of the mill's distance from the relative security of the settlement, it became the object of frequent Indian attacks. Although the mill was never destroyed by the Indians, a number of lives were lost there.[13] Presumably the mill ceased its limited operations when it was destroyed during the Revolution. Unfortunately there exists no clear understanding of what De Witt himself had initially invested in the mill, or what profits he might have obtained from it. Most likely he had sold out his interests before the mill was destroyed.

Since there exists no record of De Witt's financial situation, it can only be assumed that the profits he hoped to reap from his land venture did not materialize. Those fees which he received for the issuance of the land titles were, more often than not, in the form of goods, in services, or in his own issuance of "Guadalupe Land Office notes." The goods and services were limited however, since the total number of his colonists was small. Any profit he might have accrued was absorbed in meeting the expenses of the colony. Even such a shrewd and experienced empresario as Stephen Austin found it difficult to collect fees, accepting such things as cows, horses, mules, hogs, corn, and other products.[14]

With the immigration to his colony having ended, it became apparent to Green De Witt that any profit from the title fees would not be realized in the immediate future. That premium land which he held was also of no immediate value. These premium lands, as Stephen Austin considered them, could not all be utilized, could not be eaten, or could not be made into clothes.[15] Their value was in the future; they were speculative. "His [De Witt's] premium lands for introducing immigrants . . . were judiciously selected, and hence he left a handsome landed estate to his children, while otherwise he was a poor man, like most of his colonists."[16]

An indirect, but excellent view of De Witt's financial situation can be seen in the petition which his wife, Sarah Seely De Witt, made to the governor for a special grant. The nature of a special grant was literally an outright gift of land from the government. This grant was usually given to individuals who had performed some rewarding service for the state. The services might consist of military duty, laying out and constructing roads, and Indian fighting. However special grants were given, in some instances, to individuals who were poor or who had suffered hardships.[17] This last reason was what Sarah Seely De Witt had given for her request of the special grant.

> I, Sarah Seely, wife of Green De Witt, with a family of six children, with all due respect and in the best form of law, present the following statement: in the year 1826 I arrived in this country with my above mentioned family from the state of Missouri, one of the United States of the North. Since the year, 1826, until now I have dwelt on a sitio of land, chosen by my husband on the right bank of the Guadalupe River, opposite the town of Gonzales. My husband, before mentioned, has made improvements such as houses and out buildings for the family and has opened a rather large farm. The

family has suffered much in consequence of being in an unpopulated country on the frontier, through exposure to the incursions of the savage Indians, and for want of supplies. For these reasons and also because my husband, the said Green De Witt, *finds himself much embarassed in his affairs on account of the enterprise that he has undertaken, and because of other circumstances which have placed the family in an unfortunate situation*, I, the petitioner, with a view to acquiring and preserving a secure estate for the maintenance of myself and children, humbly beg your excellency to have the kindness to concede to me and my children in fee simple for myself and my heirs the sitio of land above mentioned on which I now live, with the understanding that all the requirements of the law in the matter will be fulfilled. Therefore I ask and beg you be so kind as to favor me by doing as above stated.[18]

De Witt endorsed the petition, thereby signifying his knowledge and consent. After his endorsement can be found some additional comments made by him which are of great interest. He pointed out that when he had married Sarah Seely, she was in possession of a considerable amount of property in Missouri. Since then he had invested the money, derived from the sale of that property, in his colonizing scheme. At that moment he had no way of reimbursing her, except by making improvements on the land which they occupied. For her security, he hoped the government would cede her the land.[19] The government did comply with the petition. A sitio, or a league of land, of 4,428 acres was granted in February, 1831. It was recorded, in her maiden name, on April 15, 1831.[20] Of the list of the special grantees, she was the only woman. "The Sarah Seely League still figures in the real estate transactions of Gonzales County today."[21]

The entire colonizing venture was, for the most part, materially and financially unsuccessful for Green De Witt and his colonists. Hopes for economic gain were frustrated by the very system which called the colony into being. When the empresario system was finally abandoned, the Mexican government did not initiate any programs which would stimulate the economy of Texas. Instead the economy remained static, and the anticipated financial gains of De Witt and his colonists were never realized. The economy as it developed under the empresario system and the subsequent Mexican policy, was merely subsistence. There was, as mentioned earlier, neither encouragement of credit and banking facilities nor encouragement for internal improvements. Many of these functions were undertaken by the colonists themselves, but, because of limited means, their efforts were limited. This can be seen in the manner of urban development in the colony. In order to facilitate the transition from a subsistence economy to a market economy, the town was essential since it provided an area where those necessary economic functions could be performed. As has been shown, the colonists of the town of Gonzales made an attempt to become the commercial hub for the De Witt colony and for a greater portion of Texas as well, but many conditions prevailed against them. The final blow to any hopes of financial gain came with the restriction upon further immigration into Texas after 1830. A larger population would have meant a greater demand for goods, services, and land.

What the colonists wanted, Mexico would not or, in many cases, could not provide. In this given situation, it can be seen how a particular attitude might very well develop in the minds of the colonists: other than relatively cheap land what else did the Mexican government provide for these expectant capitalists. On the other hand, in the United States, the frontier element was courted, aided and, at times, placated, by the federal and state government and private capital. Consequently, in the limitations of both the empresario system and in the subsequent Mexican policy may be found the seeds of the Texas Revolution. What the Mexican government did not provide, the colonists would attempt to provide themselves. This can be seen, first with attempts at separate statehood, and later, with eventual total separation.

Notes

CHAPTER I

1. Henry Folmer, *Franco-Spanish Rivalry in North America, 1524-1763* (Glendale, Calif., 1953), pp. 145-188; William Edward Dunn, *Spanish and French Rivalry in the Gulf Region of the United States, 1967-1702: The Beginnings of Texas and Pensacola* (Austin, 1917), pp. 31-47 and 59-105; Walter F. McCaleb, *Spanish Missions of Texas*, rev. ed. (San Antonio, 1961), pp. 20-27; Juan Agustin Morfi, *History of Texas, 1673-1779*, translated and edited by Carlos E. Castaneda, 2 Vols. (Albuquerque, 1935), Vol. I, pp. 114-139; Odie B. Faulk, *A Successful Failure, 1519-1810* (Austin, 1965), pp. 30-59; Rupert Norval Richardson, Texas; *The Lone Star State*, 2d ed. (Englewood Cliffs, N. J., 1958), pp. 16-17; Charles Wilson Hackett, "Policy of the Spanish Crown Regarding French Encroachments from Louisiana, 1721-1762," *New Spain and the Anglo-American West: Historical Contributions Presented to Herbert Eugene Bolton*, 2 Vols. (Lancaster, Penn., 1932), Vol. I, pp. 107-145.

2. The following is only a brief listing of the numerous tribes which inhabited the plains of Texas: Caracauyases, Taraucaues, Cocos, Venados, Taucuhues, Conchates, Texas, Ativanions, Velamcihi, Bidais, Nacogdoches, Nadamos, Nevadoches, Cadoes, Ziquani, Quichas, Tahauacanes, Tahuayses, Wichitas, Aguajes, Guitavirates, Eastern Comanches, Western Comanches, Tanicoes, Lipans, Chariticas, and Apaches. Instructions to the Representative of Texas in the Mexican Congress, January 30, 1822, Nacogdoches Archives, Texas State Library, Austin, Texas. Copies at Newberry Library, Chicago, Illinois; Herbert Eugene Bolton, ed., *Athanase de Mezieres and the Louisiana-Texas Frontier, 1768-1780. Documents Published for the First Time from the Original Spanish and French Manuscripts, Chiefly in the Archives of Mexico and Spain,* 2 Vols. (Cleveland, 1914), Vol. I, pp. 18-28; Morfi, *History of Texas, 1673-1779,* Vol. I, pp. 79-92.

3. Bernardo de Galvez, *Instructions for Governing the Interior Provinces of New Spain, 1786*, translated and edited by Donald E. Worcester (Berkeley, 1951), p. 2.

4. Herbert Eugene Bolton, "The Mission as a Frontier Institution," *American Historical Review*, XXIII (February, 1943), pp. 42-61; Herbert Eugene Bolton, "Spanish Activities on the Lower Trinity River, 1746-1771," *Southwestern Historical Quarterly*, XVI (April, 1913), pp. 339-377; Herbert Eugene Bolton, *Texas in the Middle Eighteenth Century: Studies in Spanish Colonial History and Administration* (Berkeley, 1915); Walter F. McCaleb, "Some Obscure Points in the Mission Period of Texas History," *The Quarterly of the Texas State Historical Association*, I (January, 1898), pp. 218-219; McCaleb, *Spanish Missions*, p. 31; Joseph W. Schmitz, S. M., *Mission Concepcion* (Waco, Texas, 1965), pp. 5-7.

5. The only exception was Refugio mission which was established in 1792. Carlos E. Castaneda, *Our Catholic Heritage in Texas, 1519-1937*, 7 Vols. (Austin, 1936), Vol. IV, pp. 204, 273-302; Bolton, *Texas in the Middle Eighteenth Century*, p. 377; Herbert Eugene Bolton, *The Spanish Borderlands: A Chronicle of Old Florida and the Southwest* (New Haven, 1921), p. 250; Richardson, *Lone Star State*, pp. 28-29; McCaleb, *Spanish Missions*, pp. 92-93; Faulk, *A Successful Failure*, pp. 118-120; Morfi, *History of Texas*, Vol. II, pp. 420-422.

6. Frank Wilson Blackmar, "Spanish Colonization in the Southwest," *Johns Hopkins University Studies in Historical and Political Sciences*, IV (April, 1890), pp. 7-79; Frank Wilson Blackmar, *Spanish Institutions of the Southwest* (Baltimore, 1891), pp. 130-131.

7. Castaneda, *Catholic Heritage*, Vol. IV, pp. 344-356; Schmitz, *Mission Concepcion*, pp. 5-6, 20-22, this work contains excerpts of the explicit statements of Spanish policy regarding secularization. Of interest are articles 1, which abolishes the policy of communal property, and 7, which requires the redistribution of the land among the natives in the form of 400 *varas* by 200 *varas*. Morfi, *History of Texas*, Vol. II, pp. 420-422; McCaleb, *Spanish Missions*, pp. 104-105.

8. Francois Barbe-Marbois, *The History of Louisiana, Particularly of the Cession of That Colony to the United States of America; With an Introductory Essay on the Constitution and Government of the United States* (Philadelphia, 1830), p. 171.

9. Bolton, *Anthanase de Mezieres*, Vol I, pp. 69-71; Bolton, *Spanish Borderlands*, pp. 251-257.

10. Bolton, *Spanish Borderlands*, pp. 255-257.

11. Arthur Preston Whitaker, *The Spanish American Frontier: 1783-1795; The Westward Movement and the Spanish Retreat in the Mississippi Valley* (Gloucester, 1962), pp. 21-22.

12. Lawrence Kinnaird, "American Penetration into Spanish Louisiana," *New Spain and the Anglo-American West: Historical Contributions Presented to Herbert Eugene Bolton*, 2 Vols. (Lancaster, 1932), Vol. I, pp. 214-216; "Miro to Paulus, March 7, 1789," *New Spain and the Anglo-American West*, Vol. I, pp., 232-234.

13. Whitaker, *Spanish-American Frontier*, pp. 105-106.

14. Jack D. L. Holmes, ed., *Documentos Ineditos para la Historia de la Luisiana* (Madrid, 1962), pp. 26-27; Manuel Serrano y Sanz, ed., *Documentos Historicos de la Florida y la Luisiana* (Madrid, 1912), pp. 316-320; Louis Houck, ed., *The Spanish Regime in Missouri: A Collection of Papers and Documents Relating to Upper Louisiana Principally Within the Present Limits of Missouri During the Dominion of Spain, from the Archives of the Indies at Seville*, 2 Vols. (Chicago, 1909). One of the earliest works dealing with this aspect of Spanish policy is Charles Gayarre's *History of Louisiana*, 4 Vols. (New York, 1854), Vol. III, pp. 182-183, 189-190, 199-200, and 202-203. Gayarre incorporated the dispatches of the various Spanish governors in his narrative. The dispatches were deposited in the Secretary of State's office, Baton Rouge, Louisiana, but now may be found in the Archives of Louisiana State University. Mattie Austin Hatcher's "The Louisiana Background of the Colonization of Texas, 1763-1803," *The Southwestern Historical Quarterly*, XXIV (January, 1921), pp. 169-194 gives a general, but informative, treatment of the policy. Hatcher relies primarily upon the transcripts of the *Archivo General de Indias*, Sevilla deposited at the University of Texas. In his article, "American Penetration," Lawrence Kinnaird utilized the documents of the *Archivo General de Indias, Papeles de Cuba*, Louisiana Collection of the Bancroft Library, Houck's *The Spanish Regime*, Gayarre's *History of Louisiana* and Hatcher, "The Louisiana Background. . . ." Most recently Jack D. L. Holmes has dealt with the policy in his *Gayoso: The Life of a Spanish Governor in the Mississippi Valley, 1789-1799* (Baton Rouge, 1965), pp. 23-24 and 239. Holmes has made extensive use of the documents of the *Archivo General Militar de Segovia, Museo Naval*, Madrid, Spain, Mississippi Department of Archives and History, and the Gayoso Papers at Louisiana State University and at the Missouri Historical Society.

15. "Bernardo de Galvez to Jose de Galvez, December 20, 1783," Arthur P. Whitaker, ed., *Documents Relating to the Commercial Policy of Spain in The Floridas with Incidental References to Louisiana* (Deland, 1931); "Esteban Miro to Conde de Alange, August 11, 1792," Holmes, ed., *Documentos Ineditos*, pp. 22-23; "Political Reflection on the Present Condition of the Province of Louisiana by Intendant Martin de Navarro, 1785," James Alexander Robertson, ed., *Louisiana Under the Rule of Spain, France, and the United States*, 2 Vols. (Cleveland, 1911), Vol. I, pp. 248-250.

16. Whitaker, *Spanish-American Frontier*, pp. 102-103. Whitaker has aptly described the nature and meaning of this decree by pointing out that "Toleration was utterly at varience with the whole of Spanish policy, and its grant in the case of Louisiana and West Florida shows the importance that the Spanish government attached to the development of those provinces. It was an experiment forced upon Spain by the requirements of its frontier conflict with the United States, a device adopted to aid Spain in that most vital phase of the frontier conflict, the competition for immigrants."

17. *Ibid.*, pp. 157-162; Arthur P. Whitaker, *The Mississippi Question, 1795-1803. A Study in Trade, Politics and Diplomacy* (New York, 1934), pp. 28-29, 61, 155-6, and 181-182; Kinnaird, "American Penetration of Spanish Louisiana," *New Spain and the Anglo-American West*, Vol. I, p. 218.

18. "Villemont to Minister, Sedan, France, 17 Prairial an X, June 6, 1802," A. P. Nasatir, ed., *Before Lewis and Clark: Documents Illustrating the History of Missouri*, 2 Vols. (St. Louis, 1952), Vol. II, pp. 680-687.

19. Talleyrand is referring to Louisiana and the Floridas.

20. Frederick Ogg, *The Opening of the Mississippi: A Struggle for Supremacy in the American Interior* (New York, 1904), pp. 466-467.

21. D. W. Meining, *Imperial Texas. An Interpretative Essay in Cultural Geography* (Austin, 1969), pp. 24-26; Faulk, *A Successful Failure*, pp. 144-178; Odie B. Faulk, *Land of Many Frontiers: A History of the American Southwest* (New York, 1968), pp. 75-83; Odie B. Faulk, *The Last Years of Spanish Texas, 1778-1821* (Hague, 1964), pp. 83-92.

22. Nava to Cabello, May 17, 1784, Bexar Archives, Eugene C. Barker Texas History Center, University of Texas, Austin, Texas.

23. Mattie Austin Hatcher, *The Opening of Texas to Foreign Settlements, 1801-1821* (Austin, 1927), p. 58. This is still the basic work dealing with this particular topic of Texas history for the period 1801-1821. Hatcher made use of the Bexar Archives, Nacogdoches Archives, and the transcripts of the *Archivo General de Mexico* and the *Archivo General de Indias* at the University of Texas.

24. Castaneda, *Catholic Heritage*, Vol. V, pp. 285-286.

25. Hatcher, *Opening of Texas*, p. 58.

26. Salcedo to Elquezabal, May 23, 1803, Nacogdoches Archives.

27. Hatcher, *Opening of Texas*, p. 67. The census report of 1804 shows that a total of 68 foreigners resided in Texas. Of this number 50 had resided there since 1801 and of them thirteen were Anglo-Americans.

28. Salcedo to Elquezabal, March 27, 1804, Bexar Archives.

29. Hatcher, *Opening of Texas*, pp. 77-99.

30. Gayarre, *History of Louisiana*, Vol. II, pp. 145-146.

31. Castaneda, *Catholic Heritage*, Vol. V, pp. 286-293.

32. Joel R. Poinsett, *Notes on Mexico, Made in the Autumn of 1822. Accompanied by an Historical Sketch of the Revolution, and Translations of Official Reports on the Present State of That Country* (London, 1825), pp. 151-153.

33. Miguel Ramos Arizpe, *Report to the August Congress on the Natural, Poltical, and Civil Conditions of the Provinces of Coahuila, Nuevo Leon, Nuevo Santander, and Texas of the Four Eastern Interior Provinces of the Kingdom of Mexico*, trans., annotations, and introduction by Nettie Lee Benson (Austin, 1950), p. 12.

34. The main trade route and highway in the province which connected San Juan Bautista to Nachitoches and Loredo to La Bahia.

35. Salcedo to Cordero, August 20, 1805, Nacogdoches Archives.

36. Thomas Maitland Marshall, *A History of the Western Boundary of the Louisiana Purchase, 1819-1841* (Berkeley, 1914), p. 23.

37. Hatcher, *Opening of Texas*, p. 117, footnote #61; Castaneda, *Catholic Heritage*, Vol. V, pp. 250-73; Faulk, *Last Years of Spanish Texas*, pp. 121-126; Faulk, *Successful Failure*, pp. 189-196; J. Villasana Haggard, "The Neutral Ground between Louisiana and Texas, 1806-1821," *Louisiana Historical Quarterly* 28 (October, 1945), pp. 1001-1128.

38. Castaneda, *Catholic Heritage*, Vol. V, pp. 393-96.

39. Hatcher, *Opening of Texas*, p. 118.

40. *Ibid.*, pp. 124-125.

41. Manuel de Salcedo to Nemesio de Salcedo, November 30, 1808, Bexar Archives.

42. Hatcher, *Opening of Texas*, pp. 145-146; Castaneda, *Catholic Heritage*, Vol. V, pp. 337-399; Faulk, *Last Years of Spanish Texas*, pp. 130-131; Felix D. Almaraz, Jr., *Tragic Cavalier: Governor Manuel Salcedo of Texas, 1808-1813* (Austin, 1971), pp. 31-35, 59-62.

43. Manuel de Salcedo to Nemesio de Salcedo, January 23, 1809, Nacogdoches Archives.

44. Hatcher, *Opening of Texas*, pp. 147-155.

45. *Ibid.*

46. Bonavia to Salcedo, May 17, 1810, Nacogdoches Archives.

47. Manuel de Salcedo to Nemesio de Salcedo, June 26, 1812, Nacogdoches Archives.

48. Ramos Arizpe, *Report to the August Congress*, p. 40.

49. "A filibustering expedition is an irregular, unauthorized attack which proceeds from the territory of one state against that of a friendly state. Once such an expedition merges with the armed forces opposed to that legal government, . . . it ceases to be a filibustering movement." Harris G. Warren, *A Sword Was Their Passport: A History of American Filibustering in the Mexican Revolution* (Baton Rouge, 1943), p. vii.

50. Julia K. Garrett, *Green Flag Over Texas; A Story of the Last Years of Spain in Texas* (New York, 1939); Warren, *Sword Was Their Passport*; Castaneda, *Catholic Heritage*, Vol. VI, pp. 77-112; David M. Vigness, *The Revolutionary Decades, 1810-1836* (Austin, 1965), pp. 9-14.

51. The proclamation provided that all travelers must have passports; if any inhabitant admitted a stranger, without a passport, and failed to notify the authorities, the offender was fined fifty dollars, which was payable immediately; if an offender was not capable of paying the fine, he was compelled to labor in irons at the public works; anyone who reported a stranger without a passport received a reward of twenty-five dollars; all prohibited games and fandangos were punishable by a fine of twenty-five dollars; and in issuing "fandango licenses, the official should be cautious so as not to grant them for places where they cannot be watched." Proclamation, October 15, 1814, Nacogdoches Archives.

52. Antonio Menchaca, *Memoirs* (San Antonio, 1937), pp. 19-20.

53. Virginia H. Taylor, trans. & ed., *The Letters of Antonio Martinez: Last Spanish Governor of Texas, 1817-1822* (Austin, 1957), pp. 1-2.

54. "Martinez to Apodaca, October 15, 1818," Taylor, *Letters of Antonio Martinez*, p. 185.

55. Hatcher, *Opening of Texas*, pp. 271-272.

56. Luis de Onis, *Memoria Sobre Las Negociones Entre Espana y Los Estado de America, Que Dieron Motivo Al Tratado de 1819. Con Una Noticia Sobre la Estadistica de Aquel Pais. Acompana un Apendice, Que Contiene Documentos Importantes Para Mayor Ilustracion del Asunto,* 2 Vols. (Madrid, 1820), pp. 1-2; "unsigned correspondence," 1/23/1810, Nacogdoches Archives.

57. Philip C. Brooks, *Diplomacy and the Borderlands: The Adams Onis Treaty of 1819* (Berkeley, 1939) p. 76.

58. Hunter Miller, ed., *Treaties and Other International Acts of the United States of America,* 5 Vols. (Washington, 1933), Vol. III, pp. 5-7.

59. Onis, *Memoria Sobre,* Vol. II, pp. 209-213.

60. Castaneda, *Catholic Heritage,* Vol. VI, pp. 186-187.

61. Hatcher, *Opening of Texas,* pp. 278-280.

CHAPTER II

1. The definitive biography is Eugene C. Barker's, *The Life of Stephen F. Austin, Founder of Texas, 1793-1836* (Austin, 1949).

2. For a concise account see Douglas C. North's, *The Economic Growth of the United States, 1790-1860* (New York, 1966), pp. 135-140, 177-188.

3. Houck, ed., *The Spanish Regime in Missouri,* Vol. I, pp. 368-371; Barker, *Life of Stephen F. Austin,* pp. 3-13.

4. Moses Austin to Baron de Bastrop, January 26, 1821, Austin Papers; Barker, *Life of Stephen Austin,* p. 21.

5. North, *The Economic Growth of the United States,* p. 137; chart I-XI.

6. *Ibid.,* pp. 186-187.

7. Ambrosia de Aldasora to the Ayuntamiento of Bexar, January 17, 1821, Nacogdoches Archives.

8. Moses Austin to Antonio Martinez, March 19, 1821, Nacogdoches Archives.

9. Eugene C. Barker, ed., "Journal of Stephen F. Austin on His First Trip to Texas, 1821," *Quarterly of the Texas State Historical Association,* VII (April, 1904), p. 297.

10. *Ibid.,* p. 298.

11. "Ayuntamiento of Bexar to Martinez, November 15, 1820," *Southwestern Historical Quarterly,* XXIII (July, 1919), p. 61.

12. Martinez to Lopez, February 6, 1822, Bexar Archives.

13. Instructions to the Representatives of the Province of Texas in the Mexican Congress, January 20, 1822, Nacogdoches Archives.

14. *Ibid.*

15. Lucas Alaman, *Historia de Mejico Desde los Primeros Movimentos Que Preparon Su Independencia en el Ano de 1808, Hasta la Epoca Presente,* 5 Vols. (Mexico, 1849-1852), Vol. V, pp. 447-458; Hubert Howe Bancroft, *History of Mexico, Being a Popular History of the Mexican People From the Earliest Primitive Civilization to the Present Time,* 5 Vols. (New York, 1914), Vol. IV, pp. 757-778.

16. Report of the Committee on Colonization, June 3, 1822, University of Texas Transcripts from Departmento de Fomento, Mexico. Cited in Barker, *Life of Stephen F. Austin,* p. 52.

17. *Laws and Decrees of the Republic of Mexico in Relation to Colonization and Grants of Land, More Particularly in New Mexico and California, From 1823 to 1846* (New York, 1871), pp. 2-12.

18. Report on the Conditions of Texas, May 26, 1823, Nacogdoches Archives.

19. General Law of Colonization, August 18, 1824, Nacogdoches Archives.

20. Austin to A. W. Breedlove, October 12, 1829, Austin Papers.

21. Barker, *Life of Stephen Austin,* p. 123.

22. *Ibid.*

23. Although the colonization law of the state of Coahuila-Texas contained this requirement, having been advocated and advanced by Bastrop, the national colonization law did not contain such a provision. During the framing of the national colonization law an amendment was introduced to admit only those who professed the Catholic religion, but this measure was soundly defeated with only one vote favoring it, that of the individual who introduced it.

24. Samuel Harman Lowrie, *Culture Conflict in Texas, 1821-1835* (New York, 1932), p. 58; *Life of Stephen Austin,* pp. 127-128.

25. Record of Translation of Empresario Contracts of Coahuila-Texas, 1825-1832, Spanish Archives, General Land Office, Austin, Texas.

26. Hans Peter Nielsen Gammel, ed., *Laws of Texas,* 10 Vols. (Austin, 1906), Vol. I, p. 48; Joseph M. White, comp., *A New Collection of Laws, Charters and Local Ordinances of the Government of Great Britain, France, and Spain, Relating to the Concessions of Land in Their Colonies; Together With the Laws of Mexico and Texas on the Same Subject,* 2 Vols. (Philadelphia, 1839), Vol. I, pp. 601-602.

27. Bancroft, *North Mexican States,* Vol. II, p. 72.

28. Gammel, *Laws of Texas,* Vol. I, p. 48.

29. J. Antonio Mateos, *Historia Parlementaria de los Congresos Mexicanos de 1821 a 1857,* 25 Vols. (Mexico, 1877-1912), Vol. II, pp. 377-379, 477, 482, 648; John Henry Brown, *History of Texas, From 1685 to 1892* (St. Louis, 1892), pp. 109-11. John Henry Brown was the son of Henry Brown, a resident of De Witt's colony from 1825 till his death in 1834. John Henry lived in Texas with his uncle, James Kerr. He was active in the military and in the state government till his death in 1895. Because of his father's involvement in the De Witt colony and his own participation in Texas politics he was well qualified to write an authoritative history of Texas.

211

30. Histories and genealogical records of Saint Louis and Ralls County, Missouri do not contain any information concerning the De Witts. As far as this writer has determined, there are no De Witt descendants living in Missouri today. Letter from Frances H. Stadler, Missouri Historical Society, St. Louis, Missouri, October 17, 1969; Letter from Goldena Howard, the State Historical Society of Missouri, Columbia, Missouri, November 7, 1969; and Goldena Howard to Della E. Nugent, Houston, Texas, November 7, 1969.

31. "J. C. Clopper's Journal and Book of Memoranda for 1828," *Quarterly of the Texas State Historical Association*, XIII (July, 1909), p. 67. In 1818 he moved with the family to Cincinnati where his father purchased land and built a home. In 1827 Clopper went with his father to Texas where the latter had obtained some land. It was at this time that Clopper kept his journal and recorded his observations concerning Green De. Witt and the De Witt colony.

32. Brooks County borders the Ohio River and is located in present-day West Virginia.

33. Minerva De Witt Whittington, "De Witt's Colony," Speech given before the Yoakum Rotary Club, Yoakum, Texas, February 21, 1968, p. 2.

34. *Ibid.*, p. 1; John Henry Brown, *History of Texas*, Vol. I, pp. 109-111, 341.

35. Brown, *History of Texas*, Vol. I, pp. 109-111; Mateos, *Historia Parlamentaria de los Congresos Mexicanos*, Vol. I, p. 312.

36. Minerva De Witt Whittington, "De Witt's Colony," p. 1; Edna Green De Witt, comp., *Lest We Forget* (Gonzales, Texas, no date of publication), p. 9.

37. William Trimble to Stephen Austin, June 26, 1824, Austin Papers.

38. G. Dewitt (sic) to Austin, December 6, 1824, Austin Papers. In this correspondence, De Witt mentions having seen Austin in San Jacinto. De Witt, writing from Saltillo, asked Austin to forward any letters to a Mr. Hickman, presumably an Austin agent at the state capitol.

39. Baron de Bastrop to Stephen Austin, July 16, 1825, Austin Papers.

40. Green De Witt was referring to Mexican nationals.

41. De Witt's Petition, April 7, 1825, Empresario Contracts, Spanish Archives, General Land Office, Austin, Texas. Original Document of Green De Witt's Grant, Gonzales Historical Museum, Gonzales, Texas.

42. *Ibid.* Stephen Austin's Map of Texas, 1830.

43. Original Document of Green De Witt's Grant, Gonzales Historical Museum. The grant included what are today Gonzales, Guadalupe, Caldwell, De Witt, and sections of Lavaca and Fayette Counties, Texas.

44. This stipulation was included so as to recognize and protect the Spanish land grants and those grants issued by any ayuntamiento or provincial assemblies.

45. De Witt Grant, April 15, 1825, Empresario Contracts, Spanish Archives, General Land Office, Austin, Texas.

46. Anastasio Bustamante to Iturbide, January 5, 1822, University of Texas Transcripts from Department de Fomento, Mexico, cited in Barker, *Life of Stephen F. Austin*, p. 45.

47. Peter Ellis Bean was a member of the ill-fated Nolan expedition in 1800. As one of the survivors, he was imprisoned at Acapulco. When he received his release, he took part in the revolutionary movement in New Spain. He was commissioned a colonel under Jose Maria Morelos's command and spent much time in the United States espousing the cause of Mexican independence. In 1823 he settled in East Texas. Two years later he went to Mexico to obtain compensation for his services to Morelos. He received a military commission and was named Indian agent for the Nacogdoches area. He dissuaded the Cherokees from joining the Texas Revolution. After the Revolution he left Texas for Jalapa, Mexico. He died there in 1846. Walter Prescott Webb and H. Bailey Carroll, eds., *The Handbook of Texas*, 2 Vols. (Austin, 1952), Vol. I, p. 129.

48. Stephen Austin to Governor Rafael Gonzales, June 26, 1825, and Stephen Austin to Governor Rafael Gonzales, October 17, 1825, Bexar Archives.

49. Empresario Contracts, Spanish Archives, General Land Office, Austin, Texas.

50. Henry G. Ward, *Mexico During the Years 1825, 1826, and Part of 1827. With an Account of the Mining Companies, and of the Political Events in That Republic, to the Present Day* (London, 1829); Eugene C. Barker, *Mexico and Texas, 1821-1835* (Dallas, 1928) pp. 38-40; J. Fred Rippy, "British Role in the Early Relations of the United States and Mexico," *The Hispanic American Historical Review*, VII (February, 1927), pp. 2-24.

51. Index to Spanish and Mexican Land Titles, Spanish Archives, General Land Office, Austin, Texas.

52. Vito Alessio Robles, *Coahuila y Texas*, 2 Vols. (Mexico, 1945), Vol. I, p. 30.

53. S. A. G. Bourne, *Observations on the Mexican Province of Texas* (London, 1828), p. 10.

54. Carlos Eduardo Castaneda, ed. & trans., "Statistical Report on Texas by Juan N. Almonte, 1835," *The Southwestern Historical Quarterly*, XXVIII, (January, 1925), pp. 186-206.

55. Bourne, *Observations*, p. 10.

56. United States Census, 1850, Texas; Barnes F. Lathrop, *Migration into East Texas, 1835-1860: A Study from the United States Census* (Austin, 1949), pp. 34-35.

CHAPTER III

1. Stephen Austin to Gefe del Departmento de Texas, Jose Antonio Saucedo, May 8, 1826, Austin Papers.

2. D. W. C. Baker, compiler, *Texas Scrap Book: Made Up of the History, Biography and Miscellany of Texas and Its People* (New York, 1875), p. 290.

3. Louis Houck, *A History of Missouri from the Earliest Explorations and Settlement Until the Admission of the State into the Union*, 3 Vols. (Chicago, 1908), Vol. III, p. 102.

4. Baker, *Texas Scrap Book*, pp. 290-291.

5. *Ibid*.

6. Nathaniel Cox to Stephen Austin, April 21, 1825, Austin Papers.

7. Brown, *History of Texas*, Vol. I, p. 124.

8. *Ibid*.

9. "Green De Witt to Major James Kerr, November 12, 1825," *Texas Letters* (San Antonio, 1940), p. 137; Brown, *History of Texas*, Vol. I, p. 125.

10. Both Thorn and Edwards were recipients of empresario contracts on April 15, 1825. Empresario Contracts, Spanish Archives, General Land Office, Austin, Texas.

11. "Green De Witt to Major James Kerr, November 12, 1825," *Texas Letters*, p. 137; Brown, *History of Texas*, Vol. I, p. 125.

12. Louis Lenz, "Texas Money," *Southwestern Historical Quarterly*, LVII, (October, 1953), pp. 175-180.

13. Brown, *History of Texas*, Vol. I, p. 125, note.

14. Eugene C. Barker and Ernest W. Winkler, eds., *A History of Texas and Texans By Frank W. Johnson*, 5 Volumes (Chicago, 1941), Vol. I, pp. v-vi. Frank W. Johnson was born in Virginia in 1799, and moved with his father to Tennessee in 1812. In 1817 he was a surveyor in northern Alabama, but soon went to southern Illinois and Saint Louis. There he attempted several occupations. He taught school for a while, clerked in a store, opened his own grocery store which apparently sold only coffee, sugar, salt, and whiskey. All these attempts failed and in 1821 he relocated to Saint Louis County, Missouri. He worked as a constable for a time there, but by 1824 he was involved in a lead mining operation near Herculaneum. In 1826, he hired on a flatboat scheduled to carry cargo to New Orleans. It was on this trip that he took ill. From the records of the General Land Office, it appears that a Frank W. Johnson did immigrate to Texas in March, 1831. The record reveals that he received one league of land in what is today Fayette County, Texas. Interestingly, however, that portion of Fayette County was in the confines of Stephen Austin's second contract.

15. Stephen Austin to Mrs. Emily Perry, May, 1825; James E. B. Austin to Mrs. Emily Perry, October 28, 1825, Austin Papers.

16. Green De Witt to Stephen Austin, New London, Ralls County, Missouri, March 9, 1826, Austin Papers.

17. Minerva De Witt Whittington, "De Witt's Colony," p. 62.

18. Brown, *History of Texas*, Vol. I, p. 128.

19. James Kerr to Stephen Austin, July 30, 1826, Austin Papers.

20. James Kerr to Stephen Austin, August, 1826, Austin Papers.

21. Brown, *History of Texas*, Vol. I, p. 124, note #1.

22. *Ibid*. These visitors were Henry S. Brown, Edwin Morehouse, Elijah Stapp, and Frost Thorn. Of these only Stapp and Brown returned.

23. Stephen Austin to Jose Saucedo, July 17, 1826, Austin Papers.

24. James Kerr to Stephen Austin, July 15, 1826, Austin Papers.

25. Brown, *History of Texas*, Vol. I, pp. 126-127.

26. *Ibid.*

27. Stephen Austin to Jose Antonio Saucedo, July 17, 1826, Austin Papers; Brown, *History of Texas*, Vol. I, p. 127.

28. James Kerr to Stephen Austin, July 15, 1826, Austin Papers.

29. *Ibid.*

30. James Kerr to Stephen Austin, August 8, 1826, Austin Papers.

31. See Chapter II, pp. 42, 45.

32. Green De Witt to Jose Antonio Saucedo, September 13, 1827, Spanish Archives, General Land Office, Austin, Texas.

33. Green De Witt to Stephen Austin, September 3, 1826, Austin Papers. Since De Witt did not mention his colony in particular, but referred to all the "colonies," it is suspected that he hoped to provide a service for all incoming colonists. They would be able to store and even purchase provisions from the warehouse he planned to establish there.

34. *Ibid.*

35. *Ibid.*

36. Jose Antonio Saucedo to Stephen Austin, September 21, 1826, Austin Papers.

37. Brown, *History of Texas*, Vol. I, p. 128.

38. Green De Witt to Stephen Austin, September 3, 1826, Austin Papers; Jose Antonio Saucedo to Stephen Austin, September 21, 1826, Austin Papers.

39. Index to Spanish and Mexican Land Titles, Spanish Archives, General Land Office, Austin, Texas.

40. Jose Antonio Saucedo to Green De Witt, October 25, 1826, Bexar Archives.

41. Empresario Contracts, Spanish Archives, General Land Office, Austin, Texas. Mary Virginia Henderson, "Miner Empresario Contracts for the Colonization of Texas, 1825-1834," *Southwestern Historical Quarterly*, XXXII (July, 1928), pp. 1-6.

42. Empresario Contracts, Spanish Archives, General Land Office, Austin, Texas.

43. Rafael Gonzales to Bernardo De Leon, October, 1825, Spanish Archives, General Land Office, Austin, Texas.

44. Kerr to Austin, August 23, 1826, Austin Papers.

45. Kerr to Austin, August, 1826, Austin Papers.

46. Powell to Austin, October 24, 1826, Austin Papers; Norton to Saucedo, November 8, 1826, Bexar Archives.

47. De Witt to Austin and Williams, Austin Papers.

48. Saucedo to De Witt, October 25, 1826, Bexar Archives.

49. Kerr to Austin, November 11, 1826, Austin Papers.

50. Ibid.

51. Ibid.

52. Brown, History of Texas, Vol. I, p. 128.

53. Kerr to Austin, November 11, 1826, Austin Papers.

54. Norton to Austin, December 13, 1826, Nacogdoches Archives.

55. De Witt to Austin, December 1, 1826, Austin Papers.

56. De Witt to Ramon Musquiz, Gonzales, May 8, 1829, Bexar Archives.

57. Barker, Life of Stephen F. Austin, "The Fredonian Rebellion," pp. 148-177. The Nacogdoches Archives and the Bexar Archives possess a great deal of material concerning the entire incident.

58. Resolution of Loyalty, January 27, 1827, Austin Papers.

59. Ibid.

60. Ibid.

61. Ibid.

62. Brown, History of Texas, Vol. I, p. 138.

63. James Kerr to Stephen Austin, January 24, 1827, Austin Papers.

64. Anastacio Bustamante to Jose Antonio Saucedo, December 6, 1827, Nacogdoches Archives.

65. De Witt to Saucedo, July 14, 1827, Bexar Archives.

66. Kerr to Austin, February 26, 1827, Austin Papers.

67. In addition to his duties as surveyor-general and attorney, Kerr was also De Witt's secretary. Fragments of the original "James Kerr's Ledger," Gonzales Historical Museum, Gonzales, Texas.

68. Brown, History of Texas, Vol. I, p. 129, note.

69. James Kerr to Stephen Austin, August 8, 1826, Austin Papers.

70. Lista de los Havitantes de la Colonia de De Witt en el Departmento de Texas, Ano de 1828, Nacogdoches Archives.

71. Jose Saucedo to Green De Witt, August 29, 1827, Bexar Archives.

72. Anastacio Bustamante to Jose Antonio Saucedo, August 18, 1827, Nacogdoches Archives.

73. *Ibid.*

74. Jose Antonio Saucedo to Green De Witt, August 29, 1827, Bexar Archives.

75. *Ibid.*

76. Green De Witt to Jose Antonio Saucedo, September 13, 1827, Spanish Archives, General Land Office, Austin, Texas.

77. James Kerr to Jose Antonio, Saucedo, October 18, 1827, Bexar Archives.

78. Green De Witt to Jose Antonio Saucedo, September 13, 1827, Spanish Archives, General Land Office, Austin, Texas.

79. Jose Antonio Saucedo to Green De Witt, September 28, 1827, Spanish Archives, General Land Office, Austin, Texas.

80. Jose Maria Viesca to Jose Antonio Saucedo, November 17, 1827, Nacogdoches Archives.

81. Anastacio Bustamante to Jose Antonio Saucedo, December 6, 1827, Nacogdoches Archives.

82. Green De Witt to Stephen Austin, April 3, 1827, Austin Papers; Green De Witt to Jose Antonio Saucedo, 1827, Bexar Archives.

83. James Kerr to Stephen Austin, Station on the Labaca, February 2, 1827, Austin Papers.

84. Green De Witt to Stephen Austin, Station on the Labaca, April 3, 1827, Austin Papers.

85. Anastacio Bustamante to Jose Antonio Saucedo, December 23, 1827, Bexar Archives.

CHAPTER IV

1. Lista de los Havitantes de la Colonia de De Witt en el Departmento de Texas, Ano de 1828, Nacogdoches Archives.

2. Of these nine married women, only one was a widow, and that was Elizabeth Berry.

3. Lista de los Havitantes de la Colonia de De Witt, Nacogdoches Archives.

4. For a discussion of this dichotomy in the ante-bellum south, as it effected the settlement of Texas, see Terry G. Jordan, "The Imprint of the Upper and Lower South on Mid-Nineteenth Century Texas," *Annals of the Association of American Geographers*, LVII (December, 1967), pp. 667-690.

5. *Ibid.*, p. 670, see Table 1.

217

6. This has been determined by comparing the De Witt colony census of 1828 with Titles, De Witt Colony, Spanish Archives, General Land Office, Austin, Texas. Those names which were not listed in the Titles are considered to have relocated. This, in turn was verified by the Index to Spanish and Mexican Land Titles, Spanish Archives, General Land Office, Austin, Texas, which indicated that the eleven names absent from De Witt's Titles received land in another empresario colony.

7. Index to Spanish and Mexican Land Titles, Spanish Archives, General Land Office, Austin, Texas.

8. Lista de los Havitantes de la Colonia de De Witt, Nacogdoches Archives.

9. D. W. Meinig, *Imperial Texas*, p. 95; W. W. Newcomb, Jr., *The Indians of Texas: From Prehistoric Times to Modern Times* (Austin, 1961), pp. 60-61.

10. William Kennedy, *Texas: The Rise, Progress, and Prospect of the Republic of Texas*, 2 Vols. (London, 1841), Vol. I, pp. 96-97.

11. Stephen Austin's map of Texas, 1830.

12. David B. Edward, *The History of Texas; or the Emigrant's, Farmer's and Politician's Guide to the Character, Climate, Soil, and Production of That Country: Geographically Arranged from Personal Observations and Experience* (Cincinnati, 1836), p. 33.

13. "J. C. Clopper's Journal," p. 67.

14. George R. Nielsen, "Matthew Caldwell," *Southwestern Historical Quarterly*, LXIV (April, 1961), pp. 478-502.

15. Ethel Zivley Rather had compiled one general map of De Witt's colony which shows all of the tracts of land occupied by the colonists during the years 1828 to 1831. Her map was compiled by using the titles and county maps found in the General Land Office. The Rather map gives the entire population distribution of the De Witt colony as of 1831. This writer, however, has attempted to provide five maps which show the progressive or cumulative distribution of population for the years 1828 to 1831. This writer has relied on the Rather map for a format and on the data contained in Titles, De Witt's Colony, Date of Arrival, Spanish Archives, General Land Office, Austin, Texas. Each map attempts to show what immigration and distribution occurred by the end of a given year. The map for the years 1825 to 1827 shows no location of settlement since none were permanently established. The Kerr surveying party and the Berry family were settled in the area from August, 1825 to July, 1826, but as has been recounted earlier, the first settlement was abandoned. (See Chapter III, pp. 70-73.)

16. As has been previously mentioned, the only official census of the colony was that of 1828. The population figure of 158 was arrived at by the use of data contained in Titles, De Witt's Colony, Spanish Archives, General Land Office, Austin, Texas. The data consists of a date of arrival and the number of dependents in a man's family if he were married. By this method, this writer had arrived at a total of twenty-five families as of June, 1829. However in a letter written by Green De Witt to jefe-politico, on May 8, 1829, De Witt indicated the presence of thirty families in his colony, Green De Witt to Ramon Musquiz, May 8, 1829, Bexar Archives. This difference of five families may have been due to an attempt on De Witt's part to inflate the figure or the families may have been transient.

17. Green De Witt to Stephen Austin, Gonzales, March 31, 1829, Austin Papers.

18. Titles, De Witt's Colony, Spanish Archives, General Land Office, Austin, Texas.

19. See note, #15, p. 87 & 88.

20. Green De Witt to Ramon Musquiz, May 8, 1829, Bexar Archives.

21. See note #15, p. 92.

22. Titles, De Witt's Colony, Spanish Archives, General Land Office, Austin, Texas.

23. *Ibid.*

24. *Ibid.*

25. See note #15, p. 93.

26. Jose Antonio Navarro was born in San Antonio in 1795. He was a member of the Gutierrez-Magee expedition in 1812-1813. When that attempted filibuster failed, he fled to Louisiana. In 1816 he returned to San Antonio and in 1824 became one of the representatives from Texas in the state Legislature. He received many large land grants which he used as ranch property. He was operating a general store, practicing law and active in politics in San Antonio. He became an avid promoter of Texas independence. During the Texan Sante Fe Expedition in 1841 he was taken prisoner and sentenced to death. He escaped and finally returned to Texas in 1845. Throughout the remainder of his life he was active in Texas politics. He died in 1871. See Joseph M. Dawson, *Jose Antonio Navarro: Co-Creator of Texas*, (Waco, 1969).

27. Titles, De Witt's Colony, Spanish Archives, General Land Office, Austin, Texas.

28. Gammel, Laws of Texas, Vol. I, pp. 180-182, 216; Unsigned, May 17, 1826, Nacogdoches Archives.

29. Brown, *History of Texas*, Vol. I, p. 129.

30. Baker, *Texas Scrap Book*, pp. 290-292.

31. Aldon S. Lang, *Financial History of the Public Lands in Texas* (Waco, 1932), p. 29; "Minutes of the Ayuntamiento of Gonzales, February 15, 1833," Ethel Zivley Rather, "De Witt's Colony," *The Quarterly of the Texas State Historical Association*, VIII (October, 1904), Appendix VI, p. 181.

32. Index to Spanish and Mexican Land Titles, Spanish Archives, General Land Office, Austin, Texas; Eugene C. Barker, ed., "Minutes of the Ayuntamiento of San Felipe de Austin," *Southwestern Historical Quarterly*, XXIII-XXIV (1919-1921).

33. Virginia H. Taylor Houston, "Surveying in Texas," *Southwestern Historical Quarterly*, LXV (October, 1961), pp. 204-233; Forrest Daniell, "Texas Pioneer Surveyors and Indians," *Southwestern Historical Quarterly*, LX (April, 1957), pp. 501-506; Virginia H. Taylor, *The Spanish Archives of the General Land Office of Texas* (Austin, 1954), pp. 65-68; Sue Watkins, ed., *One League to Each Wind, Accounts of Early Surveying in Texas* (Austin, 1964); Thomas Donaldson, *The Public Domain* (Washington, 1884); C. S. Woodard, *The Public*

Domain, Its Surveys & Surveyors (Lansing, 1897). The recent historiographical trends dealing with the explanation and description of various frontier types and frontier roles can readily be seen when compared with older works such as Eugene C. Barker's, *The Life of Stephen F. Austin*. In this work, the late Professor Barker devoted only a few small paragraphs to Stephen Austin's land surveyor, Seth Ingram. There can be no doubt that a work dealing with these surveyors would be an enlightening contribution to the field of frontier studies and other areas as well. Some prominent surveyors were James Kerr, Byrd Lockhart, Seth Ingram, James Gaines, and John P. Borden, who later became the first Land Office Commissioner of the Republic of Texas.

34. The word is derived from the Latin *ripa* which means "bank."

35. Clesson S. Kinney, *Laws of Irrigation and Water Rights and the Arid Region Doctrine of Appropriation of Waters*, 4 Vols. (San Francisco, 1912), Vol. I; Herbert Davenport and J. T. Canales, *The Texas Law of Flowing Waters* (Brownsville, 1949), p. 20; Walter P. Webb, *The Great Plains* (New York, 1931), pp. 432-439; Gerald Ashford, "Jacksonian Liberalism and Spanish Law in Early Texas," *Southwestern Historical Quarterly*, LVII (July, 1953), p. 12; Ira P. Hildebrand, "The Rights of Riparian Owners at Common Law in Texas," *Texas Law Review*, VI (December, 1927), p. 19; Gerald Ashford, *Spanish Texas: Yesterday and Today* (Austin, 1971).

36. Titles, De Witt's Colony, Spanish Archives, General Land Office, Austin, Texas.

37. *Ibid.*

38. Gammel, *Laws of Texas*, Vol. I.

39. *Ibid.*

40. There were twenty-five persons in the De Witt Colony who held only town lots and acquired no additional land within the colony. "List of the Lots in the Inner and Outer Town of Gonzales, Deeded by Alcaldes," Rather, "De Witt's Colony," Appendix II, pp. 168-172.

41. Gammel, *Laws of Texas*, Vol. I.

42. Titles, De Witt's Contract, Spanish Archives, General Land Office, Austin, Texas.

43. Ramon Musquiz to Alcalde of San Felipe, Goliad, May 26, 1831, Austin Papers.

44. Titles, De Witt's Contract, Spanish Archives, General Land Office, Austin, Texas.

45. *Ibid.*

46. *Ibid.*

47. Seymour V. Connors, "Log Cabins in Texas," *The Southwestern Historical Quarterly*, LIII (October, 1949), pp. 105-116.

48. A description of the hewn timber structure common in Texas may be found in the Nacogdoches Archives. However, it is "unsigned" and only the date of 1830 is given. The exact nature of this correspondence is unknown. Connors, "Log Cabins in Texas, p. 105.

49. Unsigned, 1830, Nacogdoches Archives.

50. Connors, "Log Cabins in Texas," p. 113.

51. Noah Smithwick, *The Evolution of a State, or Recollections of Old Texas Days* (Austin, 1900), p. 24.

52. *Ibid.*, p. 15.

53. *Ibid.*, p. 24.

54. Edward, *History of Texas*, pp. 45-48.

55. Smithwick, *Evolution of a State*, p. 18.

56. Edward, *History of Texas*, pp. 45-48.

57. *Ibid.*

58. Stephen F. Austin, "Description of Texas," *Southwestern Historical Quarterly*, Vol. XXVIII (October, 1924), p. 102.

59. Marilyn McAdams Sibley, *Travelers in Texas, 1761-1860* (Austin, 1967), pp. 22-24, 27-28.

60. Frederick L. Olmstead, *A Journey Through Texas; or a Saddle-Trip on the Southwestern Frontier* (New York, 1857), p. 90.

61. *Ibid.*, pp. 48-51, 78; "Minutes of the Ayuntamiento of Gonzales, Article 10, July 25, 1833," *The Quarterly of the Texas State Historical Association*, VIII (October, 1904), p. 181.

62. Edward, *History of Texas*, pp. 48-51.

63. Smithwick, *Evolution of a State*, p. 43. James Kerr had imported some milch cows, but after 1828 he was no longer residing in De Witt's colony.

64. Paul Wallace Gates, *The Farmer's Age: Agriculture, 1815-1860* (New York, 1960), pp. 209, 227.

65. Smithwick, *Evolution of a State*, p. 14.

66. Eclavos, Lista de los Havitantes de la Colonia de De Witt, 1828, Nacogdoches Archives.

67. Titles, De Witt's Contract, Spanish Archives, General Land Office, Austin, Texas.

68. Juan N. Almonte, "Statistical Report of Texas, 1835," Carlos Eduardo Castaneda, trans., *Southwestern Historical Quarterly*, XXVIII, (January, 1925), pp. 177-222.

69. Jose Maria Sanchez, "A Trip to Texas in 1828," Carlos Eduardo Castaneda, trans., *Southwestern Historical Quarterly*, XXIX (April, 1926), p. 267. Jose Maria Sanchez, a Mexican official, journeyed with General Manuel de Mier y Teran to Nachitoches to arrange a boundary between Mexico and the United States.

70. Edward, *History of Texas*, pp. 78-80.

71. *Ibid.*, p. 79.

72. *Ibid.*, p. 80.

73. Amos A. Parker, *Trip to the West and Texas* (Concord, N. H., 1835), p. 148.

74. Edwards, *History of Texas*, p. 79.

75. "Letter XV, November 6, 1831," W. B. De Wees, *Letters from an Early Settler of Texas*, compiled by Cara Cardelle (Louisville, 1852), p. 137.

76. William S. Red, *Texas Colonists and Religion* (Austin, 1924).

77. Gammel, *Laws of Texas*, Vol. I, p. 358.

78. Edna Green De Witt, *Lest We Forget*, pp. 15-16.

CHAPTER V

1. Smithwick, *Evolution of a State*, p. 21.

2. Fray Gaspar Jose De Solis, "Diary of a Visit of Inspection of the Texas Missions Made by Fray Gaspar Jose De Solis in the Years 1767-1768, Translated by Margaret K. Kress," *Southwestern Historical Quarterly*, XXV (July, 1931), p. 43; Albert S. Catschet, *The Karankawa Indians, The Coast People of Texas* (Cambridge, Mass., 1891), pp. 23-32; W. W. Newcomb, Jr., *The Indians of Texas*, pp. 60-61; Ed Kilman, *Cannibal Coast* (San Antonio, 1959), p. xii; Jean Louis Berlandier, *The Indians of Texas in 1830* (Washington, D. C., 1969), pp. 77 and 148.

3. Berlandier, *Indians of Texas*, p. 148.

4. Smithwick, *Evolution of a State*, p. 13.

5. *Ibid.*

6. De Solis, "Diary of a Visit," pp. 42-43.

7. Gatschet, *Karankawa Indians*, pp. 23-32; Newcomb, *Indians of Texas*, pp. 48, 77-78, 150-152, 308, and 327-328.

8. Barker, ed., "Journal of Stephen Austin," p. 305.

9. See Chapter III, pp. 80-81.

10. James Kerr to Stephen Austin, January 24, 1827, Austin Papers.

11. James Kerr to Stephen Austin, Station on the Labaca, February 24, 1827, Austin Papers.

12. Green De Witt to Stephen Austin, April 3, 1827, Austin Papers.

13. *Ibid.*

14. *Ibid.*

15. See Chapter III, p. 62.

16. Smithwick, *Evolution of a State*, p. 21.

17. Gatschet, *Karankawa Indians*, p. 31.

18. Treaty with the Karankawa Indians, May 13, 1827, Bexar Archives.

19. Mary Austin Holley, *Texas* (Lexington, Kentucky, 1836), p. 159; Gatschet, *Karankawa Indians*, pp. 45-51; Berlandier, *Indians of Texas*, p. 148; W. Eugene Hollon and Ruth L. Butler, ed., *William Bollaert's Texas* (Norman, Oklahoma, 1956), p. 174.

20. Smithwick, *Evolution of a State*, pp. 21-22.

21. Holley, *Texas*, p. 159.

22. Smithwick, *Evolution of a State*, p. 22.

23. Holley, *Texas*, p. 159; Gatschet, *Karankawa Indians*, pp. 45-51; Newcomb, *Indians of Texas*, p. 342.

24. Stephen F. Austin to Jose Antonio Saucedo, July 17, 1826, Austin Papers.

25. Stephen F. Austin to Mateo Ahumada, September 10, 1825, Austin Papers. Ahumada was the military commandant of Texas at that time.

26. The word Tonkawa comes from the Wichita, "tonkawey," which means, "they all stay together." The reference here means the tribal confederation of Tancaoye, Tancaguas, Tancahua, Tanquaay, Titskan, and Tonkawega. Webb and Carroll, eds., *The Handbook of Texas*, pp. 788-789.

27. James Kerr to Stephen Austin, February 26, 1827, Austin Papers.

28. *Ibid.*, the "place" means Gonzales.

29. James Kerr to Ramon Musquiz, February 11, 1828, Bexar Archives.

30. See Chapter IV, pp. 85-91.

31. Henry Stevenson Brown was the brother-in-law of James Kerr and the father of the frontier historian John Henry Brown.

32. Holley, *Texas*, p. 148.

33. Brown, *History of Texas*, Vol. I, pp. 154-156.

34. Green De Witt to Stephen Austin, Gonzales, March 3, 1829, Austin Papers.

35. *Ibid.*

36. *Ibid.*

37. *Ibid.*

38. Berlandier, *Indians*, p. 147; Newcomb, *Indians*, pp. 133-153.

39. Ernest Wallace and E. A. Hoebel, *The Comanches, Lords of the South Plains* (Norman, 1952), pp. 254-259, 264-265; Rupert N. Richardson, *The Comanche Barrier to South Plains Settlement* (Glendale, Calif., 1933), pp. 36-37.

40. Green De Witt to Stephen Austin, Gonzales, March 3, 1829, Austin Papers.

41. Green De Witt to Ramon Musquiz, April 23, 1829, Bexar Archives; E. W. Winkler, ed., *Manuscript Letters and Documents of Early Texians, 1821-1845, in Facsimile; Folio Collection of Original Documents* (Austin, 1937), pp. 77-80.

42. *Ibid.*

43. *Ibid.*

44. *Ibid.*

45. Wallace and Hoebel, *The Comanche*, pp. 33-47; Richardson, *Comanche Barrier*, pp. 24-28.

46. Bolton, *Athanase de Mezieres*, Vol. I, pp. 218-219, 297-298.

47. Ferdinand Roemer, *Texas: With Particular Reference to German Immigration and the Physical Appearance of the Country*, Oswald Muellar, trans., (San Antonio, 1935), p. 278.

48. Wallace and Hoebel, *The Comanches*, pp. 3-17.

49. Webb, *The Great Plains*, p. 138.

50. For treatment of this subject see Carolyn Thomas Foreman, *The Cross Timbers* (Muskogee, Okla., 1947).

51. *Ibid.*, p. 5.

52. Wallace and Hoebel, *The Comanches*, p. 7.

53. Green De Witt to Ramon Musquiz, May 8, 1829, Bexar Archives.

54. *Ibid.*

55. Smithwick, *Evolution of a State*, p. 30. According to Smithwick, McCoy was engaged in horse trading with the Comanches.

56. Green De Witt to Ramon Musquiz, May 8, 1829, Bexar Archives.

57. This trade, a violation of both Spanish and Mexican law, began as early as the 1790's and had been increasing steadily. Probably most of the traders, or Comancheros, were Mexican but a good number of them were Anglo-Americans. In the trading, store goods were exchanged for horses and mules which the Comanche had obtained in raids on Mexican border provinces. This trade, which inspired the Comanches to make more raids, caused the authorities grave concern. Attempts were made to suppress it, but were unsuccessful. When Anglo-American settlers arrived in Texas they realized the desirability of ending this "iniquitous traffic" if only to insure peace. The views of one of the leading Anglo-American spokesmen, Stephen Austin, possibly suggests another motive for desiring to suppress this trade. Austin suggested to the Mexican authorities various means of suppressing this trade. One means was for the government to grant a monopoly of the Indian trade to chartered companies of Texans.

58. Green De Witt to Ramon Musquiz, May 8, 1829, Bexar Archives.

59. *Ibid.*

60. See Chapter VI, pp. 89-91.

61. Jose Ruia to Antonio Elosua, May 22, 1829, Bexar Archives.

62. Green De Witt to Ramon Musquiz, May 23, 1829, Bexar Archives.

63. Vincente Filisola, *Memorias para la Historia de la Guerra de Tejas*, 2 Volumes (Mexico, 1848-1849), Vol. I, pp. 233-235.

64. Green De Witt to Ramon Musquiz, December 28, 1830, Bexar Archives.

65. See Chapter IV, pp. 91.

66. Wallace and Hoebel, *The Comanches*, pp. 33-50; Newcomb, *Indians*, pp. 90, 97-98, 163, 173, 180; Hollon and Butler, *Bollaert's Texas*, pp. 361, 375.

67. Green De Witt to Ramon Musquiz, December 28, 1830, Bexar Archives.

68. *Ibid.*

69. Edward, *History of Texas.*

70. Green De Witt to Ramon Musquiz, December 28, 1830, Bexar Archives.

71. Green De Witt to Ramon Musquiz, January 7, 1831, Bexar Archives.

72. Ramon Musquiz to Antonio Elosua, January 12, 1831, Bexar Archives.

73. Green De Witt to Ramon Musquiz, March 4, 1831, Bexar Archives.

74. Jose Antonio Navarro to Ramon Murquiz, April 30, 1831, Nacogdoches Archives.

75. *Ibid.*

76. Remigio Pisana to Antonio Elosua, August 18, 1831, Bexar Archives.

77. Jose Barberena to Antonio Elosua, September 22, 1831, Bexar Archives.

78. Brown, *History of Texas*, Vol. I, pp. 283-285.

79. Filisola, *Memoria*, Vol. I, p. 273.

CHAPTER VI

1. Ramon Musquiz to Jose Antonio Navarro, April 14, 1831, Titles, De Witt's Colony, Spanish Archives, General Land Office, Austin, Texas.

2. Brown, *History of Texas*, Vol. I, pp. 129-130, note.

3. "Map of Gonzales, Inner Town," Rather, "De Witt's Colony," Appendix VIII. The map was drawn by D. S. H. Darst in 1903. Darst had lived in Gonzales since 1831. Miss Rather, in an interview with Darst, had him draw the map for her.

4. "Map of the Town of Gonzales," Rather, "De Witt's Colony," Appendix VIII. This map was compiled and drawn by L. Chenault and L. H. Hopkins in 1892. This map was in the possession of the Harwood and Walsh Abstract Company, Gonzales, Texas. This writer has determined that the Harwood and Walsh firm went out of existence in 1914. Its interests were obtained by C. Samuel and C. A. Burchard which is the present firm of Burchard Abstract Corporation, Gonzales, Texas.

5. *Ibid.*

6. "Minutes of the Ayuntamiento of Gonzales, January 25, 1833," Rather, "De Witt's Colony," Appendix VI, p. 181.

7. "Minutes of the Ayuntamiento of Gonzales, July 10, 1833," Rather, "De Witt's Colony," Appendix VI, p. 183.

8. "Minutes of the Ayuntamiento of Gonzales, February 15, 1833," Rather "De Witt's Colony," Appendix VI, p. 181.

9. Instructions to the Representative of the Province of Texas in the Mexican Congress, January 20, 1822, Nacogdoches Archives; *Laws and Decrees*, pp. 2-12.

10. Darst, "Map of Gonzales, Inner Town."

11. "Records of the Corporation of the Town of Gonzales," Rather, "De Witt's Colony," Appendix II, pp. 168-172. These records were also acquired by the Burchard Abstract Corporation, Gonzales, Texas.

12. Green De Witt to Stephen Austin, April 3, 1827, Austin Papers.

13. Darst, "Map of Gonzales, Inner Town."

14. *Ibid.*

15. *Ibid.*

16. Webb and Carroll, eds., *The Handbook of Texas*, p. 657. it is quite possible that the placed called "Luna" was one of the "grog shops" that David B. Edward mentioned.

17. The word "kitchen" most likely refers to a restaurant.

18. Darst, "Map of Gonzales, Inner Town."

19. *Ibid.*

20. "Records of the Corporation of the Town of Gonzales," Rather, "De Witt's Colony," Appendix II, pp. 168-169.

21. *Ibid.*

22. "Map of the Town of Gonzales" and "Records of the Corporation of the Town of Gonzales," Rather, "De Witt's Colony," Appendix VIII and Appendix II, pp. 169-172.

23. Index to Spanish and Mexican Land Titles, Spanish Archives, General Land Office, Austin, Texas; "Records of the Corporation of the Town of Gonzales," Rather, "De Witt's Colony," Appendix II, pp. 168-172.

24. "Minutes of the Ayuntamiento of Gonzales, January, 1833 to December, 1833," Rather, "De Witt's Colony," Appendix VI, pp. 181-188; Barker, ed., "Minutes of the Ayuntamiento of San Felipe de Austin, 1828-1832," Vols. XXI-XXIV.

25. Joseph M. White, comp., *New Collection of Laws*, pp. 416-418.

26. Gammel, *Laws of Texas*, Vol. I, pp. 335-336.

27. C. H. Haring, *Spanish Empire in America* (New York, 1947), pp. 147-165.

28. *Ibid.*, pp. 151-156; Charles Gibson, *Spain In America* (New York, 1966), p. 97.

29. Castaneda, *Catholic Heritage*, Vol. IV, p. 223; Haring, *Spanish Empire*, p. 150.

30. Gammel, *Laws of Texas*, Vol. I, pp. 335-336.

31. White, *New Collection of Laws*, Vol. I, pp. 416-418.

32. Jose Maria Viesca to Ramon Musquiz, October, 1828, Bexar Archives; Barker, ed., "Minutes of the Ayuntamiento of San Felipe de Austin, February 11, 1829," Vol. XXI, p. 399; Brown, *History of Texas*, p. 144.

33. Barker, *Life of Austin*, pp. 110-112; Eugene C. Barker, "The Government of Austin's Colony, 1821-1831," *The Southwestern Historical Quarterly* XXI (January, 1918), pp. 223-252; Castaneda, *Catholic Heritage, Vol. IV, pp. 225-226.*

34. Barker, ed., "Minutes of the Ayuntamiento of San Felipe de Austin, February 11, 1829," Vol. XXI, p. 399.

35. *Ibid.*

36. Barker, ed., "Minutes of the Ayunatamiento of San Felipe de Austin, July 5, 1830," Vol. XXII, p. 95.

37. Friley saved Brown's life on one occasion when the latter had been injured in retreating from an Indian attack. Brown, *History of Texas*, p. 144.

38. *Ibid.*

39. *Ibid.*

40. *Ibid.*

41. Smithwick, *Evolution of a State*, pp. 84-85.

42. Barker, ed., "Minutes of the Ayuntamiento of San Felipe de Austin, September 6, 1830," Vol. XXIII, p. 187.

43. Smithwick, *Evolution of a State*, p. 85.

44. *Ibid.*

45. *Ibid.*

46. Barker, ed., "Minutes of the Ayuntamiento of San Felipe de Austin, December 17, 1830," Vol. XXIII, p. 76.

47. Barker, ed., "Minutes of the Ayuntamiento of San Felipe de Austin, September 13, 1830," Vol. XXII, p. 189.

48. Barker, ed., "Minutes of the Ayuntamiento of San Felipe de Austin, December 19, 1830," Vol. XXIII, p. 214.

49. *Ibid.*

50. Edward, *History of Texas*, pp. 190-191.

51. Ayuntamiento of Gonzales to Ramon Musquiz, November 13, 1832, Bexar Archives.

52. Gammel, *Laws of Texas*, Vol. I, pp. 335-336.

53. Ayuntamiento of Gonzales to Ramon Musquiz, June 22, 1833, Bexar Archives.

54. *Ibid.*

55. "Minutes of the Ayuntamiento of Gonzales, January 25, 1833," Rather, "De Witt's Colony," Appendix VI, p. 181.

56. *Ibid.*

57. "Minutes of the Ayuntamiento of Gonzales, February 15, 1833," Rather, "De Witt's Colony," Appendix VI, pp. 181-182.

58. "Minutes of the Ayuntamiento of Gonzales, August 5, 1833," Rather, "De Witt's Colony," Appendix VI, p. 184. The contract was made earlier but was not recorded in the "minutes." The entry, dated August 5, merely states that the contract was made (no date given), the price of the ferry, and that the ferry had been delivered and the money authorized.

59. "Minutes of the Ayuntamiento of Gonzales, July 10, 1833," Rather, "De Witt's Colony," Appendix VI, p. 183.

60. See Chapter IV, p. 89.

61. "Minutes of the Ayuntamiento of Gonzales, July 10, 1833," Rather, "De Witt's Colony," Appendix VI, p. 183.

62. *Ibid.*

63. See Chapter IV, p. 105.

64. George Rogers Taylor, *The Transportation Revolution, 1815-1860* (New York, 1951). See his Chapter II, "Roads and Bridges," pp. 15-31.

65. "Minutes of the Ayuntamiento of Gonzales, December 21, 1833," Rather, "De Witt's Colony," Appendix VI, p. 185.

66. *Ibid.*

67. "Minutes of the Ayuntamiento of Gonzales, Article 1st, January, 1834," Rather, "De Witt's Colony," Appendix VI, p. 185.

68. "Minutes of the Ayuntamiento of Gonzales, Article 2nd, January, 1834," Rather, "De Witt's Colony," Appendix VI, p. 186.

69. *Ibid.*

70. See p. 153.

71. "Minutes of the Ayuntamiento of Gonzales, Article 6th, January, 1834," Rather, "De Witt's Colony," Appendix VI, p. 186.

72. *Ibid.*

73. "Minutes of the Ayuntamiento of Gonzales, Article 7th, May 1834," Rather, "De Witt's Colony," Appendix VI, p. 187.

74. The lot on which Eggleston's store was located was owned by George W. Davis. Eggleston, no doubt, was renting it from him. "List of the Lots in the Inner Town of Gonzales," Rather, "De Witt's Colony," Appendix II, p. 168.

75. "Darst's Map of Gonzales, Inner Town."

76. "Minutes of the ayuntamiento of Gonzales, Article 7th, May, 1834," Rather, "De Witt's Colony," Appendix VI, p. 187.

77. "Minutes of the Ayuntamiento of Gonzales, Article 4th, January, 1834," Rather, "De Witt's Colony," Appendix VI, p. 186.

78. "Minutes of the Ayuntamiento of Gonzales, Article 7th, May, 1834," Rather, "De Witt's Colony," Appendix VI, p. 187.

79. See Chapter III, p. 65, note #33, and p. 66.

80. Webb and Carroll, *Handbook of Texas*, "Banks and Banking in Texas," pp. 107-108.

81. "Minutes of the Ayuntamiento of Gonzales, Article 8th, May 1834," Rather, "De Witt's Colony," Appendix VI, p. 187.

82. Thomas S. Berry, *Western Prices Before 1861* (Cambridge, 1943), pp. 486-498; Arthur H. Cole and Walter B. Smith, *Fluctuations in American Business, 1790-1860* (Cambridge, 1935), pp. 76-78, 125-127.

83. "Minutes of the Ayuntamiento of Gonzales, Article 9th, May, 1834," Rather, "De Witt's Colony," Appendix VI, p. 187.

84. "Minutes of the Ayuntamiento of Gonzales, Article 10th, May, 1834," Rather, "De Witt's Colony," Appendix VI, p. 187.

85. "Minutes of the Ayuntamiento of Gonzales, Article 11th, May, 1834," Rather, "De Witt's Colony," Appendix VI, pp. 187-188.

86. "Minutes of the Ayuntamiento of Gonzales, Article 13th, May, 1834," Rather, "De Witt's Colony," Appendix VI, p. 188.

87. Ayuntamiento of Gonzales to Juan Jose Elquezabal, December, 1835, Bexar Archives.

CHAPTER VII

1. Alaman, *Historia de Mejico;* Alessio Robles, *Coahuila y Texas;* Bancroft, *North Mexican States and Texas;* Barker, *Life of Stephen Austin;* Barker, *Mexico and Texas, 1821-1835;* Barker, "Land Speculation as the Cause of the Texas Revolution," *Quarterly of the Texas State Historical Association,* X (July, 1906), pp. 76-95; William C. Binkley, *The Texas Revolution* (Baton Rouge, 1952); Carlos Castaneda, ed., *The Mexican Side of the Texas Revolution* (Dallas, 1928); Castaneda, *Catholic Heritage,* Vol. IV; W. H. Callcott, *Santa Anna, the Story of an Enigma Who Once Was Mexico* (Norman, 1936); Herbert Davenport, "The Men of Goliad," *Southwestern Historical Quarterly,* XLIII (July, 1939), pp. 1-41; Filisola, *Memorias para la Historia;* Llerena Friend, *Sam Houston, the Great Designer* (Austin, 1954); Henry S. Foote, *Texas and Texans,* 2 Vols. (Philadelphia, 1841); George P. Garrison, *Texas: A Contest of Civilization* (New York, 1903); Frank C. Hanighen, *Santa Anna; the Napoleon of the West* (New York, 1934); Walter Lord, *A Time to Stand* (New York, 1963); Ohland Morton, *Teran and Texas* (Austin, 1948); Enrique Olivarria y Ferrari, *Mexico Independiente, 1821-1855,* 5 Vols., Vol. IV, Part I of Vicente Riva Palacio, *Mexico a State;* Vigness, *The Revolutionary Decades;* Amelia Williams, "A Critical Study of the Siege of the Alamo and of the Personnel of Its Defenders," *Southwestern Historical Quarterly,* XXXVI and XXVII (1932 and 1933); Elgin Williams, *The Animating Pursuits of Speculation: Land Traffic in the Annexation of Texas* (New York, 1949); Louis J. Worthan, *A History of Texas from Wilderness to Commonwealth,* 5 Vols. (Fort Worth, 1924); Henderson Yoakum, *History of Texas,* 2 Vols. (New York, 1855).

2. See Samuel Flagg Bemis, ed., *The American Secretaries of State and Their Diplomacy,* Vols. IV and V (New York, 1927-1929); Samuel Flagg Bemis, *John Quincy Adams and the Union* (New York, 1956); Samuel Flagg Bemis, *The Latin American Policy of the United States. An Historical Interpretation* (New York, 1943); James M. Callahan, *American Foreign Policy in Mexican Relations* (New York, 1932); William R. Manning, *Early Diplomatic Relations Between the United States and Mexico* (Baltimore, 1916); William R. Manning, "Texas and the Boundary Issue, 1822-1829," *Southwestern Historical Quarterly,* XVII (January, 1914), pp. 217-261.

3. See Morton, *Teran and Texas;* Allein Howren, "The Causes and Origin of the Decree of April 6, 1830," *Southwestern Historical Quarterly,* XVI (April, 1913), pp. 378-422.

4. Joseph L. Clark and Julia K. Garrett, *A History of Texas, Land of Promise* (Boston, 1949), p. 171.

5. Barker, *Life of Stephen Austin,* pp. 281-282. This entire problem and eventual policy is described in the *Transcripts from the Departmento de Fomento, Mexico,* contained in the University of Texas Archives.

6. See Footnote #1, also Edna Rown, "The Disturbances at Anahuac in 1832," *The Quarterly of the Texas State Historical Association,* IV (April, 1900), pp. 262-299; N. D. Labadie, "Narrative of the Fight at Annahuac," *The Texas Alamanac* (Galveston, 1859), pp. 30-36.

7. Edward, *History of Texas,* pp. 191-192.

8. "Proceedings of the General Convention of 1832," Gammel, *Laws of Texas*, Vol. I, p. 480; Brown, History of Texas, Vol. I, p. 198.

9. Gammel, *Laws of Texas*, Vol. I, pp. 475-503.

10. Ramon Musquiz to the Ayuntamiento of Gonzales, November 22, 1832, Nacogdoches Archives.

11. Ezekiel Williams, Alcalde, to Ramon Musquiz, December 16, 1832, Nacogdoches Archives.

12. Notice to the Public, signed by Thomas Hastings, Chairman of the Nacogdoches Subcommittee, January 3, 1833, Nacogdoches Archives; Stephen F. Austin, "Explanation to the Public Concerning the Affairs of Texas," *Quarterly of the Texas State Historical Association*, VIII (January, 1905), p. 240.

13. Brown, *History of Texas*, Vol. I, pp. 221-229.

14. Brown, *History of Texas*, Vol. I, pp. 228-229; Austin "Explanation to the Public . . . ," p. 240.

15. Edward, *History of Texas*, pp. 196-205.

16. It is most unfortunate that no journal or record of the Convention of 1833 was kept. If one were ever compiled, there is no record of its existence.

17. Brown, *History of Texas*, Vol. I, pp. 232-233.

18. Manuel Ximenes to the Ayuntamiento of Gonzales, May 15, 1833, Bexar Archives.

19. Ayuntamiento of Gonzales to Manuel Ximenes, June 22, 1833, Bexar Archives.

20. Austin informed the ayuntamientos of San Antonio and Nacogdoches of these promises on October 16, 1833 and October 30, 1833, respectively. Cited in Barker, *Life of Stephen Austin*, pp. 274-375.

21. Almonte, "Statistical Report," XXVIII, pp. 177-222.

22. *Ibid.*

23. Barker, *Life of Austin*, pp. 395-396; Richardson, *Texas, Lone Star State*, pp. 77-78.

24. Castaneda, *Catholic Heritage*, Vol. VI, pp. 259-260; Barker, *Life of Stephen Austin*, pp. 400-403; Richardson, *Texas*, pp. 80-81.

25. Barker & Winkler, eds., *History of Texas and Texans, by Frank W. Johnson*, Vol. I, pp. 178-186; Castaneda, *Catholic Heritage*, Vol. VI, pp. 259-261; Barker, *Life of Austin*, pp. 400-406; Barker, "Land Speculation . . . ," X, pp. 76-95.

26. Frank W. Johnson to Gail Bordern, Jr., April 15, 1835, Austin Papers.

27. There is no evidence existing which explains the circumstances surrounding his death. The descendants of Green De Witt have recorded this date in the limited family records. Edna N. De Witt, *Lest We Forget*, p. 10; Minerva De Witt Whittington, "De Witt's Colony," p. 2; Minerva De Witt Whittington to this writer, December 22, 1969; Della E. Nugent to this writer, January 5, 1970.

28. Barker, *Life of Austin*, pp. 404-405; Williams, *Animating Pursuits of Speculation*, pp. 56-57; Castaneda, *Catholic Heritage*, Vol. VI, p. 263; Richardson, *Texas*, p. 81; Vigness, *Revolutionary Decade*, pp. 144-145; Barker, "Land Speculation . . . ," X, pp. 76-95.

29. Asa Brigham to J. A. Wharton, July 19, 1835, Austin Papers. This is merely one of many examples contained in the Austin Papers which reflect the attitude of some of the colonists toward the affair.

30. Barker, *Life of Austin*, p. 407.

31. Brown, *History of Texas*, Vol. I, p. 290.

32. Edward Gritten to Domingo de Ugartechea, July 6, 1835, Bexar Archives.

33. Edward Gritten to Domingo de Ugartechea, July 9, 1835, Bexar Archives.

34. Brown, *History of Texas*, Vol. I, p. 303.

35. "Dr. J. H. C. Miller to J. W. Smith, July 25, 1835," Brown, *History of Texas*, Vol. I, p. 303.

36. Brown, *History of Texas*, Vol. I, p. 352.

37. Yoakum, *History of Texas*, Vol. I, p. 343.

38. There is yet to be written a concise history of the role of the "peace party" in Texas prior to the Revolution. There are, however a number of excellent articles and collections of documents dealing with this subject. Eugene C. Barker, "Don Carlos Barrett," *Southwestern Historical Quarterly*, XX (October, 1916); Eugene C. Barker, "James H. C. Miller and Edward Gritten," *Quarterly of the Texas State Historical Association*, XIII (October, 1909), pp. 145-153; Eugene C. Barker, "Public Opinion in Texas Preceding the Revolution," *Annual Report of the American Historical Association for the Year 1911*, Vol. I (Washington, 1913), pp. 217-228; "Conservatives and Renegades in the Texas Revolution, Documents, 1835," *Publications of the Southern History Association*, VIII (September, 1904), pp. 343-362, "Documents," *Publications of the Southern History Association*, IX (March, 1905), pp. 89-92.

39. Smithwick, *Evolution of a State*, p. 101.

40. Francisco Castaneda to Domingo Ugartechea, September 29, 1835, Bexar Archives.

41. George W. Davis to the Mina Committee of Safety, September 25, 1835, Austin Papers.

42. Francisco Castaneda to Domingo Ugartechea, September 29, 1835, Bexar Archives.

43. Rather, "De Witt's Colony," p. 150, note 3.

44. Miles S. Bennet, "The Battle of Gonzales, the 'Lexington' of the Texas Revolution," *Quarterly of the Texas State Historical Association*, II, (April, 1899), p. 315. Miles S. Bennet was the son of Valentine Bennet, a De Witt colonist.

45. It should be recalled that when the cannon was first obtained, Green De Witt had promised that it would promptly be returned upon request of the government. Ponton, no doubt, was aware of the statement but merely used this excuse as a delaying tactic.

46. Andrew Ponton to Domingo Ugartechea, September 26, 1835, Bexar Archives.

47. *Ibid.*

48. Domingo Ugartechea to Francisco Castaneda, September 27, 1835, Bexar Archives.

49. "Report of William T. Austin on the Battle of Gonzales," Dudley Goodall Wooten, ed., *A Comprehensive History of Texas, 1685 to 1897*, 2 Vols. (Dallas, 1898), Vol. I, p. 536. William Tennant Austin, no relation to Stephen Austin, came to Texas in 1830 and settled in Brazoria. He, together with his brother John, was engaged in the mercantile business. He was wounded in 1832 during the hostilities at Velasco. He was an active member in the radical party and was one of the first to answer Ponton's call for assistance.

50. Francisco Castaneda to Domingo Ugartechea, September 29, 1835, Bexar Archives.

51. *Ibid.*

52. *Ibid.*

53. "Report of William T. Austin," p. 536.

54. Bennet, "The Battle of Gonzales . . . ," p. 315.

55. Francisco Castaneda to Domingo Ugartechea, September 29, 1835, Bexar Archives.

56. *Ibid.*

57. Francisco Castaneda to Domingo Ugartechea, September 29, 1835, Bexar Archives.

58. Joseph D. Clements to Francisco Castaneda, September 30, 1835, Bexar Archives.

59. Domingo Ugartechea to Francisco Castaneda, September 30, 1835, Bexar Archives.

60. Francisco Castaneda to Domingo Ugartechea, September 30, 1835, Bexar Archives.

61. *Ibid.*

62. Bennet, "The Battle of Gonzales . . . ," p. 315.

63. *Ibid.*, p. 314.

64. *Ibid.*

65. "Report of William T. Austin," p. 536.

66. *Ibid.*

67. Webb and Carroll, *Handbook of Texas*, pp. 229-230.

68. Index of Spanish and Mexican Land Titles, Spanish Archives, General Land Office, Austin, Texas; Webb and Carroll, *Handbook of Texas*, p. 856.

69. Miles S. Bennet, "The Battle of Gonzales," p. 36.

70. *Ibid.*

71. "Report of William T. Austin," pp. 536-7.

72. *Ibid.*, p. 537.

73. *Ibid.*, pp. 537-538.

74. *Ibid.*, p. 538.

75. Smithwick, *Evolution of a State*, p. 102.

76. "Report of William T. Austin," p. 539.

77. "General Austin's Order Book for the Campaign of 1835, October 11, 1835 to November 24, 1835," *Quarterly of the Texas State Historical Association*, XI (July, 1907), p. 1.

78. Smithwick, *Evolution of a State*, p. 104; Minerva Whittington, "De Witt's Colony," p. 3; Goldena Howard to Della E. Nugent, November 7, 1969. When the army had taken San Antonio, the flag was taken into the Alamo where it was presumably destroyed. Sarah Seely De Witt's talents in flag making were employed again in 1836. She, Sam Houston, and a Mrs. Plummer designed and made the flag used by the army at San Jacinto. Minerva Whittington, "De Witt's Colony," p. 4.

79. For one of the best and most detailed accounts of the siege of the Alamo, see Amelia Williams, "A Critical Study of the Siege of the Alamo," XXXVI and XXXVII, pp. 1-44, 79-115, 157-184, and 237-312.

80. "William B. Travis to Andrew Ponton, February 23, 1836," Brown, *History of Texas*, Vol. I, p. 550.

81. *Ibid.*, pp. 550-51.

82. The list of the men from the De Witt colony may be found in the "Muster Roll" books found in the General Land Office, Austin, Texas.

83. *Ibid.*

84. Eugene C. Barker, ed., "The San Jacinto Campaign, Documents: Kuykendall's Recollection of the Campaign," *Quarterly of the Texas State Historical Association*, IV (April, 1901), p. 293.

85. Sam Houston, *The Autobiography of Sam Houston*, edited by Donald Day and Harry H. Ullom (Norman, 1954), pp. 101-102.

86. *Ibid.*

87. The *dequello* was a series of musical notes which implied that no quarter was to be given.

88. "Sam Houston to Henry Raquet, March 13, 1826," Amelia Williams and Eugene C. Barker, ed., *The Writings of Sam Houston*, 8 Vols. (Austin, 1938-1943), Vol. IV, pp. 17-19.

89. "Report of Capt. Sharp," Foote, *Texas and Texans*, Vol. II, p. 268.

90. "Darst's Map of Gonzales, Inner Town," Rather, "De Witt's Colony," VIII, Appendix VIII.

91. Barker, "San Jacinto Campaign . . . ," IV, p. 295.

92. "Sam Houston to Henry Raguet, March 13, 1836," Williams and Barker, eds., *Writings of Sam Houston*, Vol. IV, pp. 17-19.

93. Andrew F. Muir, ed., *Texas in 1837: An Anonymous, Contemporary Narrative* (Austin, 1958), pp. 89-91.

94. Webb and Carroll, eds., *Handbook of Texas*, Vol. I, pp. 268-269, 742-743, and 37.

95. *Ibid.*

Conclusion VIII

1. Edward, *History of Texas*, p. 33.

2. Garrison, *Texas: A Contest of Civilization*; Barker, *Mexico and Texas*, pp. 1-31; Lowrie, *Culture Conflict*.

3. Index to Spanish and Mexican Land Titles, Spanish Archives, General Land Office, Austin, Texas. Austin had issued 1,540 land titles by 1836. De Witt had issued 189.

4. It should be pointed out that Austin is considered a success, but the word "success" is used in its strict sense. That is, Austin was successful in introducing more settlers than anyone else. However, that was not his nor any other empresario's primary goal. The introduction of settlers was only a means to achieve personal economic advancement. Eugene Barker points out that Austin in his writings laments that he did all the work and others gained. Austin did not die a rich man.

5. Kerr to Austin, February 26, 1827, Austin Papers.

6. "J. C. Clopper's Journal and Book of Memoranda for 1828," XIII, pp. 44-80, p. 67.

7. *Ibid.*

8. Although the De Witt residence was destroyed during the Texas Revolution, the land upon which it was built is located south of the present day city of Gonzales in the area that is known as De Witt's Mound or Santa Anna's Mound.

9. Jose Antonio Navarro to the Political Chief of Bexar, April 30, 1831, Nacogdoches Archives. De Witt's letter is transcribed in the Navarro correspondence to the political chief.

10. Governor of Coahuila-Texas to Political Chief, Department of Bexar, March 23, 1831, Bexar Archives; Barker, *Life of Austin*, pp. 269-271. ". . . he [General Mier y Teran] reiterated his order to military commander to admit immigrants without distinction if they gave evidence of destination to Austin's colony; and instructed the vice-counsul at New Orleans to issue passports to those only who were going to Austin's or De Witt's colony."

11. Brown, *History of Texas*, Vol. I, p. 341.

12. Original Contract between Green De Witt and J. D. Clements, Gonzales Historical Museum, Gonzales, Texas.

13. Green De Witt to the Political Chief of Bexar, Gonzales, December 28, 1830, Bexar Archives.

14. Barker, *Life of Stephen Austin, p. 133.* There was a great number of unpaid notes found in the Austin Papers.

15. *"Austin to Padilla, August 12, 1826,"* cited in Barker, *Life of Austin, p. 104.*

16. Edna Green De Witt, *Lest We Forget*, p. 78.

17. Titles to Special Grants, Spanish Archives, General Land Office, Austin, Texas.

18. *Ibid.* (Italics in above quotation, this writer).

19. *Ibid.*

20. *Ibid.*

21. Minerva De Witt Whittington, "De Witt's Colony," p. 3.

Bibliography

Manuscripts

Austin Papers, University of Texas, Austin, Texas.

Bexar Archives, University of Texas, Austin, Texas.

Nacogdoches Archives, Texas State Library, Austin, Texas.

Manuscript Collection of the Gonzales Historical Museum, Gonzales, Texas.

Spanish Archives, General Land Office, Austin, Texas.

Primary Sources, Printed.

Alaman, Lucas. *Historia de Mejico Desde Los Primeros Movimientos Que Preparon Su Independencia en el Ano de 1808 Hasta la Epoca Presente.* 5 Volumes. Mexico: J. M. Lara, 1849-1852.

Almonte, Juan N. *Noticia Estadistica Sobre Tejas.* Mexico: Impreso Por Ignacio Cumplido, 1835.

Austin, Stephen F. "Description of Texas," *Southwestern Historical Quarterly*, XXVIII (October, 1924), 98-121.

_____. "Explanation to the Public Concerning the Affairs of Texas," translated by Ethel Zivley Rather, *Quarterly of the Texas State Historical Association*, VIII (January, 1905), 232-258.

Austin, William T. "Report of William T. Austin on the Battle of Gonzales," *A Comprehensive History of Texas, 1685 to 1897*. Edited by Dudley Goodall Wooten. 2 Volumes. Dallas: William G. Scarff, 1898.

Barbe-Marbois, Francois. *Histoire de la Louisiane: De La Cession de Cette Colonie Par la France Aux Etats-Unis de L'Amerique Septentrionale: D'un Discours Sur la Constitution Et Le Government Des Etats-Unis*. Paris: Imprimerie De Firmin Didot, 1829.

_____. *The History of Louisiana, Particularly of the Cession of That Colony to the United States of America; with an Introductory Essay on the Constitution and Government of the United States*. Philadelphia: Carey and Lea, 1830.

Barker, Eugene C., ed. *The Austin Papers*. 3 Volumes. Washington: Government Printing Office, 1924-1928.

Barker, Eugene C., ed. "Journal of Stephen F. Austin on His First Trip to Texas, 1821," *Quarterly of the Texas State Historical Association*, VII (April, 1904), 286-307.

_____, ed. "Minutes of the Ayuntamiento of San Felipe de Austin, 1828-1832," *Southwestern Historical Quarterly*, Vol. XXI (January, 1918), 299-326. Vol. XXI (April, 1918), 395-423. Vol. XXII (July, 1918), 78-95. Vol. XXII (October, 1918), 180-196. Vol. XXII (January, 1919), 272-278. Vol. XXII (April, 1919), 353-359. Vol. XXIII (July, 1919), 69-77. Vol. XXIII (October, 1919), 141-151. Vol. XXIII (January, 1920), 214-223. Vol. XXIII (April, 1920), 302-307. Vol. XXIV (July, 1920), 81-83. Vol. XXIV (October, 1920), 154-166.

_____, ed. "The San Jacinto Campaign, Documents: Kuykendall's Recollection of the Campaign," *Quarterly of the Texas State Historical Association*, IV (April, 1901), 260-343.

Barker, Eugene C. and Ernest W. Winkler, eds. *A History of Texas and Texans by Frank W. Johnson.* 5 Vols. Chicago: The American Historical Society, 1914.

Bennet, Miles S. "The Battle of Gonzales, the 'Lexington' of the Texas Revolution," *Quarterly of the Texas State Historical Association,* II (April, 1899), 313-316.

Berlandier, Jean Louis. *The Indians of Texas in 1830.* Edited and Introduced by John C. Ewers and translated by Patricia R. Leclercq. Washington, D. C.: Smithsonian Institution Press, 1969.

Binkley, William C., ed. *Official Correspondence of the Texas Revolution, 1835-1836.* 2 Volumes. New York: D. Appleton-Century Company, 1936.

Bolton, Herbert Eugene, ed. *Athanase de Mezieres and the Louisiana-Texas Frontier, 1768-1780, Documents Published for the First Time, from the Original Spanish and French Manuscripts, Chiefly in the Archives of Mexico and Spain.* 2 Vols. Cleveland: The Arthur H. Clark Co., 1914.

Bourne, S. A. G. *Observations Upon the Mexican Province of Texas.* London: William and Samuel Graves, 1826.

Braham, D. E. *Braman's Information About Texas.* Philadelphia: J. B. Lippincott and Co., 1958.

Brodie, John Pringle. *Journal of a Voyage to Mexico, 1824-1832.*

Brown, John Henry. *History of Texas, From 1685 to 1892.* 2 Volumes. St. Louis: L. E. Daniell, Publisher, 1892.

_____. *Indian Wars and Pioneers of Texas.* Austin: L. E. Daniell.

Bullock, William. *Le Mexique en 1823, ou Relation d'un Voyage Dans La Nouvell-Espagne, Contenant Des Noteons Exactes et Peu Connues Sur la Situation Physique, Morale, et Politique de Ce Pays.* 2 Volumes. Paris: Alexis-Eymery, Libraire, 1824.

_____. *Six Months Residence and Travel in Mexico; Containing Remarks on the Present State of New Spain, Its Natural Productions, State of Society, Manufactures, Trade, Agriculture, and Antiquities, etc.* London: John Murray, Albemarle-Street, 1824.

Castaneda, Carlos E., ed. & trans. *The Mexican Side of the Texas Revolution*. Dallas; P. L. Turner, 1928.

_____. "Statistical Report on Texas, by Juan N. Almonte, 1835," *Southwestern Historical Quarterly*, XXVIII (January, 1925), 177-222.

Cloppers, J. C. "J. C. Clopper's Journal and Book of Memoranda for 1828," *The Quarterly of the Texas State Historical Association*, XIII (July, 1909), 44-80.

"Conservatives and Renegades in the Texas Revolution, Documents, 1835," *Publications of the Southern History Association*, VII, (September, 1904), 343-362.

The Constitution of the Republic of Mexico, and the State of Coahuila & Texas. Containing also an Abridgement of the Laws of the General and State Governments, Relating to Colonization. With Sundry Other Laws and Documents, Not Before Published, Particularly Relating to Coahuila and Texas. The Documents Relating to the Galveston Bay and Texas Land Company; the Grants to Messrs. Wilson and Exeter, and to Col. John Dominguez, With a Description of the Soil, Climate, Production, Local and Commercial Advantages of the Interesting Country. New York: Ludwig and Tolefree, Printers, 1832.

De Solis, Fray Gaspar Jose. "Diary of a Visit of Inspection of the Texas Missions Made by Fray Gaspar Jose de Solis in the Years 1767-1768, Translated by Margaret K. Kress," *Southwestern Historical Quarterly*, XXV (July, 1931), 28-76.

Dewees, William B. *Letters from an Early Settler of Texas*. Compiled by Cara Cardelle. Louisville, Ky.: Morton & Griswold, 1852.

"Documents," *Publications of the Southern History Association*, IX (March, 1905), 89-92.

Edward, David B. *The History of Texas; or, the Emigrant's, Farmer's and Politician's Guide to the Character, Climate, Soil, and Production of That Country: Geographically Arranged From Personal Observations and Experience*. Cincinnati: J. A. James & Co., 1836.

Field, Joseph E. *Three Years in Texas. Including a View of the Texan Revolution, and an Account of the Principal Battles; Together with Descriptions of the Soil, Commercial, and Agricultural Advantages.* Greenfield: Justin Jones, 1836.

Filisola, Vicente. *Memorias Para la Historia de la Guerra de Tejas.* 2 Volumes. Mexico: R. Rafael, 1848-1849.

Foote, Henry S. *Texas and the Texans; or Advance of the Anglo-Americans to the Southwest; Including a History of Leading Events in Mexico, From the Conquest by Fernando Cortes to the Termination of the Texan Revolution.* 2 Volumes. Philadelphia: Thomas, Cowperthwait & Co., 1841.

Galvez, Bernardo de. *Instructions for Governing the Interior Provinces of New Spain, 1786,* trans. and ed. by Donald E. Worcester. Berkeley: The Quivira Society, 1951.

Gammel, Hans Peter Nielsen. *Laws of Texas.* 10 Vol. Austin: George P. Finley, 1906.

"General Austin's Order Book for the Campaign of 1835, October 11, 1835 to November 24, 1835." *Quarterly of the Texas State Historical Association,* XI (July, 1907), 1-55.

Hatcher, Mattie Austin, ed. *Letters of an Early American Traveller, Mary Austin Holley; Her Life and Works, 1784-1846.* Dallas: Southwest Press, 1933.

Holley, Mary Austin. *Texas.* Lexington, Kentucky: J. Clark & Co., 1836.

_____. *The Texas Diary, 1835-1838.* Edited with an Introduction by J. P. Bryan. Austin: University of Texas Press, 1965.

Hollon, W. Eugene and Ruth L. Butler, eds. *William Bollaert's Texas.* Norman: University of Oklahoma Press, 1956.

Holmes, Jack D. L., ed. *Documents Ineditos para la Historia de la Luisiana, 1792-1810.* Madrid: Ediciones Jose Porrua Turanzas, 1962.

Houck, Louis ed. *The Spanish Regime in Missouri: A Collection of Papers and Documents Relating to Upper Louisiana Principally Within the Present Limits of Missouri During* the Dominion of Spain, From the Archives of the Indies at Seville, etc. Translated from the Original Spanish into English, and Including Also Some Papers Concerning the Supposed Grant to Colonel George Morgan at the Mouth of the Ohio. 2 Volumes. Chicago: R. R. Donneley & Sons Co., 1909.

Houston, Sam. The Autobiography of Sam Houston, edited by Donald Day and Harvey H. Ullom. Norman: University of Oklahoma Press, 1954.

Houston, Matilda C. F. Texas and the Gulf of Mexico. London: J. Murray, 1844.

Hunt, Richard. Guide to the Republic of Texas: Consisting of a Brief Outline of the History of Its Settlements. New York: J. H. Colton, 1839.

Ikin, Arthur. Texas: Its History, Topography, Agriculture, Commerce and General Statistics. London: Sherwood, Gilbert, and Piper, 1841.

Jones, Anson. Memoranda & Official Correspondence. New York: D. Appleton & Co., 1859.

Jordan, John. Serious Actual Dangers of Foreigners & Foreign Commerce in the Mexican States. Philadelphia: P. M. Lafowicade, 1826.

Kerr, Hugh. A Poetical Description of Texas. New York, 1838.

Kimball, J. P., trans. Constitution of the State of Coahuila and Texas; Also the Colonization Law of the State of Tamaulipas and Naturalization Law of the General Congress. Houston, 1839.

Laws and Decrees of the Republic of Mexico in Relation to Colonization and Grants of Land, More Particularly in New Mexico and California, From 1823 to 1846. New York: The New York Printing Co., 1871.

Leclerc, Frederick. Texas & Its Revolution; Translated from the Original French by James L. Shepherd, III. Houston: Anson Jones Press, 1950.

Menchaca, Antonio. Memoirs. San Antonio: Yanaguana Society, 1937.

Miller, Hunter, ed. *Treaties and Other International Acts of the United States of America.* 5 Volumes. Washington. United States Government Printing Office, 1933.

Morfi, Juan Agustin. *History of Texas, 1673-1779.* Translated and annotated by Carlos Eduardo Castaneda. 2 Volumes. Albuquerque: The Quivira Society, 1935.

Morrell, Z. N. *Flowers & Fruits from the Wilderness, or Thirty-Six Years in Texas.* Boston: Gould and Lincoln, 1873.

Muir, Andrew F. *Texas in 1837: An Anonymous, Contemporary Narrative.* Austin: University of Texas Press, 1958.

Nasatir, A. P., ed. *Before Lewis and Clark: Documents Illustrating the History of the Missouri. 2 Volumes. St. Louis: St. Louis Historical Documents Foundation, 1952.*

Newell, Chester. History of the Revolution in Texas. New York: Wiley & Putnam, 1838.

Olmstead, Frederick L. *A Journey Through Texas; or a Saddle-Trip on the Southwestern Frontier.* New York: Dix, Edwards & Co., 1857.

Onis, Luis de. *Memoria Sobre las Negociones Entre Espana y Los Estado de America, Que Dieron Motivo al Tratado de 1819. Con Una Noticia Sobre la Estadistica de Aquel Paris. Acompana un Apendice, Que Contiene Documentos Importantes Para Mayor Illustracion del Asunto.* 2 Volumes. Madrid: Imprenta D. M. Burgos, 1820.

Parker, Amos Andrew. *Trip to the West and Texas.* Concord, N. H.: White & Fisher, 1835.

Poinsett, Joel R. *Notes on Mexico, Made in the Autumn of 1822. Accompanied by an Historical Sketch of the Revolution, and Translations of Official Reports on the Present State of that Country.* London: John Miller, 1825.

Ramos Arizpe, Miguel. *Report to the August Congress on the Natural Political, and Civil Condition of the Provinces of Coahuila, Nuevo Leon, Nuevo Santander, and Texas of the Four Eastern Interior Provinces of the Kingdom of Mexico.* Translation, Annotations, and Introduction by Nettie Lee Benson. Austin: University of Texas Press, 1950.

Robertson, James Alexander, ed. *Louisiana Under the Rule of Spain, France, and the United States, 1785-1807.* 2 Volumes. Cleveland: The Arthur H. Clark Co., 1911.

Roemer, Ferdinand. *Texas: With Particular Reference to German Immigration and the Physical Appearance of the Country.* Oswald Mueller, trans. San Antonio: Standard Printing Co., 1935.

Sanchez, Jose M. "A Trip to Texas in 1828," *Southwestern Historical Quarterly,* XXIX (April, 1926), 249-288.

Serrano y Sanz, Manuel, ed. *Documentos Historicos de la Florida y la Louisiana.* Madrid: Liberia General de Vicotiano Suarez, 1912.

Smithwick, Noah. *The Evolution of a State or Recollection of Old Texas Days.* Austin: Gammel Book Co., 1900.

Stiff, Edward. *The Texas Emigrant: Being a Narration of the Author in Texas and a Description of the Soil, Climate, Production, Minerals, Towns, Bays, Harbors, Rivers, Institutions, and Manners and Customs of the Inhabitants of that Country, Together with the Principal Incidents of Fifteen Years Revolution in Mexico; and Embracing a Condensed Statement of Interesting Events in Texas, from the First European Settlement in 1692 Down to the Year 1840.* Cincinnati: Conclin, 1840.

Taylor, Virginia H., trans. and ed. *The Letters of Antonio Martinez: Last Spanish Governor of Texas, 1817-1822.* Austin: Texas State Library, 1957.

Texas Letters. San Antonio: Yanaguana Society, 1940.

A Visit to Texas; Being the Journal of a Traveller Through Those Parts Most Interesting to American Settlers. New York: Van Nostrand & Swight, 1836.

Ward, Henry George. *Mexico During the Years 1825, 1826, and Part of 1827. With an Account of the Mining Companies, and of the Political Events in That Republic, to the Present Day.* 2 Volumes. London: Henry Colburn, 1829.

Whitaker, Arthur Preston, ed. *Documents Relating to the Commercial Policy of Spain in the Floridas with Incidental References to Louisiana.* Deland: The Florida State Historical Society, 1931.

White, Joseph M., comp. *A New Collection of Laws, Charters and Local Ordinances of the Government of Great Britain, France, and Spain, Relating to the Concessions of Land in Their Respective Colonies; Together with the Laws of Mexico and Texas on the Same Subject.* 2 Volumes. Philadelphia: T. and J. W. Johnson, 1839.

Williams, Amelia and Eugene C. Barker, eds. *The Writings of Sam Houston.* 8 Volumes. Austin: University of Texas Press, 1938-1943.

Winfrey, Dorman H., ed. *Texas Indian Papers.* Edited from the Original Manuscript Copies in the Texas State Archives. 5 Volumes. Austin: Texas State Library, 1959-1966.

Winkler, Ernest W., ed. *Manuscript Letters & Documents of Early Texians, 1821-1845, in Facsimile; Folio Collection of Original Documents.* Austin: The Steck Co., 1937.

Secondary Sources

Alessio Robles, Vito. *Coahuila y Texas.* 2 Volumes. Mexico, D. F.: Editorial Cultura, 1938 & 1945.

Allen, John Taylor. *Early Pioneer Days in Texas.* Dallas: Wilkinson Printing Co., 1918.

Almaraz, Felix D. *Tragic Cavalier: Governor Manuel Salcedo of Texas, 1808-1813.* Austin: University of Texas Press, 1971.

Ashford, Gerald. "Jacksonian Liberalism and Spanish Law in Early Texas," *Southwestern Historical Quarterly,* LVII (July, 1953), 1-37.

Atkinson, Mary J. *The Texan Indians.* San Antonio: The Naylor Co., 1935.

Baker, D. W. C., compiler. *Texas Scrap Book: Made Up of the History, Biography, & Miscellany of Texas & Its People.* New York: A. S. Barnes & Co., 1875.

Bancroft, Hubert Howe. *History of the North Mexican States and Texas, 1531-1800.* San Francisco: The History Co. Publisher, 1886.

Barker, Eugene C. "Don Carlos Barrett," *Southwestern Historical Quarterly,* XX (October, 1916), 139-145.

_____. "The Government of Austin's Colony, 1821-1831," *Southwestern Historical Quarterly,* XXI (January, 1918), 223-252.

_____. "Influence of Slavery in the Colonization of Texas," *Mississippi Valley Historical Review,* XI (June, 1924), 3-36.

Barker, Eugene C. "James H. C. Miller and Edward Gritten," *Quarterly of the Texas State Historical Association,* XIII (October, 1909), 145-153.

_____. "Land Speculation as the Cause of the Texas Revolution," *Quarterly of the Texas State Historical Association,* X (July, 1906), 76-95.

_____. *The Life of Stephen F. Austin: Founder of Texas, 1793-1836.* Austin: The Texas State Historical Association, 1949.

_____. *Mexico and Texas, 1821-1835.* Dallas: P. L. Turner Co., 1928.

_____. "Notes on the Colonization of Texas," *Mississippi Valley Historical Review,* X (September, 1923), 141-152.

_____. "Public Opinion in Texas Preceding the Revolution," *Annual Report of the American Historical Association for the Year 1911.* Vol. I (Washington, 1913), 217-228.

_____, ed. *Readings in Texas History.* Dallas: The Southwest Press, 1929.

_____. "Report on the Bexar Archives," *Annual Report of the American Historical Association for the Year 1902.* Vol. I, 357-363.

Bedford, Hilory G. *Texas Indian Troubles.* Dallas: Hargreaves Printing Co., 1905.

Bemis, Samuel Flagg, ed. *The American Scretaries of State & Their Diplomacy.* Vols. IV & V. New York: A. A. Knopf, 1927.

_____. *John Quincy Adams and the Union.* New York: A. A. Knopf, 1956.

_____. *The Latin American Policy of the United States. An Historical Interpretation.* New York: Harcourt, Brace & Co., 1943.

Berry, Thomas S. *Western Prices Before 1861: A Study of the Cincinnati Market.* Cambridge: Harvard University Press, 1943.

Biesele, Rudolph. *The History of the German Settlements in Texas, 1831-1861.* Austin: Press of Von Boeckmann-Jones Co., 1930.

Binkley, William C. *The Texas Revolution.* Baton Rouge: Louisiana State University Press, 1952.

Blackmar, Frank W. "Spanish Colonization in the Southwest," *Johns Hopkins University Studies in Historical and Political Sciences,* IV (April, 1890), 7-79.,

_____. *Spanish Institutions of the Southwest.* Baltimore: The Johns Hopkins Press, 1891.

Bolton, Herbert Eugene. *Guide to the Materials for the History of the United States in the Principle Archives of Mexico.* Washington, D. C.: Carnegie Institution of Washington, 1913.

_____. "The Mission as a Frontier Institution," *American Historical Review,* XXIII (February, 1943), 42-61.

_____. "Spanish Activities on the Lower Trinity River, 1746-1771," *Southwestern Historical Quarterly,* XVI (April, 1913), 339-377.

_____. *The Spanish Borderlands: A Chronicle of Old Florida and the Southwest.* New Haven: Yale University Press, 1921.

_____. *Texas in the Middle Eighteenth Century: Studies in Spanish Colonial History and Administration.* Berkeley: University of California Press, 1915.

Brooks, Elizabeth. *Prominent Women of Texas.* Akron, Ohio: The Werner Co., 1896.

Brooks, Philip C. *Diplomacy and the Borderlands: The Adams-Onis Treaty of 1819* Berkeley: University of California Press, 1939.

Bugbee, Lester G. "The Old Three Hundred: A List of Settlers in Austin's First Colony," *Quarterly of the Texas State Historical Association*, I (October, 1897), 108-117.

Butler, Ruth Lapham, comp. *A Checklist of Manuscripts in the Edward E. Ayer Collection.* Chicago: The Newberry Library, 1937.

Butterfield, Jack C. *Men of the Alamo, Goliad and San Jacinto.* San Antonio: The Naylor Co., 1936.

Callahan, James Morton. *American Foreign Policy in Mexican Relations.* New York: The Macmillan Co., 1932.

Callcott, Wilfred H. *Santa Anna, the Story of an Enigma Who Once Was Mexico.* Norman: University of Oklahoma Press, 1936.

Carroll, Horace Bailey. *Texas County Histories; A Bibliography.* Austin: Texas State Historical Association, 1943.

_____. *Texas History Theses; a Check List of the Theses and Dissertations Relating to Texas History, 1893-1951.* Austin: Texas Historical Association, 1955.

Castaneda, Carlos E. *Our Catholic Heritage in Texas, 1519-1936.* 7 Volumes. Austin: Von Boeckmann-Jones Co., 1936.

_____. *A Report on the Spanish Archives in San Antonio, Texas.* San Antonio: Yanaguana Society, 1937.

Chabot, Frederick C. *With the Makers of San Antonio: Genologies of the Early Latin, Anglo-American, and German Families with Occasional Biographies, Each Group Being Prefaced with a Brief Historical Sketch and Illustrations.* San Antonio: Artes Graficas, 1937.

Clark, Joseph L. and Julia K. Garrett. *A History of Texas: Land of Promise.* Boston: D. C. Heath & Co., 1949.

Connors, Seymour V. "Log Cabins in Texas," *Southwestern Historical Quarterly*, LIII (October, 1949), 105-116.

Crocket, George. *Two Centuries in East Texas.* Dallas: The Southwest Press, 1932.

Daniell, Forrest. "Texas Pioneer Surveyors and Indians," *Southwestern Historical Quarterly,* LX (April, 1957), 501-506.

Daniell, Lewis E. *Texas, the Country & Its Men.* Austin, 1924.

Davenport, Herbert. "The Men of Goliad," *Southwestern Historical Quarterly,* XLIII (July, 1939), 1-41.

Davis, Ellis A., ed. *The Historical Encylopedia of Texas,* Revised Edition. Texas Historical Society, 1934.

De Witt, Edna, comp. *Lest We Forget.* Gonzales, Texas.

Dixon, Samuel H. *Romance and Tragedy of Texas History.* Houston: Texas Historical Publishing Co., 1924.

Dobie, James F. *The Flavor of Texas.* Dallas: Dealey & Lowe, 1936.

Donaldson, Thomas. *The Public Domain.* Washington, D. C.: Government Printing Office, 1884.

Driggs, Howard R. *Rise of the Lone Star.* New York: Frederick A. Stokes, 1936.

Dunn, Dominick. *The Rectangular Survey System of Land Management.*

Dunn, William Edward. *Spanish and French Rivalry in the Gulf Region of the United States, 1678-1702: The Beginnings of Texas and Pensacola.* Austin: University of Texas, 1917.

Fagg, John E. *Latin America: A General History.* New York: Macmillan, 1962.

Faulk, Odie B. *Land of Many Frontiers: A History of the American Southwest.* New York: Oxford University Press, 1968.

_____. *The Last Years of Spanish Texas, 1778-1821.* Hague: Mouton & Co., 1964.

_____. *A Successful Failure, 1519-1810.* Austin: Steck-Vaughn Co., 1965.

Finlay, George P., comp. *Index to Gammel's Laws of Texas.* Austin, 1906.

Folmer, Henry. *Franco-Spanish Rivalry in North America, 1524-1763*. Glendale, California: The Arthur H. Clark Co., 1953.

Foreman, Carolyn Thomas. *The Cross Timbers*. Muskogee, Oklahoma: The Star Printing, Inc., 1947.

Friend, Llerena. *Sam Houston, the Great Designer*. Austin: University of Texas Press, 1954.

Fulmore, Zachery T. *The History and Geography of Texas as Told in County Names*. Austin: The Steck Co., 1935.

Gabriel, Ralph H. *The Lure of the Frontier, A Story of Race Conflict*. New Haven: Yale University Press, 1929.

Garrett, Julia K. *Green Flag Over Texas; A Story of the Last Years of Spain in Texas*. New York: The Cordova Press, 1939.

Garrison, George P. *Texas; A Contest of Civilization*. New York: Houghton, Mifflin & Co., 1903.

Gates, Paul Wallace. *The Farmer's Age: Agriculture, 1815-1860*. New York: Holt, Rinehart & Winston, 1960.

Gatschet, Albert S. *The Karankawa Indians, The Coast People of Texas*. Cambridge, Mass.: Peabody Museum of American Archaeology and Ethnology, 1891.

Gayarre, Charles. *History of Louisiana*. 4 Volumes. New York: Redfield, 1854.

Gibson, Charles. *Spain in America*. New York: Harper & Row, 1966.

Hackett, Charles Wilson. "Policy of the Spanish Crown Regarding French Encroachments from Louisiana, 1721-1762," *New Spain and the Anglo-American West: Historical Contributions Presented to Herbert Eugene Bolton*. Edited by George P. Hammond. 2 Volumes. Lancaster: Lancaster Press, 1932.

Haltom, Richard W. *History and Descriptions of Nacogdoches Country, Texas*. Nacogdoches News Print, 1880.

Hanighen, Frank C. *Santa Anna; the Napoleon of the West*. New York: Coward-McCann Inc., 1934.

Haggard, J. Villasana, "The Neutral Ground between Louisiana and Texas, 1806-1821," *Louisiana Historical Quarterly,* XXVIII (October, 1945), 1001-1128.

Haring, C. H. *The Spanish Empire in America.* New York: Oxford University Press, 1947.

Hatcher, Mattie Austin. "The Louisiana Background of the Colonization of Texas, 1763-1803," *Southwestern Historical Quarterly,* XXIV (January, 1921), 169-194.

_____. *The Opening of Texas to Foreign Settlements, 1801-1821.* Austin: University of Texas Press, 1927.

Henderson, Mary Virginia. "Minor Empresario Contracts for the Colonization of Texas, 1825-1834," *Southwestern Historical Quarterly,* XXXI (April, 1928), 295-324 and XXXII (July, 1928), 1-29.

Herring, Hubert. *A History of Latin America from the Beginning to the Present.* New York: Alfred A. Knopf, 1956.

Hibbard, Benjamin H. *A History of the Public Land Policies.* New York: MacMillan Co., 1924.

Hildebrand, Ira P. "The Rights of Riparian Owners at Common Law in Texas," *Texas Law Review,* VI (December, 1927), 19-49.

Holmes, Jack D. L. *Gayoso: The Life of a Spanish Governor in the Mississipi Valley, 1789-1799.* Baton Rouge: Louisiana State University Press, 1965.

Houck, Louis. *A History of Missouri from the Earliest Explorations and Settlement Until the Admission of the State into the Union.* 3 Volumes. Chicago: R. R. Donnelley and Sons Co., 1908.

Houston, Virginia H. Taylor. "Surveying in Texas," *Southwestern Historical Quarterly,* LXV (October, 1961), 204-233.

Howren, Alleine. "Causes and Origins of the Decree of April 6, 1830," *Quarterly of the Texas State Historical Association,* XVI (April, 1913), 378-422.

Hyde, George E. *Rangers and Regulars.* Denver: J. Van Male, 1933.

Jenkins, John H. *Cracker Barrel Chronicles: A Bibliography of Texas Town & County Histories*. Austin: Pemberton Press, 1965.

Jordan, Terry G. "The Imprint of the Upper and Lower South on Mid-Nineteenth Century Texas," *Annals of the Association of American Geographers*, LVII (December, 1967), 667-690.

Kemp, Louis W. *The Signers of the Texas Declaration of Independence*. Salado, Texas: The Anson Jones Press, 1944.

Kennedy, William. *Texas: The Rise, Progress and Prospects of the Republic of Texas*. 2 Volumes. London: R. Hastings, 1841.

Kielman, Chester V., ed. & comp. *The University of Texas Archives*. A Guide. Austin: University of Texas Press, 1967.

Kilman, Edward. *Cannibal Coast*. San Antonio: The Naylor Co., 1959.

Kinnaird, Lawrence. "American Penetration into Spanish Louisiana," *New Spain and the Anglo-American West: Historical Contributions Presented to Herbert Eugene Bolton*. Edited by George P. Hammond. 2 Volumes. Lancaster: Lancaster Press, 1932.

Kinney, Clesson S. *Laws of Irrigation and Water Rights and the Arid Region Doctrine of Appropriation of Waters*. 4 Volumes. San Francisco: Bender-Moss Co., 1912.

Labadie, N. D. "Narrative of the Fight at Anahuac," *The Texas Almanac*. Galveston, 1857.

Lane, Sister M. Claude. *Catholic Archives of Texas: History and Preliminary Inventory*. Houston: Sacred Heart Dominican College, 1961.

Lang, Aldon S. *Financial History of the Public Lands in Texas*. Waco: The Baylor Bulletin of Baylor University, 1932.

Lathrop, Barnes F. *Migration into East Texas, 1835-1860: A Study from the United States Census*. Austin: The Texas State Historical Association, 1949.

Lenz, Louis. "Texas Money," *Southwestern Historical Quarterly*, LVII (October, 1953), 175-180.

Lord, Walter. *A Time to Stand*. New York: Harper & Row, 1963.

Lowrie, Samuel H. *Culture Conflict in Texas, 1821-1835*. New York: Columbia University Press, 1932.

Manning, William R. *Early Diplomatic Relations Between the United States and Mexico*. Baltimore: The Johns Hopkins Press, 1916.

_____. "Texas and the Boundary Issue, 1822-1829," *Southwestern Historical Quarterly*, XVII (January, 1914), 217-261.

Marshall, Thomas Maitland. *A History of the Western Boundary of the Louisiana Purchase, 1819-1841*. Berkeley: University of California Press, 1914.

Martin, Francois Xavier. *The History of Louisiana, from the Earliest Period*. New Orleans: James A. Gresham, 1882.

Mateos, J. Antonio. *Historia Parlementaria de los Congresos Mexicanos de 1821 a 1857*. 25 Volumes. Mexico: V. S. Reyes, empresor, 1877-1912.

Mayhall, Mildred P. *Indian Wars of Texas*. Waco: Texian Press, 1965.

McCaleb, Walter F. "Some Obscure Points in the Mission Period of Texas History," *The Quarterly of the Texas State Historical Association*, I (January, 1898), 216-225.

_____. *Spanish Missions of Texas*, rev. ed. San Antonio: The Naylor Co., 1961.

McKitrick, Reuben. *The Public Land System of Texas, 1823-1910*. Madison: University of Wisconsin, 1918.

Mecham, J. Lloyd. "The Northern Expansion of New Spain, 1522-1822: A Selected Descriptive Bibliographical List," *Hispanic American Historical Review*, VII (May, 1927), 233-276.

Meining, D. W. *Imperial Texas. An Interpretive Essay in Cultural Geography*. Austin: University of Texas Press, 1969.

Moore, Francis. *Map and Description of Texas*. Philadelphia: H. Tanner, 1840.

Mukleroy, Ann. "The Indian Policy of the Republic of Texas," *Southwestern Historical Quarterly*, XXV (April, 1922), 229.

Newcomb, William W. *The Indians of Texas: From Prehistoric Times to Modern Times*. Austin: University of Texas Press, 1961.

Nielsen, George R. "Matthew Caldwell," *Southwestern Historical Quarterly*, LXIV (April, 1961), 478-502.

Norman, J. Q. Throwen. *Original Survey and Land Subdivision*. Chicago: Rand McNally, 1966.

North, Douglas C. *The Economic Growth of the United States, 1790-1860*. New York: W. W. Norton & Co., 1966.

Ogg, Frederick. *The Opening of the Mississippi: A Struggle for Supremacy in the American Interior*. New York: The Macmillan Co., 1904.

Olivarria y Ferrari, Enrique. *Mexico independiente, 1821-1855*. Vol. IV. First part of Vincente Riva Palacio's *Mexico a Trevis de los Siglos*, 5 Volumes. Mexico: Ballesca y Comp., 1887-1889.

Raines, Caldwell Walton. *Year Book for Texas*. 2 Volumes. Austin: Gammel-Statesmen Publishing Co., 1903.

Rather, Ethel Zivley. "De Witt's Colony," *Quarterly of the Texas State Historical Association*, VIII (October, 1904), 95-191.

Ray, Worth S. Austin Colony Pioneers. *Including History of Bastrop, Fayette, Grimes, Montgomery, & Washington Counties, Texas*. Austin, 1949.

Reading, Robert A. *Arrows Over Texas*. San Antonio: Naylor Co., 1960.

Red, William S. *The Texas Colonists & Religion, 1821-1836*. Austin: E. L. Shettles, 1924.

Richardson, Rupert N. *The Comanche Barrier to South Plains Settlement*. Glendale, California: Arthur H. Clark Co., 1933.

_____. *Texas; The Lone Star State*. 2nd ed. Englewood Cliffs, N. J.: Prentice-Hall, Inc., 1958.

Rippy, J. Fred. "British Role in the Early Relations of the United States and Mexico," *Hispanic American Historical Review,* VIII (February, 1927), 2-24.

Robertson, James Alexander. *List of Documents in Spanish Archives, Relating to the History of the United States, Which Have Been Printed or of Which Transcripts are Preserved in American Libraries.* Washington, D. C.: Carnegie Institution of Washington, 1910.

Robbins, Roy. *Our Landed Heritage: The Public Domain, 1776-1936.* Lincoln: University of Nebraska Press, 1962.

Rowe, Edna. "The Disturbances at Anahuac in 1832," *Quarterly of the Texas State Historical Association,* IV (April, 1900), 262-299.

Schmitz, S. M. Joseph W. *Mission Concepcion.* Waco: Texian Press, 1965.

_____. *Texas Culture.* San Antonio: Naylor Co., 1960.

Shepherd, William R. "Wilkinson and the Beginnings of the Spanish Conspiracy," *American Historical Review,* IX (April, 1904), 490-506.

Sibley, Marilyn McAdams. *Travelers in Texas, 1761-1860.* Austin: University of Texas Press, 1967.

Smith, Walter B. and Arthur H. Cole. *Fluctuations in American Business, 1790-1860.* Cambridge: Harvard University Press, 1935.

Spicer, Edward H. *Cycles of Conquest; the Impact of Spain, Mexico & the United States on the Indians of the Southwest, 1533-1960.* Tucson: University of Arizona Press, 1962.

Steck, Francis Borgia. *A Tentative Guide to Historical Materials on the Spanish Borderlands.* Philadelphia: The Catholic Historical Society of Philadelphia, 1943.

Stenberg, Richard R. "The Boundaries of the Louisiana Purchase," *Hispanic American Historical Review,* XIV (February, 1934), 32-64.

Stiff, Edward. *A New History of Texas.* Cincinnati: G. Conclin, 1848.

Taylor, George Rogers. *The Transportation Revolution, 1815-1860.* New York: Harper & Row, 1951.

Taylor, Virginia H. *The Spanish Archives of the General Land Office of Texas.* Austin: The Lone Star Press, 1964.

Thrall, Homer S. *A Pictorial History of Texas.* St. Louis: Thompson, 1883.

Tiling, Moritz P. G. *History of the German Element in Texas from 1820-1850.* Houston: M. Tiling, 1913.

Treat, Payson J. *The National Land System, 1785-1820.* New York: E. G. Treat & Co., 1910.

Turner, Frederick Jackson and Frederick Merk. *List of References on the History of the West.* Cambridge: Harvard University Press, 1922.

Vigness, David M. *The Revolutionary Decades, 1810-1836.* Austin: Steck-Vaughn Co., 1965.

Wallace, Ernest & E. A. Hoebel. *The Comanches, Lords of the South Plains.* Norman: University of Oklahoma Press, 1952.

Warren, Harris G. *A Sword Was Their Passport: A History of American Filibustering in the Mexican Revolution.* Baton Rouge: Louisiana State University Press, 1943.

Watkins, Sue, ed. *One League to Each Wind, Accounts of Early Surveyors in Texas.* Austin: Texas Surveyors Association, 1964.

Webb, Walter P. *The Great Plains.* New York: Ginn & Co., 1931.

Webb, Walter Prescott and H. Bailey Carroll, eds. *The Handbook of Texas.* Austin: The Texas State Historical Association, 1952.

Wharton, Clarence R. *Texas Under Many Flags.* New York: The American Historical Society, 1930.

Wheeler, Kenneth W. *To Wear a City's Crown; The Beginnings of Urban Growth in Texas, 1835-1865.* Cambridge: Harvard University Press, 1969.

Whitaker, Arthur Preston. "The Commerce of Louisiana and the Floridas at the End of the Eighteenth Century," *Hispanic American Historical Review,* VIII (May, 1928), 190-203.

_____. *The Mississippi Question, 1795-1803. A Study in Trade, Politics and Diplomacy.* New York: D. Appleton-Century, 1934.

_____. *The Spanish-American Frontier: 1783-1795; The Westward Movement and the Spanish Retreat in the Mississippi Valley.* Gloucester: Peter Smith, 1962.

Whittington, Minerva De Witt. "De Witt's Colony," Speech given before the Yoakum Rotary Club, Yoakum, Texas. February 21, 1968.

Wilbarger, J. W. *Indian Depredations in Texas.* Austin: Hutchings Printing House, 1889.

Williams, Amelia. "A Critical Study of the Siege of the Alamo and of the Personnel of Its Defenders," *Southwestern Historical Quarterly,* XXXVI (April, 1933), 251-287, and XXVII (July, 1933-April, 1934), 1-44, 79-115, 157-184, and 237-312.

Williams, Elgin. *The Animating Pursuits of Speculation: Land Traffic in the Annexation of Texas.* New York: Columbia University Press, 1949.

Winfrey, Dorman H., ed. *Six Missions of Texas.* Waco: Texian Press, 1965.

Wooten, Dudley G., ed. *A Comprehensive History of Texas, 1685-1897.* 2 Volumes. Dallas: William G. Scarff, 1898.

Wortham, Louis J. *A History of Texas From Wilderness to Commonwealth.* 5 Volumes. Fort Worth, Texas: Wortham-Molyneaux Co., 1924.

Yoakum, Henderson K. *History of Texas from Its First Settlement in 1865 to Its Annexation to the United States in 1846.* 2 Volumes. New York: Redfield, 1856.

Young, Philip. *History of Mexico; Her Civil Wars, and Colonial and Revolutionary Annals; from the Period of the Spanish Conquest, 1520, to the Present Time, 1847; Including an Account of the War with the United States, Its Causes and Military Achievements.* Cincinnati: J. A. & U. P. James, 1847.

Index

A

E

McCoy, Martha, 80

McCoy, Prospect, 80

McGloin, James, 89

McMullen, John, 89

Merchants, 142, 143, 156-158

Mexico, colonization laws, 42; General Colonization Law of 1824, 43; Coahuila-Texas State Colonization Law of 1825, 44, 45, 46, 47, 48; Law of April 6, 1830, 91, 161, 166, 199; Constitution of 1824, 43, 186, 188; immigration policy, 40, 42, 43, 44, 45, 46, 55, 56, 161-164, 169-171, 194-199, 201, 203; see Empresario system; Indian policy, 128-129; see Empresario system; land laws, 40, 42; General Colonization Law of 1824, 43, 173; Coahuila-Texas State Colonization Law of 1825, 44, 45, 46, 47, 48; Law of April 6, 1830, 91, 161, 166, 199; military posts, 161-163; politics, 40, 41, 42, 43, 164-165, 166, 171-174; relations with United States, 42, 43, 161; Texas Revolution, 160-193; urbanization policy, 48, 139-142

Mier y Teran, Manuel, 161

Miller, James B., 179

Miller, Doctor James H. C., 138, 144, 176

Miller, Thomas R., 142, 143, 155, 156, 183, 190

Milsap, Isaac, 190

Miro, Miguel, 119

Mission system, 16, 17, 162

Mitchell, Eli, 143, 144, 155, 158

Monclava Affair, 171-174

Monclava, Coahuila-Texas, Mexico, 110, 171-174

Money, 108, 153; see Guadalupe Land Office money

Moore, John H., 184, 186-187

Morfi, Juan Agustin, 115

Musick, James, 59, 64, 65

N

Nacogdoches, Texas, 22, 24, 162

Nash, Betty, 81

Nash, Polly, 81

Nash, Thomas, 81

Nash, William, 81, 84

Navarro, Jose Antonio, 94 n. 26, 98, 137; appointed land commissioner, DeWitt's colony, 94; forms Gonzales government, 151; surveys Gonzales, 140

Navarro, Martin, 21

Neggan, George, 190

Neill, James C., 191

Neutral Ground Agreement, 27, 30, 33

Norton, James, 67, 71, 73

O

Old Eighteen, 183

Old San Antonio Road, 105, 196

P

R

S

Turner, Winslow, 98, 143, 144, 151, 183

Turtle Bayou Resolution, 164

U

Ugartechea, Domingo, 175, 176, 177, 179-180, 183, 184, 187

United States, 21; land laws, 38, 41, 44; Louisiana-Texas boundary, 25, 26, 27, 35, 36; relations with Mexico, 42, 43, 161; relations with Spain, 19, 20, 21, 23, 25, 26, 27, 29, 30, 31, 32, 35, 36

United States Land Law of 1820, 38, 41

Upper South, 82, 83; characterizes DeWitt's colony, 105-107

Urban development, see Gonzales, Texas

V

Velasco, 162, 163, 164

Victoria, Texas, 68

Viesca, Jose Maria, 77

W

Waco Indians, 78

Wallace, Joseph Washington, 184

Ward, Henry G., 56

Water Street, Gonzales, Texas, 141, 142, 143, 144, 145

Wheat, see Agriculture

White, Robert, 190

White, Wiley, 81, 84

Wholesale trade, 156

Wichita Indians, 122, 123, 124, 126, 130, 132, 133, 134, 138

Wightman, Elias R., 81, 83

Wightman, John, 59, 64

Wilkinson, James, 26, 50

Williams, Ezekiel, 151, 183

Williams, John, 81, 83, 84

Williams, Margaret, 81

Wright, Clairborne, 190

Z

Zumwalt, Adam, 143, 144, 192

269